Charles Winchester

The Gospel of Foreign Travel

Charles Winchester

The Gospel of Foreign Travel

ISBN/EAN: 9783337212018

Printed in Europe, USA, Canada, Australia, Japan

Cover: Foto ©Lupo / pixelio.de

More available books at **www.hansebooks.com**

THE

Gospel of Foreign Travel.

BY REV. C. W. WINCHESTER, A. M.

ROCHESTER, N. Y.:
PRESS OF DEMOCRAT AND CHRONICLE.
1891.

PREFACE.

In the summer of 1890 the author spent twelve weeks on the Atlantic Ocean and on the soil of Europe, having left home, at the urgent advice of physicians, parishioners and friends, to recover from the effects of a severe illness—the first in nineteen years of labor in the pastorate.

Soon after his return, many members of his congregation began to clamor for a public recital of his experiences abroad. After due deliberation, he gave notice of a series of Sunday evening sermons on "The Gospel of Foreign Travel," stating that if the first proved acceptable, the others, as announced, would follow, to the number of eleven in all ; while if the first seemed to be uninteresting, or ill-suited to the pulpit, it would be the last. The preacher's plan was simply this : to use what he saw and experienced under foreign skies to illustrate and enforce the gospel. He did not purpose to give secular lectures, but gospel discourses—to set before his congregation the thoughts which came to him, as a student of divine truth, while he was beholding the wonders of the old world.

At the close of the first discourse, delivered November 9, 1890, there was no doubt in the mind of the preacher as to his duty, and he went forward till the one became eleven, according to the original plan, and the eleven became eighteen. The last sermon was preached April 19, 1891. From the beginning of the series to the close, congregations equal to the capacity of the church listened to the discourses, and the preacher humbly trusts that much good was accomplished.

Early in the progress of the course of sermons, their publication in book form was suggested. That suggestion has come to the author again and again. At length he decided to make a book ; and here it is. The sermons are presented, with the exception of a few slight alterations, just as they were originally delivered. The author hopes that, if the critics condescend to notice his book, they will not handle it as roughly as it may deserve, and prays that God will bless it to the spiritual good of all who may take the trouble to give it a perusal.

C. W. WINCHESTER,
Methodist Episcopal Parsonage.

Medina, N. Y., Sept. 3. 1891.

THE GOSPEL OF FOREIGN TRAVEL.

I.

OVER THE SEA.

"*Let us go over to the other side.*"—Luke, viii, 22.

On the seventeenth of June, 1890, a company of thirty-odd persons, two-thirds of the number women and one-third men, gathered in the Taylor House. Jersey City, saying to each other : " Let us go over to the other side." At seven o'clock in the evening, led by Prof. Joseph Swain of the Indiana State University, they went down to the dock of the Red Star Line, and went on board the steamship Westernland.

Imagine yourself to be a member of the party. I invite each one of you to take the voyage with us. Come with me, down into my state room. I want to stow away my baggage where it will be safe. This is the way. Down two flights of stairs we go. We pass along a narrow passage. We turn to the left. Here it is—No. 141. The door is open. An electric light is brightly burning. What do you think of such a bedroom as this? It is only eight feet long and six feet wide. Opposite the door are a wash-stand, a shelf and an oval mirror. On the floor is a good brussels carpet. On the right side are two good beds, or berths, one above the other. Mine is the upper one. On the left is a sofa. In the ceiling is a window, protected by an iron dome. Ceiling and walls are painted a brilliant white. I think this will do very well for eleven or twelve nights. Let us go back to the deck and look the ship over a little, as well as we can in the night.

Having examined the ship, we are now sitting in the saloon, writing. The room contains three long tables, fastened down, covered with thick, rich spreads, about one hundred and fifty elegant chairs and a piano. It has electric lights and about twenty little round windows, eighteen inches or two feet in diameter. On the end of the table near the door is a pile of letters and telegrams. Let us see if there is anything for us. Yes. Here is a telegram addressed to us both. It is signed by a former pastor of the Medina Church now resident in Rochester, and reads: "Wishing you health, happiness and an ideal trip." That is very kind. Thank God for the friends he has given us!

Wednesday morning finds us on deck at half-past five o'clock. At six precisely the big ship begins to back out of the slip. A little puffing, panting, blowing tug comes and helps to get her out and turn her around. Thank God for the little tugs, as well as the big ships! Both are needed, in church and state. If you cannot be a big ship, carrying immense cargoes and crowds of passengers across mighty oceans, be contented to be a little tug, doing small jobs of hard pulling in the harbors and close to the shore. If you are not willing to be a little tug, you are not fit to become a big ship.

We are standing on the forward part of the upper deck leaning against the rail above the steerage. We have just passed the Goddess of Liberty and Fort Hamilton. The wind is blowing a stiff breeze. We

are passing Staten Island, going along finely. At the
bowsprit we fly the flag of Belgium—three perpendicular
stripes, black next to the staff, then yellow
and red. At the top of the fore-mast flies the stars
and stripes. At the main masthead is a white flag
with a red star. At the mizzen masthead floats a blue
flag with white letters U. S. M.—United States Mail.

We have just passed Fort Wadsworth on Staten
Island. We have a pretty sight before us now.
About a dozen sailors in blue are up on the fore-mast,
some of them a hundred feet above the deck, shaking
out the sails and giving wings to the ship.

We must be near Sandy Hook. Everything is gay.
The harbor of New York must be one of the grandest
in the world.

The pilot has just left us and started back to the
city. We are over the bar. Sandy Hook is behind
us. The mighty Atlantic is before us. The shores
of our dear native land are rapidly receding into
dimness and nothingness.

Now we are out of sight of land. Our long voyage
of three thousand four hundred and fifty-seven miles
has begun. Where are we going? How do we
know that we are going anywhere? You say we are
going to Europe, to Antwerp; that thence we are
going to Bruges, and Brussels, and Paris, and the
Alps, and Milan, and Rome, and Florence, and
Venice, and Berlin, and London, and Edinburgh,
and Liverpool. But how do you know that
there is any such continent as Europe? How do you
know that there are any such cities as those which
you just named? Did you ever walk the streets of
Paris? Did you ever climb Mount Blanc? Did you
ever visit the cathedral of Milan? Did you ever

ascend the dome of St. Peter's? Did you ever stand on the bank of the Thames? You are compelled to answer "no." How then do you know that these places have any existence outside the fancy and fiction of fanatics and deceivers? How do you know that the Red Star Steam Ship Company is not imposing upon you in pretending to transport you to Antwerp, when there is no Antwerp, in order to get your money? If you can not answer these questions, I can answer them for you. By *faith* you know that there is such a continent as Europe, and that there are such cities as Antwerp and Rome and London. If you have not been there and seen those shores and fields and domes and towers, other men have, and you believe their testimony. Nearly all the knowledge we have in this world comes to us through the faculty of faith. If we were wholly dependent for knowledge upon our own investigation and sight, we should almost be ignoramuses and fools. But because we have faith in the intelligence and veracity of other men, and by faith accept the results of their observation, investigation and experience, we have much knowledge of worldly things, and continually grow in knowledge and wisdom.

So it is in religious things. The infidel says to the Christian: "Where are you going?" The Christian replies: "I am going to Heaven." The infidel says: "How do you know there is any such place as Heaven? Have you ever been there? Have you ever walked the streets of the New Jerusalem? Have you ever sat under the trees on the banks of the River of Life?" "No," the Christian is compelled to answer, "I never have." "Well then, how do you know but the priests, the ministers, are fooling you in order to get your money?" The Christian answers: "By faith I know that there is a hereafter; that the soul will live after death ; that there are such places as Heaven and Hell ; that there will be a resurrection of the body and a judgment seat. God, my Father, and Christ, my Saviour, have seen all these things, and I have their word and believe their testimony. I know that there is a farther shore to the ocean of death, that Heaven lies over on the other side of these waves of trial and temptation and tribulation, because the man Christ Jesus, my elder Brother, has been over there and has come back and brought me word, and I have faith in his testimony."

My friends, I want to impress on your minds the fact that the life of a man on the ocean is a life of faith; and that the Christian life is a life of faith. You cannot go to Europe without faith. You cannot go to Heaven without faith. If you would go to Europe, you must have faith in the word of others who have crossed the sea before you ; you must have faith in the ship on which you sail ; you must have faith in the machinery ; you must have faith in the compass and chart ; you must have faith in the captain and crew. If you would go to Heaven, you must have some degree of faith in Christian people and in the Christian Church ; you must have implicit faith in the chart—the Bible— and in Jesus Christ, the great Captain of your Salvation.

While we have been talking about faith, the engines have been working, and the huge ship, our floating palace-hotel, is far out on the bosom of the briny deep. How do travelers spend their time on the ocean? Eating, sleeping, walking, sitting in steamer chairs on the deck, chatting, reading, writing, playing harmless games, watching the ever-changing, never resting sea. An extract or two from the tourist's journal will tell how time goes on the ocean. " Nearly all day I have sat in my chair, in overcoat and sea-rug, on the starboard side of the ship (the south side it now is) watching the sea and chatting with many persons. The sea is a never failing source of entertainment. To-day it is as blue as blue can be, dotted all over with white caps. If an artist were to paint the sea in a picture as deep a blue as it really is now, he would be considered false to nature. Now I am sitting at the bow, just as far forward as I can get, with my back against the railing. Running my eyes along the entire length of the deck, I can see the vessel's stern, four hundred and fifty-five feet away. The sea is very beautiful this afternoon, the most beautiful it has been since the voyage began. The water near by is of the deepest blue. In the near and remote distance, the surface is flecked all over with silver. The sky is well nigh cloudless, save along the horizon. Before me on the foremast, about fifteen feet above the deck, is the 'crow's nest,' on which is a sailor at watch. Just now he blew a horn which he continually carries. At once a crowd of people come running to the bow to see if they could discover a sail. We can see one directly east, probably twenty miles away. The sea is lonely. We on the ship are, for the time, as completely separated from the rest of the world as though we were dead. If our ship should go down, no one would ever know what had become of us. But we are not separated from God. He is on the sea as much as on the land; and we are in his almighty hand. How true the words of the Psalmist : 'Whither shall I go from thy Spirit? or whither shall I flee from thy presence? If I take the wings of the morning, and dwell in the uttermost parts of the sea ; even then shall thy hand lead me, and thy right hand shall hold me.' "

Another page in the traveler's journal reads somewhat differently : "The sun went down in a cloud to-night, and there are indications of a storm. A fog has settled down upon us, and the fog-horn sounds hideously, every two or three minutes, to warn any vessel which may be passing. I fear it will not let us sleep."

I want to talk to you a little while about that fog-horn, and about another fog-horn. A fog-horn is a huge steam whistle, with a throat like the throats of an army of demons. Of all the hideous and ear-splitting sounds which I ever heard, the fog-horn's scream is the worst. You would think it might be the wailing of lost souls, undergoing torture in Dante's Inferno. You know what the fog-horn is for. When the sky is so black, or the air is so thick with vapor, that passing vessels cannot see each other's lights, the fog-horn's terrific screech reveals the vessel's position and prevents collision and wreck. The fog-horn's voice is terrific and painful ; but it means mercy and salvation. Who would strangle its cry, when a darkness which can be felt rests upon the deep? The fog-horn is sounding. Down under the decks, in one of the state-rooms, a man is trying to sleep. A hundred times, during the last hour, he has been just falling off into sweet unconsciousness, when that demoniacal screech has started him up, wide awake. "O, the hateful thing!" he angrily exclaims. Go down and ask him if he wants the fog-horn stopped. He stares at you, and says: "Do you take me for a fool? No! Let it blow! I would rather not sleep a wink till the end of the voyage, than to have the stoppage of that horn cause a collision at sea." Every person on the ship has an intense dislike for the fog-horn's voice. And yet if a vote were to be taken, everybody would hold up both hands to have it blow on as long as the fog continues.

The whole human family is sailing over the ocean of time toward the shores of eternity. For six thousand years a thick fog—the fog of sin—has covered the sea. To prevent collision and everlasting wreck, our all-wise Captain, God, has been blowing his fog-horn, to warn every man to flee from the wrath to come and to lay hold on eternal life. It is not music in a sinner's ears ; and many men are angry at it and at God, and clamor to have it stopped. In Old Testament times, Noah and Elijah and Jeremiah, and many other seers and prophets, were God's fog-horns. Noah blew a warning blast, one hundred and twenty years. The world stopped its ears and would not be warned. The result was an awful wreck, in which scores and hundreds of millions of lives were lost. Elijah was a fog-horn of terrific power. He blew a blast of loud and solemn warning in the ears of Ahab and Jezebel and apostate Israel. Instead of forsaking their sins, they found fault with the fog-horn. Ahab said to Elijah: "Art thou he that troubleth Israel?" Then they tried to silence the prophet's voice in death, that they might lie down in their sins and sleep on the verge of eternal damnation. Jeremiah knew that the ship of state was in danger of colliding with a vessel named Babylon, commanded by King Nebuchadnezzar. So he tried to warn King Zedekiah and his fellows, before it was too late. Instead of hating their sins, they hated Jeremiah and cast him into prison.

In this gospel dispensation every faithful minister is a fog-horn. These are some of the warning notes which they send out into the dark and misty atmosphere: "The soul that sinneth, it shall die ;" "The wages of sin is death;" "He that believeth and is baptized shall be saved; but he that believeth not shall be damned"; "Except ye repent ye shall all likewise perish." Many of us do not like these sounds. We do not like to hear a fog-horn, when we go to Church. We want to have the minister tell us that we are all right ; that we are sailing straight into the harbor of Heaven, when he knows that we are in imminent danger of being run down by God's ironclad war-ship "Vengeance," and sunk to the bottom of the gulf of divine wrath and indignation. If sinners in this congregation, to night, should be told what their peril is, in the very words which the Bible employs, some of them would be angry at the preacher, and would say : "Stop that fog-horn, and let us go to sleep." My friends, sailing to eternity on the ocean of time, let us be as wise as those who sail on the treacherous Atlantic Until the darkness of sin is all dispelled, let us thank God for the fog-horn, and heed its warning notes, however unpleasant they may be.

We ought to be better acquainted with the vessel on which we are sailing. She is built wholly of steel, including her masts and spars, except that her decks are wooden planks bolted down upon steel plates, and all the saloons and state-rooms are finished in wood. She is four hundred and fifty-five feet long; forty-seven feet wide, in the widest part; thirty-five feet deep; has a tonnage of five thousand seven hundred and thirty-six tons, and engines of four thousand horse-power. She burns about one hundred tons of coal every twenty-four hours, and, on this voyage, carries about five hundred souls. One night one of the engineers took me, and others, down to see the ship's machinery. We went down and down, around and around, on iron stairways, till we were twenty-two feet below the surface of the sea. The engines are two in number, and are very large. The pistons have a stroke of five and one-half feet. One has a cylinder fifty-four inches in diameter; and the other ninety-two. The smaller takes the steam from the boilers, and passes it into the second engine. Thence it passes into the condenser, is changed back into water and returns to the boilers. The engineer took us down to the very bottom of the ship and showed us the shaft which turns the propelling screw. It is one hundred and eighty-five feet long and seventeen and one-half inches in diameter. It is made of solid steel. It runs from the engines to, and through, the stern to the screw outside. We went into the furnace room. There we saw many smutty-faced beings, who looked as though they might be demons, stuffing the coal into twenty furnaces under the four boilers, and cleaning out the ashes. The place seemed like the bottomless pit. It was so hot and close that I feared I should faint. I do not understand how men can live there. But they do; and work for ten dollars a month. Down at the bottom of the ship, at the stern, we could touch both sides of the vessel at the same time, with only seven-eighths of an inch of steel between us and death. What I saw impressed me with a sense of the majesty and power of the human mind as shown in the invention and construction of such machinery and such a ship. I thought of the evolution, through the ages, of the art of ship-building, from the log raft, fastened together with ropes of twisted bark, and the rude digout, up to such a floating palace as that on which I was sailing. And yet the Westernland does not belong to the largest class of ocean steamers. She is far surpassed by the "City of New York," on which we made our returning voyage. The City of New York is indeed a floating city, with her immense saloon, her reading room, her library, her suites of apartments, her electric lights, her eleven hundred feet of unbroken side-walk, her weekly newspaper and her fifteen hundred inhabitants. If the City of New York were to be placed in the street, in front of this church, all the trees would have to be cut down to give her room ; her upper deck would be nearly as high as the highest part of this roof ; while her masts would overtop the tallest spire in this village. She has a tonnage of ten thousand tons. She has two propellers, driven by independent engines of twenty thousand horse-power. She carries six thousand tons of coal, every time she leaves her dock in Liverpool. She burns three hundred tons of coal every twenty-four hours. She sails twenty miles every sixty minutes.

As I paced the deck of "The City of New York," admiring her beauty, astonished at her greatness, feeling her motion, as she bounded along the loud-resounding sea, I said to myself: Could any man believe that this ship, so full of design, so perfectly adapted to its work, came into existence by chance? Can any man believe that that other ship, the World, came into being by chance? Compare the two. The City of New York has a tonnage of ten thousand five hundred tons. The world has a tonnage of ten quadrillion tons. The City of New York carries fifteen hundred passengers. The world carries fourteen hundred million passengers. The City of New York sails over the waves twenty miles an hour. The world sails among the stars more than sixty thousand miles an hour. The City of New York has been sailing on the Atlantic about two years. The world has been sailing through infinite space at least six thousand years. The City of New York must have frequent repairs. The world has never gone into dry dock and has never been repaired. The City of New York trembles when she moves, and, if the sea is rough, she shakes up her passengers till they are deathly sick. The world moves three thousand times as fast as the swiftest ocean steamer, and yet her motion is so steady and smooth in calm and storm, that it took her passengers several thousand years to discover that she moved at all. Now, if the little steamer City of New York was designed and built and launched by some intelligent being, how much more evident it is that this great world was designed and created and launched into space by some being of infinite wisdom and power. If that man would be a fool who should say: "The ocean steamer came by chance," surely he is a greater fool who say: "There is no God."

Over on the other side of the Atlantic Ocean lie

the continent and islands of Europe, with such splendid cities as Antwerp and Brussels and Paris and Rome and London and Edinburgh. But I ought to speak to you of another ocean and continent and city, which mortal eyes have never seen. Over on the other side of the ocean of time lie the continent of eternity and the evergreen plains and mountains of heaven. There stands a city whose walls are jasper, whose gates are pearls and whose streets are transparent gold. Men go to Europe for business, pleasure and health. They go to make money, to have a good time, to prolong life. We cannot all take a trip to Europe. To many of us that is a beautiful dream, which will never be realized. But we can all take a trip to Heaven. There we shall be immensely rich—" heirs of God and joint heirs with Jesus Christ." There in God's presence, we shall have "fulness of joy," and, at his right hand, " pleasures forevermore." There we shall not only be rich, but shall live for ever and ever. Contrast that side with this. On this side are darkness, disappointment, doubts, fears, crime, sin, death. On the other side are light, rest, joy, love, purity, eternal life. On this side the ground is strewed with withered flowers, and faded leaves, and broken columns, and blasted fruit. Everywhere we see ashes, and smouldering ruins, and bleaching bones, and grinning skulls, and tombs, and graves. This world is one vast Golgotha. Death and despair are written on every earthly thing. On the other side are flowers which never wither, and leaves which never fade, and fruit which never blasts. That world is one vast Eden. We talk about the beautiful fields and parks of England, the palaces and pictures of France, the cathedrals and temples of Italy, the mountains and glaciers of Switzerland, the castles and sculptures of Germany. But these things are nothing, and less than nothing, compared with the beauty and glory and magnificence of Heaven. You may never ride through Hyde Park in London; but you may ride in God's chariot along the banks of the River of Eternal Life. You may never see the palace of Versailles; but you may live eternally in the palace of Jehovah. You may never stand beneath the dome of St. Peter's; but you may stand before the throne of God. You may never look at the dazzling, snow-clad peak of Mt. Blanc; but you may "see the King in His beauty." You may never see a castle on the Rhine; but you may own a mansion in the Celestial City. Every one of you may take a trip to Heaven. Come, let us start to-night. Come, "let us go over to the other side."

There are many steamship lines between this country and Europe, and every line has many steamers. There is the Cunard line. All its steamers have names ending in ia, like the Etruria, the Umbria and the Britannia. There is the Inman line. All its steamers are named from cities, like the "City of Paris" the "City of Chicago," the "City of New York." There is the White Star line. All its ships are named with words ending in ic, like the "Britannic" and the "Teutonic." There is the Red Star line. All its ships are named with words ending in land, like the "Westernland" and the "Nordland." There are many other steamship lines which I have not the time to name. If you take a European trip, you may choose between a dozen lines and a hundred ships. But there is only one line by which you can sail to Heaven, and only one ship. The name of that line is the "Gospel line," or the "Red Cross line;" and the name of the ship is the "Church." The flag which floats at the top of her every mast is a red cross on a white field. If you go to Heaven, you must go by the way of the cross.

When I tell you that the only ship in which you can sail to Heaven is the Church, I do not mean the Methodist Church, or the Baptist, or the Presbyterian, or the Episcopal, or the Roman Catholic Church. I mean the Church of Christ, the Holy Catholic Church, that great spiritual society which includes every soul in every land and age who loves and serves the Lord Jesus Christ. This ship, the Church, sometimes called the Old Ship Zion, is the largest vessel ever built. She is large enough to carry every human being at once, and give every one a first-class state-room. She has no steerage passengers. She is the strongest ship ever built. She is built of steel, or something stronger and tougher than the best steel ever cast or forged. In the largest ship-yard in the world, where five thousand men find employment, in Glasgow, I saw eight huge steel monsters on the stocks, each five hundred feet long. The sound of the hammers on their metal ribs was perfectly deafening. The old ship Zion was built in a larger ship-yard than Glasgow.ever saw, and her rivets were driven home by patriarchs, prophets, apostles, martyrs, and angels, under the supervision of the Supreme Architect of the Universe. She is the safest ship that ever sailed. She is so strong that no storm can ever wreck her, no collision can shake her, no ice-berg can crush her. And then her captain is Jesus Christ—" The Wonderful, the Counselor, the

Mighty God, the Everlasting Father, the Prince of Peace." If you embark on this vessel, and do not leave her, you are absolutely sure to reach the haven of eternal rest and joy. Best of all, this salvation is free. My ticket to Antwerp cost me sixty-odd dollars; and from Liverpool to New York I paid seventy-five. But you can have a free ticket to Heaven by the Red Cross line. Jesus, by his blood shed on Calvary, has paid the passage of every human soul from this world to that kingdom which is over on the other side. All you have to do is to come on board, just as you are. Come, will you not ship for glory this very night?

Friday morning, June 27th, I came on deck at seven o'clock. At about nine o'clock we caught sight of the Cilly Islands. The first thing we saw was a tall light-house rising above the waves. At about ten we sighted Land's End, England, and, soon after, Lizard Point. There our ship was sighted from the shore, and the news of our arrival was flashed under the sea to New York. All day we sailed in the English Channel. For hours we were close to the English coast. We could see the green fields of grass and grain, and the grazing cattle and numerous farm houses. After nine days without any glimpse of land, how our hungry eyes feasted on that sight. Saturday morning the white cliffs of Dover were in sight. We were in the narrow strait between England and France, and could see Dover, with its old castle on a hill 220 feet above the water.

At three o'clock we were in the German Ocean, at the mouth of the River Scheldt. There we lay, waiting for the tide, till eight o'clock Sunday morning. At eleven our good ship reached her dock, at Antwerp, and our long voyage was joyously over.

So, I thought, it will be by and by with the faithful Christian. The last storm will be over, the last trial will be past, the last temptation will be overcome, the last cross will be laid down. Land will be in sight. The domes and spires of the eternal city will rise before him. It will be Sabbath morning—the Sabbath of eternal rest. Amid a throng of welcoming saints and angels and old familiar friends, he will step upon the golden wharf, and be forever at home.

II.

ANTWERP, BRUGES, AND BRUSSELS.

"*Go * * * * and see the land, what it is; and the people that dwelleth therein * * * * and what cities they be that they dwell in * * * * "* Numbers xiii, 17 —19.

These words are a part of Moses' instructions to the committee of twelve, whom he sent to spy out the land of Canaan. We, on the Red Star Steamer Westernland, went across the ocean to see the land, what it is and the people who dwell therein, and what cities they be that they dwell in. The first land on which we stood was the little kingdom of Belgium, and in that kingdom we saw three cities, Antwerp, Bruges and Brussels.

Antwerp is a city of about two hundred thousand inhabitants, situated on the right, or eastern, bank of the River Scheldt, fifty miles from its mouth. It has a find harbor, which will admit the largest vessels, and is the greatest sea-port on the continent of Europe. It registers six thousand vessels every year. It carries on an enormous trade with Great Britain and Germany, and with the inland towns and cities. It is strongly fortified, and is the principal arsenal of Belgium. Antwerp was founded twelve hundred years ago, and has passed through many vicissitudes. Four times the dogs of war have howled before its gates. Four times it has suffered the horrors of siege and pillage. Four different nations, in modern times, have swayed the scepter over its inhabitants—Spain, France, Holland and Belgium. Its people are mostly of Flemish stock, resembling the Dutch. They speak two languages—Dutch and French. In Dutch they call their town Antwerpen; in French Anvers.

Many magnificent public buildings, numerous splendid churches, stately and antique houses and a profusion of ornamental trees render Antwerp a very interesting and picturesque city. It is the cleanest city I ever saw. I did not see a street which did not seem to be almost perfectly free from dirt of every kind. I hardly saw a spot where a person could not walk without shoes and scarcely soil his stockings, either on the side-walk or in the middle of the carriage drive. But while the streets are clean, they have the fault of being very narrow and crooked. They wind and twist around in every direction, and cross each other without any kind of order. They are as much worse than the streets of old Boston as you can think. The houses are very queer. Their gables are turned toward the street, and their roofs are covered with the oddest-looking tiles. The shape of the house fronts is much like that of a big box with a lot of little boxes piled on top so as to form two flights of steps, ascending from each side toward the middle. I suppose we saw hundreds of such houses which have been occupied for five and six hundred years, and even longer.

But I am getting ahead of my story. We landed at Antwerp, on the magnificent stone quay which the Great Napoleon built three-quarters of a century ago at a cost of $2,600,000. After attending to our baggage, we formed a procession, thirty strong, and marched to the Hotel du Commerce, near the Bourse. My immediate traveling companion and myself were assigned to the same room—a very quaint, old, interesting place. The bed was very high and had a canopy over it. The only thing to give light, in the absence of the sun, was a tallow candle, in a brass stick with a handle like that of a frying pan. The furniture was all old-fashioned, as if it had been made five hundred years ago. But every thing was clean and good, and we liked the place all the more for being old and odd.

After dinner, at about two o'clock Antwerp time (which would be eight forty-five, New York time) I went to the Bourse, a grand massive building, where the exchange of the city is carried on, and, from an office in one of the upper stories, sent a cablegram to my Medina home. Including the address, it contained four words, and cost me seven francs. The message was written at two o'clock, and was delivered at the parsonage in Medina, three thousand eight hundred miles distant, at about half-past one. In other words, my little message, of one word, outstripped the sun in his stately march, and, according to two time-pieces both correct, was in the hands of my wife before it left my fingers. That fact, it seems to me, is a beautiful comment on one of the promises which God has written for us in his book. In the sixty-fifth chapter of Isaiah, and the twenty-fourth verse, we read: "It shall come to pass, that before they call, I will answer; and while they are yet speaking, I will hear." This is one of a thousand places in which the Almighty has promised to hear and answer prayer. Only here he promises to receive and answer our petitions before we send

them. Do you believe in prayer? Do you believe
that God will hear you, if you pray out of an honest
and sincere heart? If you do not, I am sorry for
you; I think you must be one of the most unhappy
persons in the world. Some people say that God
cannot answer prayer; that prayer is impossible.
Fifty years ago men would have said that it was
impossible to send messages along a wire by means of
electricity; and a man who should have proposed to
do what I did do – send a dispatch under the ocean
from Antwerp to New York—would have been
hurried away to the nearest insane asylum. But
whatever men might have said then, electric teleg-
raphy is a fact; and, whatever infidels may say now,
prayer is a fact. I trust you will not accuse me of
egotism and pride, when I say that I have tried and
proved both. If puny, ignorant, finite man has been
able to invent an arrangement by which a husband,
on one side of the Atlantic, can send a message to
his wife, on the other side of the Atlantic, in less than
no time; why cannot the almighty, infinite God con-
trive an arrangement by which a needy child, on
earth, may send a message to his Heavenly Father,
and get a speedy reply? I am very glad that the
electric telegraph has been invented and that ocean
cables have been laid, because they benefit commerce
and promote the peace of nations; and also because
they help to make us understand how God can hear
and answer prayer. "Before they call I will answer;
and while they are yet speaking, I will hear." That
divine promise was illustrated in the receipt, at
Medina, at half-past one, of a cablegram which I
sent from Antwerp, at two. It has also been fulfilled,
over and over again, in the experience of Christians,

in all ages and lands. It cost me one dollar and forty cents for only one word. I want you to try God's great prayer cable, which he has stretched from his throne to every man's door. It will cost you nothing. You can send as many words as you please. You can use it all day and all night, free of charge. Its frequent use will make you rich in joy and love and all spiritual good.

The grandest building in Antwerp is the cathedral. It is a superb old building, the erection of which was commenced in 1352, and finished in 1616. So you see its newest portion is two hundred and seventy-five years old, while its foundations were laid more than five hundred years ago. It is a magnificent structure of the Gothic style of architecture. It is not only grand, but beautiful. Externally the chief attraction is the Gothic tower, four hundred and two feet high, containing a chime of ninety-nine bells, the largest of which weighs eight tons, while the smallest is only fifteen inches in circumference. The upper part of the tower, as well as the lower, is wholly of stone; and yet it is so richly and delicately carved that Charles V. used to say that it ought to be preserved in a glass case, and Napoleon is said to have compared it to a piece of Mechlin lace It is the most beautiful church tower I ever saw. I ascended it to the altitude of three hundred feet—which is as high as anyone can go—by a spiral stair-case of 515 stone steps. The view from that elevation is very fine, taking in the whole city, wide stretches of beautiful fields and miles and miles of winding river. The ground plan of the cathedral is a cross, three hundred and eighty-five feet long and two hundred and twenty-two feet wide in the widest part. It covers fourteen times as much space as this church in which we are assembled. Its arched ceiling, one hundred and fifty feet high in the highest place, and five times as high as the highest portion of this ceiling, is supported by one hundred and twenty-five columns. The building does not contain wood enough to make a tooth-pick, except the doors. All is stone. The chief attractions of the interior of the Antwerp Cathedral are the famous paintings by Peter Paul Rubens, the "Elevation of the Cross," and the "Descent from the Cross." The former is two hundred and eighty years old ; and the latter, two hundred and seventy-eight. At the close of a short children's service, Sunday afternoon, the pictures were uncovered and we sat down to study them.

The "Elevation of the Cross" is on the left, or north side of the altar ; the other picture is on the right side. The painting at which we are looking now represents the living Christ, spiked to a rough wooden cross, which nine or ten muscular executioners are tugging to raise. The sufferer's hands and feet are streaming with blood, and the body droops as it hangs with all its weight upon the lacerating nails. The agony on the Saviour's face is more than human. As the eyes are turned upward, there is more than mortal majesty in the look. We feel that it is the dying God at whom we are gazing. The scene is so real, that our imagination carries us back through the centuries, and we seem to be standing on Calvary, that April morning, with the crucifixion actually taking place before our eyes. It is so cruel, so dreadful, that we cannot endure the sight. As we turn away, with tears of pity in our eyes, we repeat to ourselves the old hymn :

> "Alas! and did my Saviour bleed?
> And did my Sovereign die?
> Would he devote that sacred head
> For such a worm as I?

My friend, whoever you may be, can you look at that picture, can you see Jesus lifted up on the cross, without hating your sins, which drove those nails, and resolving that henceforth you will live for him who died for you?

The "Descent from the Cross" is considered Rubens' finest work, and is one of the great pictures of the world. We sat before it, that Sunday afternoon, I cannot tell how long—till we were wholly lost in the scene before us. I wish I could make you see the picture. Shall I try? There it is. See! the figures are as large as life. The coloring is rich and vivid—just like reality. It is the evening of the crucifixion day. Armed with authority from Pilate, the disciples have come to take down the lifeless body of their beloved Master. The nails have been extracted. The body is half-way down. It looks exactly like a corpse. Death absolute, hopeless, is written in the faded majesty of that peaceful, weary face. The eyes are closed. The head hangs down on the right shoulder. Every limb and muscle is relaxed. Two rude ladders stand leaning against the cross. In the very front of the scene John is standing, with one foot on the ladder and the other on the ground, supporting almost the entire weight of the dead Saviour in his strong, loving arms. O, what love and sorrow are written on his face! Peter stands at the top of the ladder leaning over the right arm of the cross. With his left hand he steadies himself; with his right he grasps the left arm of the dead; with his teeth he holds one edge of a large linen cloth in which the corpse is to be wrapped. Such earnestness of effort is just what we should expect from Peter. Half-way down the ladder is Nicodemus, trying to help John, who seems so strong as to need no help. On the other side are two men on a ladder. One leans far over the arm of the cross from behind, and grasps one corner of the linen sheet. The other, whom, by his dress, I recognize as Joseph of Arimathæa, has a hand under the Saviour's right shoulder. On the ground, in front, on her knees, I see Mary Magdalene, holding, as though she would kiss it, one of the Saviour's pierced feet. Behind her is the other Mary. Standing, leaning forward with outstretched arms, as though she would clasp her son to her bosom, with a look of unutterable sorrow in her face, is the Virgin Mother. In her, this moment, is fulfilled the prophecy of the aged Simeon: "Yea, a sword shall pierce through thy own soul also."

As you look at the dead Christ descending from the cross, I want to repeat in your ears what you have heard a hundred times. He died for you. God so loved you that he gave his only begotten Son to save you from your sins by his death. The All-wise saw that there was no way by which you could possibly be saved without the agony and blood and death of the incarnate God. An infinite sacrifice has been made in your behalf. If you will not accept a salvation which infinite Love has purchased at so great a price, you deserve to suffer the pains of perdition for ever and ever.

Scores of thousands visit Antwerp and Antwerp Cathedral, every year, on purpose to see that picture. I believe that eternity will reveal that scores of thousands have been brought to Christ by looking at the "Descent from the Cross." With what emotions we left the house of God that afternoon. We carried away impressions which will abide with us through time and eternity. It would pay you to cross the Atlantic just to spend one hour in Antwerp Cathedral, looking at Rubens' immortal painting.

At six o'clock, that same Sabbath afternoon, we went to St. Paul's Church to attend a special service held in honor of that great apostle on his feast day. We heard the grandest sacred music which I ever heard. I have no time to describe it, and I could not, if I should spend an hour in the attempt.

On the way back to our hotel, we passed the City Hall. In front of the building stands a group of statuary representing a mythical hero, named Salvius Brabo, killing a giant. The giant, as the story goes, used to hold possession of the River Scheldt, at its mouth, and compel all sailors entering to pay him a heavy toll, or have the right hand cut off and cast into the river. Salvius killed the giant and cut off his hand. In the statue, he is in the act of throwing the giant's hand into the river. From this act the city took its name; *ant* meaning hand, and *werpen* to throw—Antwerpen, Antwerp, to throw the hand.

Looking at the prostrate bronze giant, I thought of another giant, who wrings an enormous toll from this Republic—two thousand million dollars every year—and cuts off the right hand of self-support and beneficent industry from hundreds of thousands of American citizens. How long will the children of Pilgrim Fathers and Revolutionary sires submit to such ruthless tyranny? When will God, in answer to the prayers of his people, send us a champion like

Salvius Brabo, who shall cut off the giant's hand and head, and cast them, and him, into the sea of oblivion? We left Antwerp, at half-past eight Monday morning.

A ride by rail of seventy-two miles, directly west, brought us to Bruges, which is a strange old town of fifty thousand inhabitants one-fourth of whom are paupers. Bruges was once a very great commercial center; but it is now in the decline. It is only seven and a half miles from the North Sea, with which it is connected by two canals. It derives its name, which means bridges, from the numerous bridges which span these commercial water-ways. We walked from the depot to the "Hotel Pannier d'Or," so named from a gilded basket on the top of a gabled point like those of the old houses at Antwerp.

We first visited the "Belfry," made famous by one of the poems of Longfellow. It is three hundred and fifty-two feet high. We went up three hundred and sixty-two winding stone steps to the chime of bells. They are forty-eight in number, and range from a huge old monster down to a little baby about as large as a quart pail. Four times an hour the chimes ring without human hands, playing ninety-six different tunes every day. The chimes are rung by means of a huge brass cylinder like the barrel of a hand organ. The tune is written on the cylinder by driving pegs into its surface, which pegs play against levers as the cylinder revolves by clock-work. The pegs are moved, and the tunes changed, once a year. The cylinder weighs 19,966 pounds. This odd, old belfry was begun six hundred years ago and finished five hundred years ago. Through all the generations, since its erection, the people of Bruges have joyously listened to the melody of its bells, never wearied by the sounds because of the rich variety of the tunes.

It seems to me that that old belfry is a type of an older belfry erected by divine power, eighteen centuries ago, on Mount Calvary. If the shape of the belfry of Burges is odd, the shape of God's belfry is odder still, for it is like a huge cross uplifted in sight of the nations. In God's belfry, which, in spite of wicked men and devils, will stand forever, is a wonderful chime of bells. They are gospel bells. They ring out the good news of salvation to all mankind. They play such an endless variety of tunes, composed by celestial artists, that the listener's ear is never wearied, and he never complains of monotony. The more the human heart receives of the gospel the more it longs to have.

"Salvation! O the joyful sound!
What pleasure to our ears!
A soverign balm for every wound,
A cordial for our fears."

Listen and you will hear the melody of those celestial chimes even now. Let me repeat what the bells are saying: "Come unto me, all ye that labor and are heavy laden, and I will give you rest. Take my yoke upon you and learn of me and ye shall find rest unto your souls." Now I hear a louder, heavier peal: "Ho every one that thirsteth, come ye to the waters, and he that hath no money; come ye, buy and eat; yea, come, buy wine and milk without money and without price." Now it grows soft and sweet. "The Spirit and the bride say, come. And let him that heareth say, come. And let him that is athirst, come. And whosoever will, let him take the water of life freely." "Come! come! come! Freely! freely! freely!"

You may never hear the bells of Bruges. But you can hear, you do hear, the gospel bells. If you will listen, they will charm your soul and draw you away from the path of sin into the fellowship of saints and into the joys of Heaven.

The other points of interest which we visited in Burges, are the Cathedral, the Church of Notre Dame, where we saw an immense number of fine paintings and statuary, and the Palace of Justice. In the last named we saw a room which contains the most wonderful wood carving, probably, in the world, cut by a political prisoner, who labored at it seventeen years and thus purchased his liberty. It is one of the walls of the court-room, above the fireplace, and represents Charles V. in the centre, with his paternal ancestors Mary and Maximilian, on the left, and his maternal ancestors, Ferdinand and Isabella, on the right. All the figures stand out as large, and as natural, as life, in solid English oak.

As I looked at that wonderful creation of human genius, and thought of the prisoner artist, I said to myself: I was a prisoner once, all mankind were prisoners; but Christ has given us freedom without any desert or working on our part. We are free from sin and condemnation, if we cease from our works and trust in the finished, perfect work of Christ.

We left Bruges at six in the afternoon, and, after a journey by rail of sixty-four miles, in a southeasterly direction, reached Brussels, the beautiful capital of Belgium. It has a population of nearly half a million. It is called "Little Paris." It is remarkable for the number and richness of its antique buildings, and ranks among the finest cities in Europe. It is also noted for its manufacture of the finest lace in the world. Among its chief edifices are the Hotel de Ville, or City Hall, the Cathedral, the Royal Palace, the Palace of Fine Arts, the Palace of Justice and the Bourse.

Of all these buildings I saw the exterior; of some the interior. The Hotel de Ville interested me most, because of its surpassing beauty and also because, directly in its front, I saw the spot where the Christian patriots, Counts Egmont and Hoorn, were beheaded, in the year 1522, by the orders of the cruel Duke of Alva. Shall I tell you all about it? No. You may read it for yourself in "Motley's Dutch Republic." If our young people would read such books more, and trashy books less, they would have wiser heads and purer hearts.

But my chief aim in going to Brussels was to visit the battle-field of Waterloo. In company with two other members of our party, I left the city at ten o'clock, Tuesday morning. In an English coach, with an English driver, we rolled out of the metropolis, toward the south, on our ride of twelve miles. We soon found ourselves driving along the skirts of a beautiful park, which, ere long, became the forest of Soignes and was with us all the way to the field of Waterloo. It was into this forest that Napoleon intended to drive Wellington's army, and scatter it among the trees. But the God of battles willed otherwise. A ride of an hour and a half, over a stone pavement, brought us to the village of Waterloo. Two miles farther on, we came to the battle-field. We obtained a good dinner at a hotel near the spot where Napoleon's "Old Guard" was annihilated, after which our coachman drove us about three-quarters of a mile further south and left us at Hougomont. Hougomont is the most interesting spot at Waterloo, especially to a student of Victor Hugo. It was, and is, a chateau, or a collection of farm buildings with garden and orchard, surrounded with a strong wall of masonry. It is just as it was seventy-five years ago, except as the storm of battle and the hand of time have disfigured it. June 18, 1815, Hougomont was held by the right wing of Wellington's army. About three-quarters of a mile away, at La Belle Alliance, was the center of the hosts of the great Emperor. It was his purpose to capture Hougomont and then double up Wellington's right upon his centre, and overwhelm his whole army. At eleven in the morning he launched a heavy force upon the chateau. But the English were too much for the French. All day long, with short lulls, the hurricane of war raged around this quiet rural retreat. Once the French succeeded in getting into the orchard, but they could not hold it. At the close of the day fifteen hundred corpses lay within the walls of Hougomont. We looked into the old well, into which many bodies—some still alive, it is said—were thrown after the battle. We were invited into the farm-house, and were shown bullet-holes in the thick plank door. I purchased some relics of an old woman living there.

We walked across the fields to the Lion Mound. As on that bloody day seventy-five years ago, the ground was covered with growing wheat. I think I never before saw so luxuriant a growth of grain. It is said that Waterloo has produced more and better wheat since fifty thousand men watered its soil with their blood. It was hard to make ourselves believe that that peaceful plain had ever been a battlefield. Slowly we made our way along the path, plucking roses, poppies and bending heads of wheat. At length we were near the spot where the battle ended at eight o'clock on that pivotal day. There a huge mound has been built, two hundred feet in height and, perhaps, a quarter of a mile in circumference. Under it are buried tens of thousands of dead of both armies. On its summit stands a colossal bronze lion, weighing twenty-eight tons. We went up to the lion's feet and surveyed the historic field. Facing south, we see directly in our front, about a mile away, Napoleon's center at La Belle Alliance. A mile, or more, at the west of that point an old tree marks the French left. A mile east of Alliance, at Frechemont, is the French right. Just behind us, on Mt. St. Jean, is Wellington's center. Hougomont is his right. A mile to our left is Wellington's left at Papelot. A little in front of Wellington's line half way between St. Jean and Papelot, is La Haye Sainte, a cluster of farm buildings similar to Hougomont, where a bloody drama, like Hougomont's, was played on that summer day. Over across those fields to the east, and out of those woods, came Blücher, bringing succor to the almost broken duke. Behind us, from east to west, in front of Mt. St. Jean, runs the sunken road, now level with the plain, scraped to build this mound, into which Napoleon's cavalry plunged, in ignorance of the topography of the country—the front ranks forming a bridge over which those behind rode against the English squares. Thus we fought over the battle, in imagination, that beautiful summer afternoon.

We stand to-day on a battle-field greater than Waterloo. This whole world is a battle-field. Two immense armies, compared with which the hosts of Napoleon and Wellington were mere corporal's guards, are here contending fiercely for the mastery. Waterloo lasted from eleven in the morning till eight at night. This battle has been raging six thousand years. On one side are darkness, error, barbarism, superstition, ignorance, infidelity, intemperance, impurity, vice, sin, hell, Satan. On the other side are light, truth, civilization, enlightenment, knowledge, faith, temperance, chastity, virtue, holiness, heaven, God. The right of God's army holds Hougomont. That is the family. Satan has been trying for ages to annihilate truth and righteousness by capturing and destroying the family. That is one of the things which he is trying hard to accomplish now. The left of God's army is at La Haye Sainte. That means the Church. There some of the fiercest fighting has been going on, all through the ages. Satan knows that if he can capture and corrupt the Christian Church, the victory will be his all along the line. The center of the army of truth, virtue, civilization and righteousness rests at Mt. St. Jean. That means Calvary, the doctrine of the incarnation and vicarious atonement of Jesus Christ. If Satan can only destroy that great, central, pivotal truth, he knows that he will have the whole world in his power. So he hurls his heaviest battalions against Calvary and the cross of Christ, as Napoleon hurled his "Old Guard" against Mt. St. Jean. But the victory will surely be on the side of truth and right. As Napoleon could not pound to pieces the English squares, so Satan cannot crush the bristling, thundering flaming squares of God's eternal righteousness. I am here to tell you that the truth will conquer; sin will have its Waterloo. The time is near when error and infidelity and intemperance and sin of every kind will be trampled down and annihilated under the steel-shod cavalry of the wrath of Almighty God.

Blücher saved the day at Waterloo. Truth has her Blücher. He is coming yonder, in the east. I see the dust of his tramping hosts, rising above the tops of the trees. He will soon be in sight. His portrait is painted in the Book of Revelation. You will know him when he appears. He rides a white horse. " His eyes are as a flame of fire, and on his head are many crowns; and he has a name written that no man knoweth but he himself. And he is clothed with a vesture dipped in blood; and his name is called the " Word of God." Christ is that great Captain's name. On which side are you in this great conflict? You are not, you cannot be, neutral. You are on truth's side, or error's side—God's side, or Satan's side. I exhort you to get on God's side, that, when the battle ends, as soon it will, you may receive a crown of eternal life and reign with God for ever and ever.

III.
PARIS.

" We were in that city abiding certain days."—Acts, xvi. 12.

In this text "that city" really means Philippi, a Roman city in ancient Macedonia. But, using these words of inspiration merely as a motto for the present discourse, I venture to call "that city" the capital of France, and to read the text: "We were in *Paris* abiding certain days." If you ask how long we were abiding in Paris, I answer, four days and a half. We arrived there Wednesday, July 2, at five o'clock in the afternoon, after a railway journey of two hundred and twenty miles from Brussels, and left Monday morning, at eight o'clock. Four days and a half were too short a time to see Paris, and three-quarters of an hour are too short a time to describe Paris. But I will do the best I can.

Paris is the grandest and gayest and most beautiful city on the globe; with one exception, it is also the largest. It is situated in the northern part of the Republic of France, on both banks of the River Seine. The length of the river, as it winds about through the city, within the corporate limits, is seven miles, and it contains two islands, named the Island of the City and the Island of St. Louis. On the former of these, which is the larger of the two, the city was founded more than eighteen hundred years ago, and named Lutitia. From a little island village, inhabited by semi-savages, it has grown until now it covers thirty square miles of territory and has a population of nearly two and one-half million souls. Running entirely around the whole city, a distance of twenty-one miles, is a strong military wall of earth and masonry. Beyond the wall is a ditch, forty-eight feet wide, filled with water. Beyond the ditch are sixteen forts so placed as to command every approach to the city. Wall, ditch and forts together cost twenty-eight million dollars.

Paris contains many wonders. One of these is its beautiful, serpentine river. For miles and miles it is bordered and held in place by double walls of the most solid masonry, with a broad walk between the upper and lower walls, and is spanned by twenty-three bridges of the most substantial and graceful material and form. The river also affords a most convenient and delightful means of communication between the different parts of the city, by fairy-like boats, which are flying back and forth all the time, driven by steam.

Another of the wonders of Paris is its broad and magnificent avenues and streets, paved in the most scientific and thorough manner, cleaned almost as carefully as a parlor floor, and lined with large and stately buildings. As its third wonder I would name its public buildings and religious and memorial edifices—palaces, art-galleries, temples of music, halls of industry, marts of commerce, courts of justice, cathedrals, mausoleums, columns, towers, monuments and triumphal arches. In this respect Paris stands without a rival among the cities of the world. But its greatest wonder is the life which flows through its streets, and rolls around its palaces and dashes over its parks and gardens. What vivacity! what restlessness! what mirth! what gayety! what ecstasy of glee! The city on the Seine seems to enjoy one long festival, stretching through days and weeks and months and years and generations. And yet all is not joy. Paris is the gayest city in the world ; but it records more suicides than any other. Above all others Paris is the city of pleasure ; but its pleasure most often turns to pain, and its dance of dissipation most frequently becomes the dance of death. Of all cities Paris is most devoted to amusements ; but it is likewise the city in which there are the most sad and mournful scenes. Paris is Europe's greatest " center of civilization ;" but it is also the greatest focus of revolutions, plots and conspiracies.

Paris is indeed the most beautiful city in the world ; but truth compels me to add. it is the most wicked city in the world. On the surface all is fair and clean and solid and admirable. Just below there is very much which is bad and vile and rotten and loathsome. The one thing which is needed to make Paris a heaven on earth is the pure religion of Jesus Christ, as taught in our Holy Bible, in the hearts and lives of all her people.

At half-past eight o'clock, Thursday morning, we left our hotel, on the Rue de Saint Roch, on the north side of the Seine, and walked down to the Rue de Rivoli, which runs parallel to the River at a distance of about one-quarter of a mile. The Rue de Rivoli is one of the handsomest streets in Paris. It is one mile and three-quarters long. Between it and the river lie the Garden of the Tuileries and the Palace of the Louvre. The latter place was our objective point.

The Louvre was built for a royal palace. It is now

one of the largest and finest art galleries in the world. It is several stories high. Its architecture is grand and imposing. It contains one hundred and fifty magnificent halls. To merely walk through its rooms one must travel more than a mile and a half. It covers twenty acres of ground. It is crowded with the rarest and richest treasures of the most gifted painters and sculptors. The contents of its smallest and poorest room would more than buy all the art on the American continent.

We will enter. But first I will show you something on the outside. Do you see that beautiful arched window, overlooking the street, in the first story? They call that the window of Charles IX. The stones in that arch could tell you a tragic story, if they had a tongue. Three hundred years ago, and more, King Charles IX. lived in this palace. He had many thousand subjects called Huguenots. They were the most intelligent, virtuous and loyal people in all his realm. But he feared and hated them because they differed from him and their fellow countrymen in religion. Instigated by a woman, his mother, Catharine de Medicis, he planned their massacre. Their leaders and principal men were invited to Paris, and to this palace, to witness the marriage of the king's sister. A solemn pledge was given, and confirmed with an oath, that not a hair of their heads should be touched. They came. All was mirth and seeming friendship at the palace. At midnight the bell of the Church of St. Germain tolled in the festival of St. Bartholomew. That was the preconcerted signal for the massacre to begin. The assembled guards issued out of the court of this royal abode, and spread through the city, murdering every

Huguenot they could find. Till morning, and all the day long, the fiendish butchery continued, until the gutters of Paris actually flowed with blood, and the pavements were piled with corpses. From the capital the massacre spread through the kingdom. When no more Huguenots could be found the bloody carnival ceased ; but not till one hundred thousand of France's noblest sons and daughters had been slain.

Now what I have been coming to is this : In that very window King Charles, who had planned the massacre, sat, during a portion of St. Bartholomew's day, with his shot-gun in his hands, shooting Huguenots as they ran frightened through the street, trying to escape from their relentless persecutors. Why do I speak of such terrible crimes, committed far back in those barbarous generations? Because I want to ask you a question. If there is a hereafter—and no one in this house doubts that there is—where is the soul of that infamous monarch, who made a target of innocent men and women from that window? Is he in heaven? Could the angels get along with him there? Would you want to go to heaven, if such monsters of crime are made welcome in its palaces? Does not every principle of justice demand that they shall be punished for the deeds done in the body? If Charles IX, dying impenitent, has gone to heaven, is not God an accomplice with him in the murder of the Huguenots? I do not believe that any man could stand in front of the window of Charles IX. in the Louvre and read, or recall the story of the massacre of St. Bartholomew and then say : "I do not believe there is any such place as hell." If there is no hell, there ought to be one for the eternal imprisonment of the royal villain who sat in that window, with his shot-gun, three hundred and eighteen years ago, the twenty-fourth of last August.

I cannot tell you one hundreth part of what we saw in the Louvre. It contains two thousand pictures and acres of statues. Hour after hour we wandered through the successive chambers—through a paradise of art. As we could not closely study every picture, or even one in a hundred, we gave our time almost exclusively to the works of the great masters, such as Titian, Rubens, Raphael, Da Vinci, Paul Veronese and Murillo.

We saw seventy-five pictures by Rubens. Chief among them is a series of twenty-one, representing the life of Marie de Medicis, the wife of King Henry IV, and the mother of Louis XIII. Most of them are very large. Altogether they would suffice to carpet the entire floor of this room. I make that comparison, because it is convenient, although it seems almost a sin to think of putting such glorious creations of human genius to such an ignoble use. And then reflect that all that canvass was painted, not in coarse splashes but with delicate touch, by one man, whose works are scattered in rich profusion all over Europe. I cannot give you an adequate idea of the marvelous conception of these pictures, their gorgeous coloring and their perfection of detail. The life of a queenly woman is here depicted before the eye, more perfectly than you could read it in a hundred books.

One of the most celebrated pictures in the Louvre is Murillo's greatest work, sometimes called the "Immaculate Conception," and sometimes the "Assumption of the Virgin Mary." The artist got his idea from the twelfth chapter of Revelation, where the inspired dreamer saw a " woman clothed with the sun and the moon under her feet." You see an exquisitely pure and beautiful woman (the figure is as large as life) with long golden hair, wearing a robe of more than snowy whiteness and a mantle of such blue as no one but the great Spanish artist was able to paint. She is lifted up among the clouds far above the sin and sorrow of earth. She stands on a fleecy cloud, with one draped foot on the crescent moon. Her crimson-tinted, alabaster hands are laid upon her bosom. Her face beams with holy, heavenly joy. All around, above and below is a circle of cherubs—beautiful, glorified children—the flowers of heaven. Such is the Catholic conception of Mary, the Mother of God, the Queen of Angels the Empress of Heaven. Though you do not accept that idea, you cannot look at Murillo's great master-piece without feeling your soul lifted toward heaven and God. That picture cost more than one hundred thousand dollars when purchased for the Louvre ; millions could not buy it now.

I took great pleasure in looking at a painting, by the same artist, called " The Kitchen of the Angels." It represents the cooking department of a poor monastery in Spain, with a company of angels busily engaged in getting dinner for the monks. The story is that the monks were reduced almost to starvation. It was a time of general scarcity. What little they had had, they had given away to those whom they considered more needy than themselves. There was not a crust or a crumb left in their pantry. Filled with hunger, they went out in the morning to visit the sick, and comfort the sorrowing, and save the sinning. They forgot themselves in their solicitude for others.

Faint and weary, they returned to the monastery at the dinner hour, wondering who would feed them, but trusting that in some way the Lord would provide. When they came into the refectory, they found a sumptuous repast waiting for them, on the table, smoking hot. There was something about the food, or some celestial odor in the air, which told them that the angels had been their cooks.

That picture had a lesson for me. I tell it now to you. I hardly need to tell it. You know what it is. Trust in God. He has promised to take care of you, so long as you trust and obey him. Some of his promises are these: "Trust in the Lord and do good; so shalt thou dwell in the land, and verily thou shalt be fed;" "The Lord God is a sun and shield; the Lord will give grace and glory; no good thing will be withheld from them that walk uprightly;" "They that seek the Lord shall not want any good thing;" "My God shall supply all your need, according to his riches in glory by Christ Jesus;" "All things work together for good to them that love God." These words do not mean that you are to do nothing for yourself · that you are to lie in bed and expect the angels to come and make your fire, and provide and cook your breakfast. You are to do all you can for yourself. You are to be "diligent in business, serving the Lord." You are to do all you can for the glory of God and the good of humanity. After all that, and in all that, you are to leave all your care and anxiety with God and believe that he will see that you have everything you really need. That picture says to you, and to me; "Don't worry! Don't borrow trouble about the future! Don't have an anxious thought about your temporal affairs. If God cannot take care of you in any other way, he will send down a company of angels to cook your food, taken from unseen larders, and place it on your table.

We visited the department of sculpture. We saw the world's choicest treasures in marble and bronze. There is one statue which surpasses all the rest. One of the guide books says: "If the tourist has but one hour to devote to the Louvre, one-fourth should be given to the Venus de Milo." That is the name of the statue at which I now ask you to look. It is many hundred years old. No one knows the sculptor's name. It was found in the island of Melos. Some old Greek buried it two thousand years ago. The French government purchased it for twelve hundred dollars. As many millions could not buy it now. It is the draped figure of a beautiful woman, in snow-white marble, with both arms broken off. That is all it is. There is very little about it to describe. And yet it is so wondrously, so indescribably beautiful, that it commands the supremest admiration of every beholder.

Do you not wish that you had the power to take a block of shapeless marble and hew out of it a form of such exquisite beauty and perfection? You never can carve a Venus de Milo. There never will be another statue the equal of that. But I will tell you what you can do. There are many rough and ugly blocks of humanity lying all about us. By prayer and earnest effort, you may acquire such skill in Christian work that you can carve, out of these unpromising specimens, characters of such moral and spiritual beauty that they will shine in God's kingdom for ever and ever, the admiration of saints and angels. I want to say to every Sunday-School teacher, to every "King's Daughter," to every Young Men's Christian Association worker, to every Christian: You can be a spiritual artist if you will. To work on character is an infinitely higher profession than to work on marble. With the help of the divine artist, I am sure you can save, and beautify, and develop, and prepare for eternal glory, one soul, beside your own. The world is full of material, inviting your effort. God is full of power, promising you aid. Heaven is full of honors and crowns for those who aim at the highest usefulness here.

We must leave the Louvre. It is a perfect wilderness of art. All I ever saw before, in this department of human effort, is absolute nothingness in comparison. To attempt to describe what I saw would be like counting the drops of the ocean, or telling a blind man what a sun set is like.

Friday was Independence Day, in America. In Paris we were not aroused from our morning sleep by the blowing of tin-horns and the firing of artillery. The only indications that the "Glorious Fourth" had come were the display of American flags in many parts of the city and the wearing of such flags by members of our party, your speaker among the number.

One other thing I had almost forgotten. As we walked along the Rue de Rivoli that morning, thirty strong, on our way to the Pantheon, we astonished the natives by lustily singing, "Marching Through Georgia." That may not have been very genteel; but our hearts were so bubbling over with patriotism that we had to do something to relieve the strain. We were strangers in a strange land. Our citizenship was in America. We gloried in that citizenship. We were proud to display our country's flag, and sing our country's songs and let everybody know that we were Americans.

The Christian is a stranger in a strange land. He is a pilgrim here below. His home is on the other side the flood. His citizenship is in heaven. As he marches through this world, he should show his colors, everywhere, and all the time ; he should sing the songs of Zion ; he should be proud to have everybody know that he is a Christian.

The Pantheon is a very imposing edifice, standing about half a mile from the river, on the south side. Its shape is that of a Greek cross with equal arms 370 feet long and 276 wide, with a dome 272 feet high. It is embellished, within and without, with an immense number of statues ; and its interior walls are hung with paintings, mostly historical, of great size and beauty. We were led down into vast subterranean vaults, where are the tombs of many of the greatest men of France. We saw, among others, the sarcophagi of Victor Hugo, Voltaire and Rousseau. The remains of the last two—detested for their infidelity—have been removed, whither no one knows. The dust of the first will never be disturbed, because he feared God and loved his fellow men. Hugo and Voltaire are good illustrations of that Scripture text which says : "The memory of the just is blessed : but the name of the wicked shall rot." Men will bless the memory of Hugo, as long as the world endures, because his life was a blessing to mankind. Voltaire was a curse to the world as long as he lived, and his name will be a stench to the end of time.

In the afternoon, with the "stars and stripes" in

our button-holes, we went fourteen miles, by rail, to Versailles. Versailles is the name of a city, and of a palace and park, or garden. Louis XIV. created the town and built the palace at an enormous expense, as a summer residence for his court. Thirty-six thousand men and six thousand horses were employed at one time in forming the terraces of the garden, leveling the park and constructing a road to Paris, and an aqueduct a distance of thirty-one miles. The palace covers many acres. Its front is fourteen hundred feet long. A large part of the structure is an art gallery. We went through this. We could not do much more than glance at its hundreds on hundreds of pictures and statues. The latter are mainly representations of the kings and queens and princes and generals of France. The former embody the history of the French people. The pictures are simply magnificent. They bewilder and confuse. They are all large, and some of them immense. One, the "Taking of the Smalah of Abd el-Kader," is seventy feet long and sixteen feet high. There are many which are from thirty to fifty, by sixteen. There are literally miles on miles of pictures, any one of which would make a gallery in America.

From the gallery, or museum, we were taken through the royal apartments. They are so grand and superb that it is useless for me to attempt to describe them. I did not imagine that anything could exist so beautiful, this side of heaven. We saw the bedroom of the King, and the bed in which Louis XIV. died. The mural decorations are superb and the furniture is in tortoise shell and gilded bronze. As I glanced around the apartment—so much more gorgeous than anything that I had ever seen that my presence there almost seemed a dream—I said to myself: I wonder if the old tyrant, who sat on the throne of France seventy-two years and died in that bed, found death any less bitter for meeting his fate in such a beautiful place.

My friend, do you know what will make a death bed easy and a dying pillow soft? I will answer my question in the words of a hymn, whose author tried his own medicine nearly a hundred and fifty years ago :

"Jesus can make a dying bed
Feel soft as downy pillows are,
While on his breast I lean my head
And breathe my life out sweetly there."

Do not spend all your life building a palace and making a sumptuous bed in which to die. Live for Christ and humanity, though it be in poverty and obscurity. Then it will not matter when or where you die; for the Son of God will smooth your pillow and hold your fainting head, and the angels will transport your liberated spirit to its eternal home in the palace of heaven. "Let me die the death of the righteous, and let my last end be like his!" In this bedroom of Louis XIV. we saw a tapestry picture of the Grand Monarch, which cost one hundred and sixty thousand dollars.

We saw the private apartments of Marie Antoinette, from which she was dragged by a Parisian mob, after the death of several of her guards, to prison and execution. We saw the " Gallery of Mirrors," a splendid hall two hundred and forty feet long. On one side of the hall are seventeen large arched windows, commanding a beautiful view of the garden and its ornamental sheets of water. Opposite the windows are as many mirrors in gilded niches. The ceiling is covered with paintings of great richness and harmony. In this hall King William of Prussia was proclaimed Emperor of Germany in 1871, after the taking of Paris.

From the palace we went into the garden. I never imagined Paradise, before the fall, to be as beautiful as this place. The gardens were laid out by Le Notre, the most famous landscape-gardener of his time. They consist of groves and walks and terraces and flower-beds and lawns and pools and streams and fountains and statues. I never saw any thing of the kind before that would bear any comparison with this.

On the way back to Paris, with my bewildered brain full of the splendors and beauties which I had seen, I thought of another city and palace and garden, of which I had read in the oldest book in the world. The city has a circumference of six thousand miles. The wall which surrounds it is built of jasper. Each of its twelve gates is a solid pearl. Its streets are paved with transparent gold. Its garden has a crystal river of liquid life; and trees whose leaves are medicine for all diseases, and whose fruits ripen every month. Its light is the glory of God. Its palace is the house of him to whom all the beautiful things in this world are but the coarse embroidery of his foot-stool. I suppose what the old Book says about that place is only a faint picture of an infinitely glorious reality. That reality I am resolved to go and see. I am commissioned by my king, to invite every one of you to go with me. King Louis XIV. died in the palace of Versailles. You may become a king, and live and reign in the pa'ace of heaven, for ever and ever. What I saw at Versailles made me long to see Heaven. I pray that what I have told you about Versailles may make you long to see the city and palace which Christ has built for the sons and daughters of the Heavenly King.

Saturday morning we took a Seine boat near the Royal Bridge and went down the river, about three miles to the Exposition Grounds. The grounds and buildings are much superior to those of our "Centennial" at Philadelphia, unless it be that our buildings were larger. We did not go into any of the buildings except the Eifel Tower. That structure is so familiar to everybody, through the pictures seen and the newspaper articles read, that I need give no description. I will merely state that it is built almost entirely of iron; it has room on its several platforms for many thousands of people; it is the highest building ever erected; its summit is one thousand feet above the ground. We all went up to the second platform, three hundred and fifty feet from the ground. A few of the company (I was not one) went to the top. The ascent was made by elevators. It was a pleasure to know that we were riding in an American elevator.

I have since regretted that I did not go to the top of the Eifel Tower. I lost a magnificent view, I know, and, I must confess, I lost a measure of my self-respect. I had three poor excuses for not going any farther than the second stage—first, it would have cost me two francs, and I happened to have an economical streak that day; second, the wind was blowing very hard and I was afraid, my judgment told me the tower could not blow down, yet I was afraid; third, the ministerial brother with whom I was traveling did not wish to go. Please remember these flimsy excuses; I cannot call them reasons. I am ashamed to confess them; but I have an object in view.

God has built a tower on this earth, which vastly surpasses the Eifel Tower, in every respect. It is built on the "Rock of Ages." The material of which it is composed is as enduring as eternity. It is large enough to hold the whole human family, on each of its many platforms. It is lighted with the electric lamps of divine truth. Its elevator is operated by that omnipotent power which created the earth and sent the planets and suns swinging through infinite space. If you ask how high God's tower is, I answer: I do not know. But it reaches far above the dust, mists and clouds of this world. It is so high that from its upper stages you can see such sights as those who grovel on the earth never dreamed of. It is so high that from its top you can step off into Heaven, where God has his throne. God invites us all to ascend his tower. He commands us to step into his elevator and be lifted up out of sin, into holiness; up out of unrest, into peace; up out of sadness, into joy; up out of fear, into love; up out of our life, into his life; up out of earth, into heaven. The great majority of Christians have ascended no farther than the first platform. A large, but smaller number, are on the second platform. A few have gone far up, up, up into the high experiences of the love of God. The great world of irreligious people have got no nearer heaven and eternal life than to stand on the ground, under and around the tower, and look up. Where are you my friend?

To Christians on the lower platform of an unsatisfactory religious experience, and to the prayerless, unregenerated multitudes on the ground of no religious experience, I say: Look up! go up! Get into God's great, free, gospel elevator and let him lift you up into purity, and peace, and joy, and perfect love, and everlasting bliss! There are three foolish, flimsy excuses which you make—like mine—for stopping on the second platform of the Eifel tower. First, it will cost you a few paltry pennies of self-denial and the surrender of some darling sin. You cannot afford to give up the world to gain eternal life. Second, you are afraid. You do not know what you are afraid of. Your judgment tells you that there is nothing to fear. You are afraid to do right. Third, you do not go up because others stay down. You have not the courage to go to heaven alone. When it was too late, I was sorry that I did not go to the top of the Eifel Tower. When it is too late, when "the harvest is passed, the summer is ended, and" you "are not saved," you will most bitterly regret that you did not go up God's great gospel tower as high as omnipotence could lift you. "Now is the accepted time; now is the day of salvation."

I have only begun to show you Paris, and I must draw my discourse to a close. I wish I had time to take you to the Hotel des Invalides—or Soldier's Home, as we should call it—and show you, under the gilded dome of its chapel, the huge polished red granite, sixty-seven ton sarcophagus, which holds the remains of the great Napoleon.

You ought to visit the churches of Paris; especially the cathedral of Notre Dame, and see its grand interior, and climb one of its twin towers and stand—as I did—under its sixteen ton bell, which it takes eight men to ring.

It would delight you to go through the Palace of the Luxembourg, and its splendid gallery of modern art. I should like to tell you about the Parisian Sabbath, with its busy shops and hurrying crowds and military parades and almost empty churches, that you might learn to prize your American Sabbath and resolve to preserve it in its purity.

You must take one more walk with me, and then we will turn our backs on Paris. We went one afternoon along the Rue de Rivoli to the Place de la Concorde, where stands the Obelisk of Luxor, brought from Egypt in 1833. It stands on the very spot where the guillotine stood in the days of the French Revolution, where 2,800 persons were beheaded. At this spot begins the grandest avenue in the world—the Champs Elysées—which runs one mile and a third west to the Arc de Triomphe de l'Etoile. We walked the entire length of this avenue both ways. It is impossible for any description to do it justice. It is lined with lawns, trees, flower-beds, fountains, statues and palaces, and swarms with life and splendor. At about its middle stands the Palace of Industry—one of the first exposition buildings—on the south, and the Palais de l'Elysée—the residence of the President of the Republic—on the north. Near the western end of the avenue the church of the Madeleine looks down upon it from the north; and the Hotel des Invalides, across the river, from the south.

The Triumphal Arch, at the western terminus of the Champs Elysées, is a monument of Napoleon's victories. It is called Arc de Triomph de l'Etoile, or the Triumphal Arch of the Star, because it stands at a place where twelve beautiful streets radiate like the points of a star. It is a glorious structure, the largest of the kind in the world, one hundred and sixty feet high, one hundred and forty-six wide and seventy-two deep. It is covered with statues and carvings, and with the names of one hundred and forty-two battles, and of as many generals who fought under the banners of France.

As I stood there, that afternoon, under that magnificent arch, looking down to the Obelisk of Luxor and the Garden of Tuileries, I thought of another avenue which mortal feet have never trod. It runs from the farther bank of the River of Death up through the City of God. It is paved with crystaline gold. It is flanked with battlements of radiant pearl. It is lined with palaces of dazzling light—the many mansions of which Jesus has spoken in his word. On it walk immortals, clad in spotless white, with palms of victory and crowns of glory. On it ride the chariots of God, with wheels of lightning and horses of fire. At its farther end, spanning the eternities and rising into the immensities, stands a triumphal arch. It is covered with the names of the battles in which the Great Captain of our Salvation fought for us, and with the names of his soldiers who "overcame by the blood of the Lamb and the word of their testimony."

If, in this life, you are a good soldier of the cross, you will walk up that avenue; you will stand under that arch; you will see your name written there; you will receive a crown and a palm; a palace will be assigned to you; and, through eternity, you will live in perfect and ever-increasing glory and joy.

IV.

SWITZERLAND AND THE ALPS.

" Before the mountains were brought forth, or ever thou hadst formed the earth and the world, even from everlasting to everlasting, thou art God."– Psalm XC, 2.

In saying over this text in your minds I wish you to put heavy emphasis on the word *mountains*. "Before the *mountains* were brought forth, thou art God." I have chosen these words as the text of the present discourse, because I purpose to take you among the mountains, and we shall need some such language to express the religious emotions which will stir our hearts when we come to stand in the presence of those sublimest works of the Almighty.

We left Paris Monday morning, July 7, at eight o'clock, and were on the rail all day. For some hours our journey lay through a rich, rolling country exhibiting every evidence of great fertility and thorough tillage. The places where the train stopped were mostly small villages. The exceptions were Fontainbleau, where is a palace, once the favorite residence of Napoleon and Josephine, thirty-seven miles from Paris, and Dijon. At the latter place we changed cars and had to wait an hour. We employed the time in walking about the town. It is a place of considerable importance, having about forty thousand inhabitants, once the capital of the kingdom of Burgundy.

During the Franco-German war it suffered siege and bombardment. We visited a very old cathedral which we found undergoing extensive repairs; also a delightful public garden or park.

As we flew southward from Dijon, the country grew more hilly, and many elevations appeared crowned with ruins of castles. Still farther to the south, or south-east, we saw distant mountains —the Juras— the natural boundary between the republics of France and Switzerland, and the scenery grew decidedly romantic and picturesque.

At ten o'clock at night we got off the cars at the village of Vallorbes, in Switzerland, three hundred and one miles from Paris. We obtained comfortable quarters at a queer old tavern, where we found the strangest mixture of old things and new. For example, in our room we had no light but that of candles, but might have summoned a servant by ringing an electric bell. When we looked out of the window the next morning, we saw mountains all about us, and began to realize that we were getting into the region of the Alps. At seven o'clock we left for Lausanne, on Lake Geneva, twenty-nine miles from Vallorbes. As we flew onward, the scenery grew more rugged and the mountains more lofty.

Lausanne is a beautiful city of thirty thousand inhabitants. It is a great summer resort. It has many good educational institutions. It is famed as the place where Gibbon wrote his "History of the Decline and Fall of the Roman Empire," and Byron his "Prisoner of Chillon." We had no time to see the sights of Lausanne. Without delay we embarked on a beautiful steamer, called the "France," for the city of Geneva. We had a most delightful sail of twenty-nine miles.

The scenery, all the way, was surpassingly beautiful and grand. The best views were on the southern side. From the shore rose beautiful green slopes, sprinkled with farm-houses and villages, just behind which towered lofty mountain peaks and ranges.

Ere long we were in Geneva. Geneva is a beautiful city of fifty thousand inhabitants, situated on both banks of the Rhone, at the point where it issues out of the lake. Its industry is nearly confined to the manufacture of watches, jewelry and music-boxes. Geneva is interesting to our Presbyterian friends as the home of John Calvin, and to all English-speaking Protestants as the place where an important translation of the Holy Scriptures into our mother tongue was made. During the sixteenth century, so many religious refugees, from Italy, Spain, France and England, found a home within its walls that it was justly called the "Rome of Protestantism."

We had less than an hour in Geneva. A rail-road ride of twenty-six miles brought us to Cluses, a small town chiefly inhabited by watch-makers, 1590 feet above the level of the sea. I need not say that we saw splendid scenery on this route. We were all the time winding around among the mountains and along their slopes, the summits of the more distant ones being covered with snow. We kept flying from one side of the car to the other, according as this window or that presented the finer view.

At Cluses we took the diligence for Chamonix twenty-seven miles distant. This was a ride long to be remembered. Twenty-six of us rode in one large triple-decked coach, or diligence, drawn by five horses. Beside us there were the driver and two footmen—twenty-nine in all in one carriage. The road twisted around and around, ever up, up, up, in the midst of the grandest scenery I ever saw, for we were getting into the heart of the Alps. On both sides of the narrow valley rose cloud-piercing, snow-capped mountains, adorned on their rugged sides with frequent glaciers and water falls. We kept exclaiming: "Beautiful! splendid! grand! sublime! glorious!" till our language broke down, and we were actually weary of the grandeur of Nature's works. We had been visiting man's cathedrals and art-galleries. Now we were in God's all-glorious temple, beholding the works of his own infinite hands.

We did not reach Chamonix till after night had settled down upon us. My ministerial comrade and myself went immediately to the "Hotel de la Poste," and to rest, in as good beds as were ever made, in a large and elegant room. When we awoke, it was broad day-light, and the sun was streaming in at our windows. Though we did not know it, we were about to experience the greatest joy of our natural lives. Throwing open our windows towards the south, we saw the sublimest spectacle our eyes had ever beheld. Before us, as far as we could see from right to left, were the mountains of God, with snow-clad summits gleaming in the sun, so intensely bright that we could hardly endure to look. One stood king among his fellows. My first exclamation was: "glorious!" I never saw anything that so lifted me out of myself, and seemed to lift me above the world and almost into heaven, as those dazzling, sky-piercing mountains. Tears of wonder and joy burst from my eyes. My whole frame quivered with over-powering emotions. I was in an ecstasy of amazement and delight. We did not then suspect that we were looking at Mt.

Blanc. We were. That peak, which looked so near that we would have said that we could climb to its summit in an hour, was the king of the Alps—12,275 feet above where we stood, two and three-fourths of a mile above the sea and so distant that a man needs three days and two guides to climb to its brow and return. There stood Mt. Blanc, as he had stood since the morning of creation; and there we stood looking at him—two American travelers, praising God for the sight and for the brightest morning since our landing on European soil.

We were in the far-famed Vale of Chamonix, 3,445 feet above the level of the ocean. It is a charming place. The poets and painters have not exaggerated its charms. It is very fertile — supporting four thousand inhabitants — frequented in summer by thousands of travelers from all parts of the world and framed all around with mountains of indescribable grandeur.

My experience at Chamonix and in the "Hotel de la Poste" seems to me to symbolize that spiritual experience which we call conversion. The weather had been cloudy and damp ever since we landed at Antwerp. It had rained more or less every day. Much of the time, in Paris, it had poured. We reached Chamonix in the night. It was very dark when I went to sleep in the hotel. But Wednesday morning I suddenly found myself under a cloudless sky, in the most dazzling sunlight, face to face with the mountains of God lifting their summits—as it seemed—into the very heaven of heavens.

The natural man—the sinner—has been in spiritual darkness ever since he landed, out of the eternity past, upon these shores of time. If he has seen any thing, it has been dimly, as in a fog. Life has been to him one long rainy day. By and by he turns his face towards the highlands of divine illumination, the Switzerland of purity, love and truth. He studies that great guide-book and time-table—the Bible. He gets on board the gospel train. He starts for the sunny South. The mountains begin to appear, with shadows and blackness around their bases and some whiteness on their tops. The mountains get higher. The air grows purer. Heaven seems nearer. He gets into God's great diligence of prayer, drawn by heaven's white horses of faith. He ascends higher and higher. He thinks he is getting up into the better life, the real life, the life of God. But darkness comes down upon him. Not knowing where he is, and tempted to believe that there is no light and salvation for such a wretched sinner as he, he nevertheless throws himself, with all his weight, upon the divine mercy and promises, as the weary American tourist threw himself upon that bed in the "Hotel de la Poste." Then he rests, without any light or joy or consciousness of the divine presence. Morning comes He springs to his feet. By an act of faith he throws open the shutters of his soul. Instantly his whole being is flooded with light and joy and glory. Every cloud has vanished from his sky. He is in Chamonix's flowery vale of conscious salvation. All around him are the snow-white mountain peaks of God's unspeakable love; and towering above all the rest is the Mt. Blanc of perfect assurance that God loves him. He knows that all his sins are forgiven; that his name is written in heaven; that he is a new creature in Jesus Christ.

My friend, have you had that experience? Thousands have. It is for you. You can have it, if you will. You may never see the physical, Alpine Mt. Blanc; but, with the eyes of your soul, you may see the Mt. Blanc of the divine reconciliation, and know your sins forgiven.

I think I never saw anything so white as the snow on those Alpine peaks, flooded with the beams of the morning sun. As I looked and looked, and wondered and rejoiced, and turned away with dazzled, swimming eyes, I thought I could see a new force and beauty in that promise in Isaiah : "Though your sins be as scarlet they shall be *as white as snow*," and those words of the Psalmist, when he says to God : "Wash me and I shall be *whiter than snow*." What! can God wash my heart, naturally so sinful, and make it whiter than the snow on yonder far-off mountain summit? Yes! That is his word.

" *What* can wash away my sins ?
Nothing but the blood of Jesus."

The crimson blood of Calvary's Lamb, applied by faith to the heart of the vilest wretch that ever lived can wash it whiter than the whitest Alpine snow.

Wednesday morning we all armed ourselves with alpenstocks (sticks of wood about five feet long, pointed with sharp iron) and started for a large glacier, called the Mer de Glace. A hard climb of several hours brought us—some on foot and some on mules—to the Mer de Glace Hotel, 6,303 feet above the level of the sea. After a good rest, and a lunch of bread and chocolate, we went down, some hundreds of feet, to the edge of the glacier.

Do you know what a glacier is? Hours would be required to tell all about glaciers. A few sentences will give a general idea of their origin and nature.

On the tops of all mountains which rise far above the line of perpetual winter, snow accumulates in enormous quantities. Being unable to melt, it is gradually consolidated into ice, by pressure and cold, and begins to slide down the mountain side. As it moves slowly, but irresistibly, along it tears away masses of rock and breaks them into pieces, large and small. Some of these pieces it grinds into gravel, sand and powder; others it tosses right and left, forming rows of debris on both sides of the ice stream, called moraines. The middle of the glacier moves faster than the sides; the top moves faster than the bottom. Consequently the ice is split into numerous crevasses, and is heaved up into ridges and hillocks and peaks. The lower portions of the glacier yield to the melting influences of the sun and the rain, supplying the crevasses with roaring torrents, and sending out streams, large and small, into the valleys below. The glacier terminates exactly where the melting of the ice equals the supply pushed down from the snow reservoirs of the higher mountains. The largest glaciers are about thirty miles long, and two or three miles wide, in their widest places. Their rate of motion varies from summer to winter and from the middle to the sides. It may be roughly estimated at about one inch an hour.

So you see a glacier may be called a river of ice. The name of the one which we visited means a *sea* of ice. It seemed to me like a stormy sea suddenly frozen, and cleft with frequent crevasses of unknown depth.

It was with considerable trembling that I ventured upon its surface. I was told that I must have woolen socks over my boots to keep from slipping, and a pair was offered me, for money, at the hotel. But I refused them, and, grasping my alpenstock with both hands, and heading the party, I launched out from the shore. At the first dive, I came near sliding off into a crevasse. Walking, sliding, creeping, crawling, running, jumping, I made my way towards the western bank. On the edge of numerous crevasses I paused, and, leaning on my alpenstock, looked far down into the icy depths and listened to the thundering torrent, and wondered what would become of my corpse if I should tumble in. I thought of friends far away and said to myself: If I can help it, I will not die here like a fly in a pitcher of ice water. After about twenty minutes of the sharpest looking and most intense straining of nerves and the most rigorous exercise of muscles that I ever experienced, I found myself on solid ground, shouting back to my comrades who were half way across.

That glacier had two lessons for me. The first was a lesson of *trust in the word of God*. Without my alpenstock, with its tough shaft supporting my weight, and its iron point sticking into the ice, I could never have crossed the Mer de Glace. Had I attempted the passage, unarmed, my body would now be sleeping in the sands of some river, or in the mysterious depth of that great crystal tomb.

What his alpenstock is to the tourist, crossing a glacier, the Bible is to the Christian, traversing this unfriendly world. The glacier—cold, rough, slippery, and seamed with frequent crevasses—represents the world through which the Christian must journey to get to heaven. The world is cold enough to freeze all spiritual life. It is rough enough to discourage the stoutest heart. It is so slippery that no man can stand in his own strength. It has deep crevasses of temptations into which the most wary and sure-footed are in danger of falling. It has roaring torrents of lust and sin, fierce enough to sweep away the strongest wills. No man can cross this glacier, called the world, without the alpenstock of God's word—the Holy Bible. Leaning on that, by daily study and meditation, and thrusting some sharp-pointed text into every difficulty of life, you may climb every hillock, and steer your feet down every incline, and leap over every crevasse, and joyously reach the shore of eternal deliverance. He who journeys through this world carefully, thoughtfully, leaning, with intellect and heart, with study and obedience, on God's Holy Bible, will be sure of a happy and successful life.

The other lesson which Mer de Glace taught me was *the power of combined units.* The glacier is one of the mightiest manifestations of power which this world contains. It tears away the stony flesh of old mother earth. It grinds the hardest rocks into powder. It strews valleys with the wreck of mountains. It makes and unmakes lakes and rivers at will. It has produced nearly all the soil which gives food to man and beast. Nothing can stay its course. And yet, the glacier is nothing but a vast collection of snow-flakes, combined and consolidated. There is no power, which we can perceive, in a single snow-flake. But there is power, almost infinite, when enough snow-flakes combine to form a glacier.

One man or woman, acting alone, is much like a snow-flake. One good man, or woman, acting alone, can never reform the world and break ancient evils into pieces. But if all the good people in the world would combine and consolidate, nothing could resist their onward push ; Satan's kingdom would be torn down, and evil customs and institutions would be ground into gravel and sand. If all Christians would forget their differences and unite their forces, they could pulverize the rum traffic and reduce intemperance to fine dust which the wind could drive away. When will the scattered snow-flakes of sectarian and partisan division and weakness unite in the irresistible glacier of the world's salvation? Such thoughts passed through my brain, as I stood on the western moraine of the Mer de Glace, leaning on my alpenstock, waiting for the rest of the party to come up.

We went down into the valley on the glacier's western side. The descent was by a narrow path, on the face of the mountain. One part of the path is called the "Mauvais Pas," or the "Bad Path." For half a mile we had to walk on the narrowest imaginable ledge, with the mountain rising almost perpendicularly above our heads and falling away a thousand feet below. The only way we could get along at all was by clinging to an iron railing fastened to the rock. All our company traversed the Bad Path in safety and reached the valley, where a smooth high-way brought us to the village of Chamonix and to our hotel.

We saw many curious sights on the road. We saw women working in the fields, and tugging along the way with hugh bundles of wood, or hay, on their heads. Wherever we went in Europe, we saw women toiling in the fields and streets, doing the work which in this country belongs to the men. Why are American women exempt from severe out-door labor? I think it is because a purer and more advanced type of Christianity prevails here than in Europe. If Christ, the Virgin's son, the friend of woman, should be driven out of America, heavier burdens would immediately be piled on woman's shoulders ; and, ere long, she would become the beast of burden and slave, which she now is in all non-christian and heathen lands.

Woman owes more than man to the Christian religion. Every man ought to be a Christian. Every woman is under double obligation to give her heart to Jesus Christ. The greatest monster of ingratitude and wickedness in the world is a female infidel.

We saw other unusual sights that afternoon. We saw men cutting grass with broad scythes, about two and a half feet long, fastened to straight handles. We saw women washing in big troughs, made for the purpose, with water running through, rubbing the garments on smooth boards laid across the troughs. We saw a woman driving three cows, holding a basket of yarn on her left arm, and knitting with all her might. Everybody has to work in that country, and work all the time. We saw great numbers of cows feeding by the road-side and in the fields, each animal wearing a bell suspended to her neck by means of a leather strap about six inches wide. Through all the valley, the evening air was resonant with the music of these tinkling bells. We passed frequent crucifixes and crosses, where inscriptions invite the passer by to stop and pray. Thus we reached our hotel, after an excursion twelve miles long.

Before we leave Chamonix, I must show you a beautiful work of art. Standing in an open space near our hotel, is a piece of sculpture, in bronze, on a granite base, representing a French scientist, named Saussure, and an Alpine guide, named Balmat. It commemorates the first ascension of Mt. Blanc ever made, effected by these two men in 1787. It was erected just one hundred years after that event. Saussure stands, in tourist's costume, with spy-glass and alpenstock, eagerly looking towards the mountain top. On his face is an expression of noble ambition and high resolve. At his right hand stands Balmat, the guide, with a coil of rope around his waist, ready to start, looking as though he could almost fly. His left hand is on Saussure's shoulder. With the index finger of his upraised right hand he points straight at Mt. Blanc's snow-capped peak. Summer and winter, in sunshine and fog, by day and by night, whenever there is sufficient light to reveal them, that finger and those faces tell the visitor where the king of mountains is standing. I think there is more inspiration in that statue than in any other that I ever saw. I could not look at it—and I studied it long and earnestly, many times—without feeling a strong desire to rise into a higher plane of intellectual and spiritual living. It always said to my soul: "Up! up! Attempt something high and great for God and humanity!"

What Balmat was to Saussure, and what Balmat's statue is to every beholder, some men, whom we know, are to all among whom they live. I could give you the name of such a man. He can always be depended upon. His integrity is as unbending as a statue of bronze. He could no more do a mean and dishonest act than the sun could reverse its course through the heavens. He is always the same, in all seasons of the year, and all days of the week. He is always in his place, at church, and everywhere else. He is always ready to give a reason for the hope that is in him. His testimony is always straight and clear for God and the truth. By word and act, by profession and living, he points the way to the mountain-top of holiness, to the gate of heaven. He is not like a church-spire always pointing and never going. Like Balmat, the Alpine guide, he points and goes. He points and leads the way.

Multitudes of men and women—some of them church-members too—are nothing but noisy weather-cocks, rattling in the breeze and whirling with the wind. My friend, why not stand for truth and righteousness, like a statue of bronze? Why not be a high-souled guide, leading multitudes to the Alpine summits of purity and eternal life? You can, if you are so determined, by the grace of God.

Thursday our whole company were to go to Martigny. There are two passes out of one valley into the other. One is called Tete Noire; and the other Col de Balme. Fifteen of the party—myself being one - decided to take the latter. That meant a walk of fifteen miles. The others chose the other route and to ride in carriages. We set out at quarter to eight in the morning, and all rode together —that is, in the same procession—seven miles to Argentiere. Then ten women and five men began to climb. It was climbing too, much of the way of the most difficult kind. At eleven forty, after two hours of "*excelsior*,' we reached the Col de Balme, 7,225 feet above the level of the sea, and 3,262 feet above the place where our climb began.

We were weary; but felt amply repaid for our effort by the magnificent views we had of the grandest mountain scenery. We found a *chalet*, into which we hurried to escape a storm which we saw approaching

Soon the storm of wind and rain and hail burst

upon the house. We were in the very midst of the cloud. The rain and hail did not have to fall, unless it might be a few inches; they were manufactured right on the spot. We were in the very nursery of the Storm King, where his demons are born and trained for their work of destruction. The throne of old Jupiter Tonans was just in front of the door of the *chalet*. It was terrific, yet delightful—an experience never to be forgotten. There, nearly a thousand feet higher than the summit of Mt. Washington in New Hampshire, we warmed ourselves at a good fire and ate a refreshing lunch of bread, butter, cheese, honey and hot milk. After lunch some of us went out and had a game of snow-balling. Think of that! snow-balling the tenth day of July!

Then we started down the mountain, on the eastern side. The ascent had been hard for heart and lungs. The descent was hard for feet and legs. But we had many delightful experiences to relieve the tedium. We had found flowers all the way long. That afternoon we found a field of many acres, on the mountain side, which was one vast bed of wild blossoms of many kinds. On that, and the previous day, one of our ladies collected more than seventy different varieties of wild flowers. A rapid descent of an hour and a half, and an ascent of three-quarters of an hour, brought us to the spot where we could see the beautiful Rhone valley, and the city of Martigny, lying two thousand feet below us. Two hours of further effort brought us, greatly exhausted, to the Hotel de Mount Blanc in Martigny. An old guide, whom we met at the hotel, told us that no lady had ever before made that journey in one day. That made us proud of our nine American women.

Friday morning we left Martigny and went by rail, one hundred and forty-three miles to Visp. There we changed to a new road up the Visp valley toward Zermatt. After riding six miles, as far as the road had been finished, we walked—a part rode on mules—from Stalden to St. Nicholas. The day was hot, the road rough, and we became very weary. After dinner we rode in carriages twelve miles to Zermatt, when we took rooms at the Hotel Zermatterhoff. Zermatt is a little village with many large hotels, 5,315 feet above the level of the sea, at the foot of the far-famed Matterhorn.. The place owes all its importance to its location. Scores of thousands of visitors come here every summer to see the Matterhorn and its glaciers.

There is nothing in nature that suggests God, as much as mountain scenery. It does not seem to me that a man, born and living among the Alps, could possibly be an atheist. If he should stand, as I did that Wednesday morning, looking at Mt. Blanc, from the hotel window at Chamonix, and should say, "there is no God," it seems as though all the mountains which shut in that valley would answer back, in one thundering chorus "There is a God. You are a fool, if you say there is no God who created us."

The one attribute of deity which, above all others, the mountains proclaim is his eternity. God is eternal. He never began to be ; he will never cease to be. Can you comprehend that thought? Your existence is a straight line, beginning back there a little distance. God's existence is a circle, without beginning or end. That may be hard to believe. But it is harder to believe in the eternity of matter ; and one or the other must be the truth. We all believe in the eternity of God. We can all repeat the Old Testament text: "Before the mountains were brought forth or even thou hadst formed the earth or the world, even from everlasting to everlasting, thou art God."

Another truth I want to leave with every one of you. Before every human being stretches an eternity of existence. We began to be; but we shall never cease to be. Now comes the awfully solemn question: Where do you expect to spend eternity? Eternity! eternity! eternity! If all the Alps were ground up into separate grains of sand, and an immortal bird should come once in a million years and carry away a single grain, the last grain would at length disappear. At that far-off point, the lifetime of your soul would be just commenced.

Where do you expect to be when the glaciers have worn away the loftiest mountains, and the moon has become tired of shining, and the sun is nothing but a blackened cinder? You will be somewhere, in bliss or woe, in glory or shame. Where will you be? God has put you in this world on purpose that you may prepare for eternity. Are you using your God-given powers and opportunities in such a way as makes it probable that you will have a happy eternity? Eternity! eternity! Where do you expect to spend eternity?

V.

OUT OF SWITZERLAND INTO ITALY.

"*And an highway shall be there, and a way, and it shall be called the way of holiness; the unclean shall not pass over it; but it shall be for those: the wayfaring men, though fools, shall not err therein.*"—Isaiah xxxv., 8.

I have chosen this verse as the text of the evening because it speaks of a highway, a road, and I wish to tell you about a wonderful road by which I went out of Switzerland into Italy. But we are not quite ready to leave the region of the Alps. Before you start for Italy, you must see more of the strange and wonderful sights of Switzerland.

At the close of last Sunday evening's discourse we were at Zermatt. We reached that place Friday evening, July 12. Zermatt is a little village of about five hundred inhabitants, 5,315 feet above the level of the sea. It lies in a green valley with pine-clad slopes, above which rise lofty, snow-crowned mountains. In no other place is the traveler so completely admitted into the heart of the Alpine world—into the very sanctuary of the "Spirit of the Alps." Zermatt consists of a few narrow, winding streets, a dozen little stores, a post-office, a bank, a Roman Catholic church, an English church, a few scores of small, mean dwellings, and three large and elegant hotels. The hotels all belong to one man; and all have the same rates for entertainment. We selected the one which bears the name Zermatterhoff. Its piazzas and windows, on the south and west, command a magnificent view of the huge rock-pyramid of the far-famed Matterhorn. To see the Matterhorn and its glaciers, we had come to Zermatt. We merely glanced at the mountain that night. We were too hungry and weary to care for anything but food and bed. We could see more beauty in a good dinner than in a dozen of the highest mountains ; more satisfaction in a soft pillow than in a hundred of the roughest glaciers. We went to bed, intending to spend Saturday in climbing toward the summit of the Matterhorn, and in visiting one or more of the many glaciers which adorn its rugged sides. But when we awoke, in the morning, it was raining, and a dense fog filled all the air so that we could not see a mountain or anything else. We were greatly disappointed. However, we concluded that the foul weather was a blessing sent to compel us to take needed rest. We spent the day in writing, reading and roaming through the village. We rummaged every store and examined all the curious things exposed for sale. Our admiration was greatly excited by an immense variety of elegant carvings in wood, for which the Swiss are famous throughout the world. We purchased a few of the smaller and cheaper articles, and coveted—I trust in no wicked spirit—a multitude of the larger and more expensive ones.

Sunday morning dawned clear and bright, though cold ; and the Matterhorn stood exposed, in all his majesty, with a mantle of fresh snow thrown over his shoulders. That dark, foggy, rainy Saturday, that would not let us see the mountain which we had traveled long, weary miles on purpose to see, had a lesson for me, which I will tell to you. It was a lesson of *faith* and *trust*. Though we could not see the mountain, we knew it was there ; and we firmly believed that we should see it, if we only waited long enough. The most faithful Christian experiences many dark days in the course of his journey through this world. Though he may have been delivered, once for all, from the darkness of sin and guilt, he never will be wholly delivered, in this life, from the darkness of temptation and sorrow and mental depression and physical infirmity. He must expect to see some gloomy, foggy, rainy days. If he is what and where he ought to be, he lives all the time in the Zermatt of pardon and salvation, right at the base of the snow-clad Matterhorn of divine love and power and protection. Sometimes, for days and weeks and months, not a drop of rain falls, not a cloud obscures the sky, not a streak of mist darkens the landscape. He can see the mountain all the time. He feels the presence of God. He is conscious of the divine favor. He can " read his title clear to mansions in the skies." Satan seems to be dead. No temptation vexes his soul. His heart is filled with peace and joy. By and by the weather changes. Darkness gathers all about him. The conscious presence of God is withdrawn. Fierce temptations assail his soul. He is tempted to believe that God has forsaken him ; or that there is no God, who cares for human creatures. A terrible feeling of depression comes upon him, driving all joyous emotions from his breast. Perhaps, to make the darkness still blacker, some overwhelming sorrow comes upon him, and the tempter hisses in his ear, " God has abandoned you, God hates you ; curse God and die." I have given you an extreme case, perhaps ; but every Christian in this house has seen such days of darkness, if not quite so dark. You remember the story of Job. He had enjoyed a long period of uninterrupted prosperity. He had lived for years where he could see the dazzling summit of the mountain of God's special love and favor. He was loaded down with temporal and spiritual blessings. He owned seven thousand sheep, and three thousand camels, and five hundred yoke of oxen. He was the richest man in all that country. He had seven sons and three daughters. Hosts of friends thronged around him. He possessed everything that heart could desire.

But there came a terribly stormy day. The mountain of God's presence was completely hidden. All his property was swept away. They told him that all his children were dead. A filthy and painful disease seized his body. His friends turned against him. And even his wife looked upon him with hatred and contempt. That was the darkest and most stormy day ever put on record. And yet the mountain of God's love and protection was there, if Job could not see it. The old patriarch held fast his integrity. He would not give up his trust in the Almighty. In the beginning of his troubles he said : "The Lord gave, and the Lord hath taken away ; blessed be the name of the Lord." When the darkness of his sorrow was blackest, he exclaimed : "Though he slay me, yet will I trust in him ! " He held on ; he waited ; he trusted in the Invisible. By and by the storm ceased ; the darkness passed away. The mountain was there. God was there. A brighter day shone upon the man of Uz than he had ever seen before.

What do you do, what ought you to do, my Christian friend, when the darkness of temptation, or sorrow, or mental depression, or physical weakness comes upon you, so that you can see nothing and feel nothing of the care and love of God? You ought to do what we, American tourists, did that rainy day at Zermatt. You ought to rest and wait— wait till the storm and darkness are over. You ought to say, "The mountain is there, just the same as though I could see it. God loves me, just the same as though I could feel it. As the mountains are round about Zermatt, so the Lord is round about his people from henceforth, even for ever."

We needed that rainy day at Zermatt. It was a blessing to us. In the developement of our character we all need rainy days as well as days of sunshine. There is much beauty and truth in Longfellow's little poem "The Rainy Day:"

"The day is cold, and dark, and dreary;
It rains, and the wind is never weary;
The vine still clings to the mouldering wall,
But at every gust the dead leaves fall,
And the day is dark and dreary.

My life is cold, and dark, and dreary;
It rains, and the wind is never weary;
My thoughts still cling to the mouldering past,
But the hopes of youth fall thick in the blast,
And the days are dark and dreary.

Be still, sad heart! and cease repining;
Behind the clouds is the sun still shining;
Thy fate is the common fate of all,
Into each life some rain must fall,
Some days must be dark and dreary."

How did we spend that bright Sunday at Zermatt after the rainy Saturday? Some of the company, who had left their religion on the other side of the ocean, went up on the mountain side to see the glacier which the rain hindered us from seeing the day before.

The rest of us went to church. In the morning we went to the Episcopalian Church; in the afternoon we went to the Catholic Church. There was no one among us who belonged to either of these communions. But we acted upon this principle: Go to church somewhere. On God's day, go to God's house. If you cannot find the church which you consider the best for you, go to the next best. Do not brand yourself a *heathen* by refusing to worship anywhere. Go to some place of worship every Sabbath day. When not at church, I spent most of that day sitting on the veranda of the hotel, or at one of the windows, with my eyes fastened on the mountain top. The sight was fascinating, and I could not get enough of its beauty and grandeur. In the German language it is called the Matterhorn; in the French Mt. Cervin. It has an altitude of 14,825 feet above the level of the sea, and 9,510 above Zermatt. Mt. Blanc surpasses it by 905 feet.

Come and stand with me and look at this monarch of the Alps. At our right is a long mountain ridge, edged with snow, running northward beyond our vision. On our left is a line of snow-crowned peaks. In front is a third mountain spine, stretching across, with ravines between it and its companion ranges. Its upper portions are white with snow, while its lower parts are black with forests and rocks. Out of the top and back part of that cross ridge, the Matterhorn shoots up toward the sky. It seems to terminate in a sharp point. It curves a little toward the east. Its shape is much like that of the horns of a yearling animal of the bovine species. For a distance of four thousand feet down from its apex, it is nothing but bare rock. I mean, bare of soil and trees. It is always covered with snow. To-day it wears a fresh mantle of whiteness, which it received yesterday, while we were getting rain.

The Matterhorn is exceedingly difficult of ascent. Over yonder, close under the walls of that little Catholic church repose the remains of two Englishmen who lost their lives up on that slippery peak, on the fourteenth day of July, 1865. They belonged to a party of seven—four tourists and three guides. They succeeded in gaining the summit, and proudly stood there, the first human beings who had ever looked down from that solitude. On the descent, as they were creeping along, fastened to the same rope, one of them lost his footing, not far from the top, and, with three others, was precipitated, down the almost perpendicular face of the mountain, four thousand feet. The breaking of the rope saved the lives of one tourist and two guides.

Since then the way has been made less difficult, by blasting the rock at the most dangerous points and by attaching ropes and iron rods. And yet lives are lost almost every summer, in scaling that throne of perpetual winter. Would you like to attempt the ascent? If you have a clear head, steady nerves, a strong heart, sound lungs, tough muscles and an iron will, you may. If you lack any one of these, to undertake to climb the Matterhorn would be certain death. If you go, you must secure two or three trusty and experienced guides ; you must expect to be gone two days, at least ; and, even in the midst of summer, you must take the risk of encountering storms of wind and snow and ice, such as you never dreamed of down here where the Creator intended you to live. If you were as determined to gain heaven as some men have been to reach the summit of that mountain, and would dare and endure as much as they, I should know that eternal life would be yours.

Going to heaven is much like going to the top of the Matterhorn. In both cases you must climb; in both cases, you must have a guide; in both cases, you must be fastened to your companions in toil and danger. The guide is Jesus Christ, who, centuries ago, went up and blasted the rocks, and hewed out a path, and fastened cables and rods, and stained the snow with his blood. He has come down, and offers his services to lead you to the very summit of glory and immortality. Some men try to climb to heaven without the Guide. They all perish in the attempt; for Jesus says: "I am the way and the truth, and the life: no man cometh unto the Father, but by me." When men scale the Matterhorn, they go in companies, all fastened to one stout rope, so that, if one falls, the others can hold him up. Christians climbing toward heaven must be fastened together with the rope of common church-membership, so that the strength of all is the strength of every one.

"Blest be the tie that binds
Our hearts in Christian love."

Some men try to scale heaven alone, without the help of the Church. They may succeed; but where one gains the summit, a hundred fall and perish by the way. We all need the rope, the Church. We all must have Christ, the Guide. There is one striking point of dissimilarity between climbing that Alpine peak and climbing the mountain of holiness and heaven. In a majority of cases, to attempt the former is certain death; resolutely to attempt the latter means eternal life.

Sunday evening, after dinner, at about six o'clock, I was in my room, in the fourth story of the hotel, when I heard some one running up stairs. He bounded up from floor to floor and from landing to landing, as a chamois would bound over the rocks, pursued by an Alpine hunter. As soon as his feet struck the last step, he yelled out in the most excited manner : " Come, quick ! quick ! quick ! the Alpine glow ! the Alpine glow ! " It was my room-mate. I knew what he meant. I was out of the room in a flash ; and down the stairs, and out in the open space in front of the house, in four flashes more. There was the Alpine glow, indeed, of which I had heard so much and never could comprehend. How shall I describe it ? The sun was out of sight behind the western mountains, but was shining on the snow-clad eastern peaks. The snow was no longer white. What its color was I cannot tell. It was not golden ; it was too red for that. It was not red ; it was too golden. It was a sort of mixture of the colors of the ruby. and the sunrise, and amber, and gold, and fire. It was a color which I never saw before—a color which no artist ever spread on his canvas, or mixed on his palette It was simply glorious. The artist who could paint an accurate picture of those mountains, as they then looked, would outrank Rubens and Murillo and Raphael.

The sensation produced on my mind was strange and unearthly. I thought of the time when Elisha was in Dothan, and the army of Syria came to arrest him, and God opened the eyes of the frightened servant of the prophet, and "he saw, and behold the mountain was full of horses and chariots of fire round about Elisha." It seemed to me that all the flaming cavalry of the army of heaven had encamped on those Alpine peaks. Then I thought : No, that is not it. That is not the army of heaven up there ; it is heaven itself. All heaven has come down. God's throne is there ; and all the angels and all the redeemed and glorified spirits of earth.

Of all visible things nothing ever made the heavenly world so real, and brought it so near to me, as that Alpine glow. In a few minutes it had faded away. But its impression will abide forever in my mind. The one great lesson which the Alpine glow had for me was : " Look up ! " In the valley we could not see the sun. It was evening. The shades of night were creeping over the ground. The gloom was thickening fast. But on the eastern mountain tops was a brightness greater than that of morn and noon. If we looked down, it was night. If we looked up, it was glorious day. So it is all through this world. If we look down, we see shadows, darkness, night. If we look down we see sorrow, discouragement, death. If we continually look down we shall sink into blank despair. But if we look up, the light of heaven, reflected from the mountain peaks of eternity, shines into our faces, and into our hearts. To every discouraged one, to every sorrowful one, to every sinful one I say : " Look up ! look up ! Yonder is the Alpine glow of eternal hope, and joy, and salvation."

Monday morning, July 14, we left Zermatt, at seven o'clock. Our objective point was Milan in Italy. Before us was a journey of one hundred and fifty-seven miles. First, we had to retrace our course northward, twenty-four miles, to Visp. In doing this we rode, in carriages, in the bright sun-light, under a perfectly cloudless sky, twelve miles to St. Nicholas. Then, with the exception of two or three ladies, we walked, six miles to Stalden. If you ask how the two or three ladies, who did not walk, got over the road, I answer: on the backs of mules. Coming and going, we saw scores of these animals, moving along the narrow, stony path, under huge burdens of trunks and boxes and bundles, or saddle-loads of living freight, the drivers trudging at their sides and continually urging them on with words and blows. This is the only way by which baggage and food, for tens of thousands of travelers, can reach the great hotels of Zermatt. Soon there will be a rail-road (we saw an army of Italians pushing it to completion) and the poor people are bitterly mourning because their mules will be useless, and their chief means of support will be cut off.

While we are taking our six miles' walk I shall have a good opportunity to tell you something about Switzerland and the people who live among the Alps. Switzerland is a federate republic much like our own, made of twenty-five states or cantons. Its law-making power is a Congress of two houses. The executive power is in the hands of a Council of seven, elected, for three years, by Congress. The president of the Council, elected from and by the Council for one year, is the President of the Republic. Four languages are spoken in Switzerland. Nearly three-fourths of the people speak German; a little less than one-fourth, French; about one hundred and fifty thousand out of nearly three millions, Italian; and only thirty-eight thousand, Roumansch. Fifty-nine per cent. of the inhabitants are Protestants; and forty-one per cent. Catholics. The capital of Switzerland is Berne. Its flag is a white Greek Cross in the center of a red field. The inhabitants of the mountainous portions of Switzerland are, for the most part, very poor. For a living they depend on their cows, and goats, and bees, and what little they can produce in the line of grain and vegetables. Wherever there is a patch of soil which can possibly be tilled, you see a cottage, in midst of grass, or grain, or garden-plants. You see houses hanging on the steep mountain slopes, in the most inaccessible places, and you wonder how any creature without wings could ever get up or down.

Alpine houses are of three kinds. Some are like our log houses, only they are built of squared timber. Some are built of a strong framework covered with planks. Some have a framework of wood, filled in with brick or stone. Frequently you will see a one-storied house, such as I have just described, standing on an under story of rough stones. The roofs are almost always covered with flat stones, of all sizes and shapes, piled on in many overlapping layers. Usually the cows sleep under the same roof as their owners; and, almost invariably, a large pile of manure lies immediately in front of the house. A common sight is a little barn, standing on the top of four posts, about six feet from the ground. You would laugh to see those people getting in hay. A man lies down on his face, with a wooden framework strapped to his shoulders. The women cover him all over with the fragrant fodder. Then they help him up; and you see a huge hay-cock walk to the barn, climb the stairs and disappear through the door. Peasant life among the Alps is one long, desperate struggle for existence. You ought to thank God that you were born under better skies.

From Stalden we rode by rail to Visp. At Visp we changed cars and rode eastward five miles, up the Rhone valley, to Brieg. Brieg is a little town. The only thing which gives it prominence is the fact that it is the northern terminus of the famous "Simplon Road," which runs southeast, one hundred and twenty-eight miles, to Milan, and ends at a triumphal arch of white marble, built as a fitting goal and monument of so grand a work of engineering skill.

We reached Brieg at half-past two. Very soon after I started, with four others of our party, and three strangers, in a coach drawn by five horses, to ascend the road. The others came on after us in similar conveyances. We had an exceedingly enjoyable ride. I wish I could paint it, and the scenery, in words. The road, already referred to, was constructed by order of the great Napoleon, in 1800 to 1806, to connect Italy with Switzerland and France. The ascent from Brieg to the summit of the pass is 4,345 feet, or an average of 290 feet to the mile. It winds around the mountains and along their almost perpendicular sides, ever up, up, up, along the verge of frightful precipices, across more than six hundred bridges of solid masonry, through many tunnels piercing the everlasting rock, past ten houses of refuge for sick and weary travelers, always in sight of snow-clad peaks, and, at the top of the pass, above the limit of perpetual snow.

The road, through its entire length, is thirty feet wide—wide enough for two teams to pass on the run —and as smooth and hard as the best city pavement, except possibly, some asphalt streets. It also has, on the precipice side, nearly all the way, a massive stone parapet, to keep carriages from running off, and, where that is wanting, large stone posts, six or eight feet apart. As we wound around the mountains, we could see the valley, far below; the summits, thousands of feet below; the glaciers, shining in the sun; scores of foaming cataracts, leaping and tumbling in white robes, or veils, down the rocks; and, over all, as perfect a dome of blue as was ever seen. It was a scene never to be forgotten and never to be adequately described. In one place we went through a long tunnel, or gallery, over which plunged a large cataract. Above our heads we could hear it pounding the rock, and, through a broad arch in the tunnel's rocky side, we could see the sun-light piercing the foaming waters with thousands of arrows painted in the rainbow's sevenfold glory.

Fifteen miles of such travel brought us to the top of the pass. There we paused in front of the Hospice. It is a large building with a lofty flight of steps, founded by Napoleon for the gratuitous entertainment of travelers, kept by a community of monks. As we sat in the carriage, we had the pleasure of seeing many of the benevolent monks; also a dozen or more of their noble St. Bernard dogs, employed in the winter to seek out and rescue freezing travelers lost in the snow.

A further ride of six miles, with an average downward grade of 289 feet to the mile, brought us to the Hotel Fletschhorn, in the little village of Simplon, where, in winter, they have eight months of continuous snow. Though it was the middle of summer, the night was very cold. But we found a good fire of wood, in an old-fashioned fire-place; a hot supper; and a soft warm bed; and were content.

Tuesday morning, at an early hour, we left Simplon. Two wagons bore the whole party. Both wagons and horses were decidedly superannuated. But they answered our purpose. The horses had nothing to do but to steer the vehicle. The driver had nothing to do but direct and hold up the horses with the reins, and manage the brake. The descent was steep, the road very winding and the rate of motion exceedingly swift. It was terrific, as we swept around the curves and along the brink of deep ravines; but I suppose there was no danger. For two or three miles we rode through a narrow pass, where there was just room for the road and a rapid river, with the mountain rising straight up for fifteen hundred feet or more. The scenery was bold, wild, startling.

Nine miles of rapid riding, and a descent of 2,245 feet, brought us to the Italian boundry line, marked by a large stone pillar. We were in sunny Italy and were glad; but would have been better pleased, if it had been a little less sunny. Ten miles more, through dust and heat, and we were at the pretty little city of Domodossola. At half-past two we took the train for Milan, eighty-seven miles distant.

The country through which our route lay is fertile and well cultivated, but not so beautiful as the fields of France. Everywhere the farmers were haying. All the grass is cut by hand. We did not see one mowing machine. We saw great numbers of oxen—most of them white—drawing the hay to the barns. The weather was very hot; and we were glad when we reached Milan, at nine o'clock. We drove directly to the "Hotel Biscione and Bellevue." On the way we passed along some of the best streets and got a flying view of the famous cathedral.

Do you remember the text of this discourse? I could not blame you, if you have forgotten every word. Here it is : "And an highway shall be there, and a way, and it shall be called the way of holiness; the unclean shall not pass over it ; but it shall be for those : the wayfaring men, though fools, shall not err therein." It seems to me that the "Simplon Road," on which I have been taking you, represents the way of holiness, the road to heaven, mentioned in the text. The Simplon Road was constructed by a great conqueror, Napoleon Bonaparte, for his soldiers to march on. The highway of holiness was built by that mighty Conqueror, who vanquished sin, death and hell, Jesus Christ, for the soldiers of the cross to march on to eternal victory and fadeless renown. The Simplon Road is so thoroughly built that it is likely to last many centuries to come. The road to Heaven was built for the ages, and will be open, in perfect condition, till the last traveler has gained his everlasting home. The Simplon Road is so smooth and even and perfect there is no possibility of losing it, or mistaking some other route for this. The way of gospel salvation is so plain that a fool— a man with half a mind—can find it and safely reach its end. The Simplon Road leads from cold, rugged Switzerland, to beautiful, fertile, sunny Italy. The way of holiness leads from this cold, barren, unfriendly world to the summer land of eternal sunshine and joy. The Simplon Road begins at the little village of Brieg, and ends in a triumphal arch in the magnificent city of Milan. The way of holiness begins at repentance and faith and ends under the arch of immortal glory in the jasper-walled, golden-paved city of God. The Simplon Road runs through the finest scenery, and affords constant pleasure to the surprised and delighted tourist. The way to Heaven is a delightful route. The only really happy people in the world are those who travel through the delightful scenery which lines its every mile and rod. Everything about the Simplon Road was designed for safety the perfect road-bed, the parapet, the bridges, the tunnels, the refuges, the Hospice, the monks, the dogs. The road to Heaven is safety itself. Millions of angels fly back and forth along its entire length to protect those who walk therein. All things work together for their good. So long as they keep in the way they are as safe as though they were already in Heaven.

Come friends, let us all set out for Heaven. This Christian way is the only road out of sin, and temptation and sorrow and death into purity and freedom and joy and eternal life. If you do not travel this way, you will by and by lie down in unending sorrow, shame and remorse

I have tried to make you know how we went out of Switzerland into Italy. I hope you will always remember the Simplon Road. I hope that whenever you think of the Simplon Road, you will also think of that other highway, the way of holiness, which leads to Heaven and unending joy.

VI.

MILAN.

"*The situation of this city is pleasant.*"—II Kings ii, 19.

These words were spoken of Jericho, the City of Palm Trees, more than twenty-seven hundred years ago. They are true to-day of the city of Milan in Italy.

Milan—called Milano in the musical language of the Italians—is the chief city of the province of Lombardy. It lies in the center of the great fertile plain of the river Po, between the Alps and the Apennines on the north and south respectively, and the Adriatic and Ligurian seas on the east and west. The mountains are in plain sight from the city, which sits like a diamond in the midst of a massive emerald, surrounded with a border of sparkling amethysts. Surely "the situation of this city is pleasant."

Milan is built in a circle, its largest church, the Cathedral, being the central point. The city is surrounded by a wall seven miles in circumference; and immediately outside the wall a fine, broad thoroughfare makes the circuit of the town. Piercing the wall are twelve gates, the most striking being the Porta Simpione, on the north-west, where the great Simplon Road comes in, here commemorated by a magnificent triumphal arch, finished fifty-four years ago.

The streets of Milan are, for the most part, broad and very clean. It has many magnificent buildings. It carries on extensive commerce through a system of canals which connect it with the river Adda on the east, the Po on the south, the Ticino on the west, and with the lakes Maggiore and Como on the north. It is celebrated for its extensive manufactories of silk and woolen goods, and gold and silver ware ; also for its large trade in books, pictures and music. Its population is about three hundred and twenty-five thousand.

Milan has had a very checkered history. Two hundred and twenty-two years before Christ it was seized by the Romans. Since then it has been held by Goths, Romans, Goths, Lombards, Franks, Germans, Spaniards, Austrians, French and Austrians. It has been a foot-ball, kicked about by the despots of Europe for centuries, with brief periods of peace and independence. In the year 1162 it was utterly destroyed by Frederick Barbarossa, Emperor of Germany. It was, however, speedily rebuilt ; and is now a splendid modern city, with a few old buildings, growing and prospering and rejoicing under the government of free and united Italy.

As you were told last Sunday evening, we arrived at Milan Tuesday, July 15, at nine o'clock in the evening, and went directly to the " Hotel Biscione and Bellevue." After supper, comrade and I went out, a few rods from the hotel, and viewed the Cathedral by moon-light and star-light. We walked around it, and looked up at its statue-crowned pinnacles, and ascended its platform of seven marble steps, and felt of its massive doors, and passed our hands over the Scripture scenes which adorn the lower part of its sculptured front, and thanked God that we had lived to see that miracle in stone, and almost wondered if it was not a dream that we were there.

Wednesday morning, when we looked out of our window, the first object which caught our eye was the Cathedral tower rising above the roofs of the intervening buildings. After breakfast we walked to the Cathedral square and took the horse-cars to the Church of Santa Maria della Grazie. We walked through the church and saw some very interesting frescoes. But our minds were on something better than all that. Adjoining the church is a convent bearing the same name. A fee of twenty cents a head purchased admission into the convent refectory, or dining-room. There, painted on the plastered wall, we saw what remains of Leonardo Da Vinci's greatest picture, the "Last Supper." The Cyclopedia Britannica calls it "the third most celebrated picture of the world." It was painted for the monks, to adorn the room where they took their meals, nearly four hundred years ago. It has suffered such shameful treatment that it has been almost ruined. First it was badly disfigured with smoke from the adjoining kitchen. Then a door was cut through it and the wall. Subsequently it was covered over with a thick coat of whitewash. Lastly it suffered all sorts of ill-usage from the convent being used as a barrack for cavalry. The whitewash and smoke have been removed so far as possible. The picture is but poorly preserved, but retains enough of its original perfection to command the admiration of the world.

The man who had charge of the room told us that

the painting is 8.7 meters long and 4.8 high, which would be about 34 by 18 feet. It has become the typical representation of the sacrament of Christ's Supper for the whole Christian world. I doubt not that every person in this congregation has seen a copy. The moment selected by the artist is just after the utterance of the words: "Verily, verily, I say unto you, that one of you shall betray me." The picture expresses the effect of the Saviour's sad statement on the different auditors. Next to Christ, on his right, is John. He has just been addressed by Peter, who makes signs to him that he should ask of whom the Lord spoke. John raises himself up to reply, with an expression of mingled sadness, sweetness and gentleness on his face. Peter, leaning from behind, is all fire and energy. Judas, next to Peter and John, looks dark and hateful. With his right hand he clutches a bag of money. Knowing full well of whom Jesus spoke, he starts back amazed, overturning the salt. Andrew, with his long gray beard, lifts up his hands, expressing the wonder of a simple-hearted old man. James the Less, behind Andrew, reaches over and lays his hand on the shoulder of Peter, while his face exclaims: "Can it be possible? Have we heard aright?" Bartholomew, at the end of the table, has risen from his seat. He leans forward with parted lips and a look of eager attention. He is impatient to hear more. On the left of our Saviour is James the Greater. His arms are outstretched, and he shrinks back, as though he would repel the thought. Thomas is behind James. He holds up his right hand threateningly as much as to say: "If there be such a wretch among us let him look out for himself."

Philip, young and handsome, lays his hand on his heart, as if to protest his innocence and love and truth. Matthew is next. He has more elegance than the rest, as though he belonged to a more educated class. He turns to Jude and points to our Saviour as if he would say : "Do you hear what he says?" Simon and Jude, old men, sit together at the end of the table. Jude expresses consternation ; Simon, with both hands outstretched, a painful anxiety.

Of course the center of attraction in this picture is Jesus. As you look in his face you see intellectual elevation, dignity, purity, and God-like majesty, suffused with the most profound sorrow. There is this difference between the Master's countenance and the countenances of his disciples. The former expresses sadness and yearning love ; the latter, surprise and indignation. The former shows calmness and repose; the latter, the greatest agitation : The former is divine ; the latter are nothing but the faces of good men. Between the best mere man who ever lived and our divine Christ, there is a difference almost infinite. The head of Christ, in that picture, is better preserved than any of the others, as though it had been miraculously saved from the sacrilegious destruction of twelve generations.

That famous old painting, which admiring thousands visit every month, represents the institution of the chief ceremony of the Christian religion. That ceremony is called by various names—the Lord's Supper, the Eucharist, the Holy Communion and the Mass. Different theories are held concerning its nature and meaning. Some say that the bread and wine, after having been duly consecrated by the officiating minister, are the actual flesh and blood of Christ. That is called transubstantiation. Others hold that Christ is really and truly present in the consecrated elements, although they are, as before, nothing but bread and wine. That is called consubstantiation. Others still affirm that the Lord's Supper is nothing but an act of commemoration, a visible sign of the body and blood of Christ. All Christians, however, except the Quakers, agree in this: the Lord's Supper is a sacrament; it was instituted by divine authority; it is binding on all believers; every person who comes to the Lord's table in the right condition of mind and heart meets his Saviour and receives a peculiar spiritual benefit.

My friend, if you have never been to the table of your adorable Redeemer, you do not know how many and how great blessings you have missed. My most earnest and sincere advice to you is to get into such a spiritual condition, by the help of God, that it will be right for you to come to the Holy Communion, and then come whenever you have the opportunity.

Do you see that dark, Satanic face at the table, three places from the Saviour's right hand? Has the presence of Judas at the Lord's table any meaning for you? It has for me. It means that I should not stay away from the Lord's table, or refuse to become a Christian, because there are hypocrites and bad men in the Church. One in twelve of Christ's apostles was a villain of the blackest dye. What wonder then that there are unworthy men among the professed followers of Jesus to-day. Their badness does not justify you in refusing to do good. Their treason against the divine Master does not excuse your disloyalty to him. Peter and John did not leave the table because Judas was there. I will not leave the Church because there may be Judases among its members. Whenever I am invited to the Holy Communion, I will go though I have to kneel at the very side of the Devil himself.

Leonardo da Vinci, the painter of that sublime picture, was one of the greatest men who ever lived. Of all mankind he seems to have the best right to be called a universal genius. He was the most accomplished painter of his generation, and one of the most accomplished of the world. He was a distinguished sculptor, architect, musician and writer. He was a great mechanician, engineer, anatomist, botanist, astronomer, chemist, geologist, geographer and explorer. It is the fashion in these days to say that it makes no difference who a man's father is, if he only has the right kind of a mother; that great men never transmit their greatness to their children; that great men always have great mothers. It may therefore be interesting to know that da Vinci's father was an accomplished lawyer, while his mother was from the ignorant, degraded, peasant class.

A very interesting story is told of the origin of da Vinci's most famous painting. In some way he had incurred the hatred of a powerful and wicked priest, who procured his arrest and condemnation to death. He was however promised life and liberty on condition that he would paint a satisfactory picture of the Last Supper on the wall of the refectory of the monastery where he was confined, within a certain time. He began the task, working for his life. The painting progressed. But could he finish it before the day, appointed for his execution in case of failure? The hateful old priest would come in every day and tauntingly tell him that he could not; that he must die. The night before the fatal day arrived. The picture was completed except the head of Christ and that of Judas. These the artist had attempted, again and again, but could not execute to his satisfaction. It was night. To-morrow morning he must die, unless he should receive help from Heaven. So he prayed long and earnestly. While at prayer he had a vision. Christ appeared to him, and he saw the Saviour's face. He arose and painted it, without difficulty, and to his entire satisfaction. Then he thought that nothing would be so suitable for the traitor Judas as the face of his enemy, the malignant priest. So he painted that, and his work was done. In the morning the picture was pronounced perfect, and the artist's life was spared.

So that picture teaches a lesson about prayer. It teaches us that God hears and answers prayer, as the Bible declares, and that we may pray for temporal as well as spiritual blessings. Prayer is the mightiest agency in the universe. It moves the Almighty hand that moves the world. It has not lost one ounce of its power since the first man offered the first petition. God was just as able and willing to answer prayer in Da Vinci's time as in Elijah's. He is just as able and willing to answer prayer in our time as in Da Vinci's. If there is anything which you think you need, either spiritual or temporal, ask God for it, with a firm faith in his goodness and power, and he will give you the very thing for which you ask, or something else, which his infinite wisdom sees will be better for you. Every day God answers prayer for temporal blessings.

There were three or four copies of the Last Supper in the room with the original. One was but just commenced. Another, less than half the size of the original, was offered us for the snug little sum of two thousand dollars.

From the Convent of Santa Maria della Grazie we went to the far-famed Cathedral. In attempting to describe it to you, I have on my hands a most difficult task. How can I describe the indescribable! How can I, with my poor gift of speech, do what has taxed the powers of the most gifted word-painters in the world! Since childhood I had longed to see the Cathedral of Milan. I wanted to see it more than any other building under the skies. My expectations had been raised very high. Would I be disappointed? I had read many glowing descriptions. Would I find the reality less glorious? I want to tell you, most emphatically, that I was not disappointed. When I came to see that magnificent temple with my own eyes, I found that the half had not been told.

With two exceptions it is the largest church in the world. St. Peter's at Rome is the largest; and the Cathedral of Saville, in Spain, stands second in size. The Milan Cathedral was one hundred and thirty-four years in building. It was completed, or nearly so, three hundred and ninety years ago. Under Napoleon Bonaparte much additional work was performed upon it; and further decorations and repairs are constantly going on. In shape, its ground plan is a Latin cross. Its length is 480 feet; and its width, 183. The tower, which rises from the junction of the arms of the cross, is 354 feet high. It covers as much ground as eighteen churches like this, put together. Looking at its exterior, you see nothing but white marble of the purest variety. It is a mountain of marble, carved into forms of the most exquisite beauty and grace. The roof is a forest of Gothic turrets, ninety-eight in number, each adorned with the most elaborate carvings, and with the most beautiful statues. The entire exterior is a vast assemblage of human forms in snow-white stone. Think of it! thirty-five hundred statues—that is the count—on the outside walls and roof of the church! Wherever there is any place to put a statue, there a statue is to be found. Every one of the side windows has eight large statues, on brackets, on the outside casing.

The whole structure is so cut with the artist's chisel that it looks more like frost-work than stone. Dazzling white in the noonday sun, and yet more beautiful in the silver light of the summer moon, it is a marvel of workmanship. The Milanese, with pardonable pride, regard it as the eighth wonder of the world. It is a piece of jeweler's work magnified a million times. It perfectly astonishes and bewilders the beholder, from the moment his eye rests upon it until he climbs to the highest attainable balcony of the tower, upon the summit of which stands the figure of Christ commanding the marvelous work to God.

The ascent to the roof is made by a broad, white marble staircase of 158 steps. We went up and walked about amid a forest of statues and an endless variety of pinnacles, flying-buttresses, carvings and tracery. From the marble roof, we went up the tower, and looked down upon the mighty fabric, and asked ourselves: "Are we in the world, or have we been transported to fairy land?" We went through the interior. The floor is a stone pavement of mosaic in marble of different colors. The ceiling is stone, supported by fifty-two stone columns, and is so delicately carved that, as you gaze up at it, it looks like the finest and richest lace. As you walk up and down the aisles, elegantly adorned chapels open on either side. The transepts are full of statues. In all, the interior contains 700 statues. One of the most striking is St. Bartholomew, the flayed martyr, with his skin thrown over his shoulder, the very marble seeming to quiver with the fidelity of the artist's chiseling.

We went down under the floor into a crypt of octagonal shape, about twenty-five feet in diameter. The walls of the room are solid silver, except the panels, which are tapestry of the most expensive kind. It is the tomb of St. Charles Borromeo, a Roman cardinal and Archbishop of Milan, who died in 1584, and was written among the saints in 1610. The attendant opened a silver casket, embossed with gold and precious stones, and showed us, through glass, the embalmed body of the archbishop, dressed in a robe of silver and gold, holding a jeweled staff. All we could see of the body itself was the head.

What kind of a man was this Bishop Borromeo whose memory is honored with such a splendid tomb? He was a man of great piety, virtue and benevolence. He lived for the good of those over whom he had been appointed a spiritual shepherd. Though occupying a position almost as high as the proudest monarch, he was not ashamed to go about doing good. In the year 1576 the city and diocese of Milan were visited by the plague, and tens of thousands died. The good Bishop went about giving directions for the care of the sick and burying the dead, shunning no danger and sparing no expense.

He also visited all the parishes where the contagion raged, distributing money, providing accommodations for the sick and reproving those priests who were cowardly and remiss in their duty. Worn out with these exhausting labors, he died at the early age of 46. The love and gratitude of his people built for him this costly and magnificent tomb. It was richly deserved.

You cannot expect such a burial ; but, better than that, you may so live that, when you die, your memory will be enshrined in the grateful, loving hearts of multitudes whom your good deeds have blessed and saved. A thousand times better than a silver coffin, in a marble mausoleum, is one soul which we have helped to win to Christ and everlasting life.

From the Cathedral, or Duomo, as the Italians call it, we went to the "Palace of Science and Art." There we saw an immense collection of paintings and statuary. Among the latter the chief attraction, to us, was a marble representation of Napoleon, in the costume of a Roman emperor, by Canova.

Among the works on canvas, we saw, with admiration, a large number of fine paintings by Luini. But the chief of the paintings were Rubens' Last Supper and Raphael's Sposalizio. Before the latter of these I wish to detain you for a few minutes. It is one of Raphael's best works. It is called the "Sposalizio." That word means marriage. It is the marriage of the Virgin Mary. It is not a very large picture ; but it is exceedingly vivid in its conception and rich in coloring, and every stroke of the brush shows the hand of a consummate master. The place of the marriage is one of the temple courts at Jerusalem. In the background is the central portion of the house of God—a fourteen-sided, two-storied, dome-roofed building. In the fore-ground is the bridal party. In the center, facing you, is the high-priest in gorgeous robes. At his right is the bride ; at his left, the groom. Joseph is in the act of putting the marriage ring on Mary's finger. The hand which she extends to receive the golden circle is the right, and not, as with us, the left. The bride looks young, modest and beautiful. At her right and a little advanced stands a beautiful matron, her mother. Just behind are four younger ladies. The groom is a noble, dignified man, considerably older than the bride. In his left hand he carries a slender wand, or cane. At his left are five young men, richly dressed. They are Mary's rejected suitors. Each carries a stick, like the one in Joseph's hand. The suitor in front is breaking his wand across his knee, in token of indignation or despair.

What, I asked myself, was the artist's purpose in painting this picture ? My conclusion was : to exalt and glorify the holy estate of matrimony. Next to the Church, marriage is the holiest institution on earth. It was "instituted of God in the time of man's innocency, signifying unto us the mystical union which is between Christ and his Church." It is one of God's best gifts to the human race. It is a blessing to man. It is an equal blessing to woman. Without it this world would be a sink of pollution, too loathsome to be named. There are many ways in which marriage is dishonored in these days. First, a set of so-called reformers are doing all they can to talk down and write down marriage. Not long ago they brought about, in the newspapers and magazines, a discussion of the question, "Is marriage a failure?" Some of them declare that marriage is a failure; that it is a curse and a slavery to woman; and that it ought to be abolished by law. This sowing is springing up in a harvest of evil all over the land. Marriage is dishonored by the prevalent instruction, given to girls and young ladies, that a life of independence in business, or a profession, is far nobler than marriage and the presidency of a home.

Marriage is dishonored by the easy divorce laws, and causeless divorces, which prevail in many of the states of this Union. The Bible names only one sufficient ground for annulling the marriage contract· That man or woman who contracts a second marriage, so-called, while a former companion is living, unless he or she be the innocent party in a divorce for adultery, is an adulterer, and cannot enter the kingdom of God. Every adulterer dishonors marriage, and grossly insults its Author; and, till he repents, the red-hot wrath of Almighty God abides upon him. We all dishonor marriage when we knowingly tolerate adulterers, seducers and fornicators in our churches, admit them into our society and vote for them when candidates for any office.

To dishonor marriage, in any of these ways, is to help to abolish marriage. When marriage is abolished, this world will be a perfect hell. I think that Raphael painted the marriage of the mother of our blessed Lord and Saviour to honor marriage. If I could, I should like to hang a good copy of Raphael's "Sposalizio" in every school-room, and parlor, and court-house, and church, and office, and hotel, and railway station throughout the land

Wednesday afternoon my comrade and I spent another hour in the Cathedral. I should like to spend an hour there every day for the remainder of my life. Most reluctantly we tore ourselves away. We had to leave that sublime temple behind us; but we carried away its glorious impress in our hearts.

Thursday morning we took the cars for Genoa, which the natives call Genova. The ride was long—104 miles—slow, hot and exhausting. We passed through no fewer than twenty tunnels, one of them two miles long. The last fifteen miles were almost one continuous tunnel.

We did not see much in Genoa. There was not much to see. Near the station stands a noble statue of Columbus, who was born only five miles from the city, presenting America, in the form of an Indian maiden, to the old world.

Some of the streets of Genoa are exceedingly narrow. I measured one—a chief business street—and found it two and one-half times as wide as the length of my cane. Another was so narrow that I could lay my hands on two opposite buildings at the same time.

Friday afternoon I began to be very sick with headache and fever. At about eight o'clock in the evening we all walked down to the harbor near by, and were rowed a long distance, in two large boats, across the bay to the steamer "Marsala." I noticed that all the oarsmen, in all the boats I saw, rowed with their faces toward the bows. We had a fine view of the city as we left it.

We found the steamer quite a large and well built one. But it was dirty, and was crowded with Italian steerage passengers of the filthiest description. They were human vermin. They swarmed through their own quarters and all over the ship. They smelt and looked worse than an average American hog. We sailed at nine. I was in my berth before that, in the same state room with five other men.

I was sick when I came on board. When we got well out to sea, the water was rough and I was terribly sea-sick. Every one in our party was sea-sick. The water dashed in at the ports so that they had to be shut. That made the air very hot and close. It seemed to me that I should die. I almost wished that I might. The only thing that made life sweet was the hope of seeing loved ones far away. At length I got some relief.

At half past seven the next morning we were at Leghorn—called by the Italians Livorno—where we lay till late in the day, taking on and putting off cargo. Soon after we sailed, the sea-sickness came back, and I passed another wretched night.

Nearly all day Sunday I lay on deck. Late in the afternoon the beautiful bay of Naples appeared; but it had little beauty for my sick eyes. The shore grew nearer, and ere long old Vesuvius was in sight, sending up a cloud of smoke many hundreds of feet in height. We passed through swarms of vessels of many kinds and reached our anchorage. A boat rowed us to the dock, and carriages took us through many fine streets to a good hotel. I went to bed at once, and lay there that night and all the next day.

During that Monday while the rest of the company were enjoying a visit to Pompeii, I lay on my back at the hotel in Naples, trying to say to God—yes saying—"Thy will be done." The next morning, as gently and easily as possible, I was borne to the railway station and given a whole seat in a good car.

After a journey of one hundred and twenty-five miles, I was in Rome, as we had come, 766 miles from Milan, and 5,600 miles from home. I could have been homesick and utterly discouraged. I was desperately sick. It was the bluest time I ever saw. It looked as though I should never see a better day. Why had I not stayed at home? How had I dared to come into that dreadful climate of Southern Italy, in July, against the advice of all the guide books.

But I had a friend who could help me. I had been telegraphing to him by the prayer cable nearly all the time for three days. At Rome I received an answer. It read: "All things work together for good to them that love God." I accepted that message as from God to me. I believed it. I rested upon it. It gave me peace and comfort.

In concluding this discourse, I commend these words to every one of you. God is the sovereign ruler of this world. If you love him, if you have given him your heart, every event in your life, everything that is done to you, everything that happens to you, and all your honest blunders are parts of a complicated machine, which the Almighty operates for your benefit. If you love and trust him, you are as safe from all real harm as though you were in heaven. Outside the Bible, all books put together are not worth one-thousandth part so much as that one sentence. "All things work together for good to them that love God."

VII.

OLD ROME.

"*I must also see Rome.*"—Acts xix, 21.

Paul was a great traveler. He was a traveling preacher. He was traveling and preaching all the time. He had visited nearly all the great cities of the world. He was very familiar with Jerusalem, and Damascus, and Antioch, and Tarsus, and Ephesus, and Philippi, and Thessalonica, and Corinth and Athens. But the queen of cities, the capital of the world, the center of universal dominion he had never seen. He felt greatly dissatisfied on that account. He longed to go and preach the gospel on the docks of the Tiber, and in the Forum, and before the gates of Cæsar's palace. So he said to his companions in travel: "I must also see Rome."

I felt much as Paul did. When I first contemplated taking a trip across the sea I said to myself: If I go to London and Edinburgh and Paris and Milan, "I must also see Rome." I would rather see Rome than any other city, than all other cities put together. If I cannot see Rome, my trip will be a disappointment and a failure. When old travelers and all the guide books said to me: "You must not go to Rome in the summer; if you go, it will be at the risk of your life," I answered: "I must also see Rome." When we reached Italy, and found how hot it was, and knew that the farther we went to the south the hotter it would be, I said : " I must also see Rome." When I was taken sick in Genoa, and knew not but it was the Italian fever, and the question was raised whether I should return to the healthful atmosphere of Switzerland, and wait for the company there, or press forward into unknown dangers, I still said : " I must also see Rome."

At last I was in Rome, but could not see Rome. From Tuesday noon till the next Monday morning I could not even look out of my window ; but lay in bed, in extreme weakness and severe pain. Friday morning the entire party save myself, departed for Florence.

Monday morning, July 28, I was taken in a carriage, hardly able to hold up my head, to the railroad station, and thence, by rail, eighteen miles and carriage two miles, to Genzano, a village of five thousand inhabitants, among the Alban Hills, near the ancient site of Alba Longa. I felt the change of air and was stronger and better ere I had been in the place twenty-four hours.

After nine days of good nursing, good air, good food and good rest, I felt able to resume my travels. Then I said : I will not try to follow the party in their wanderings through Germany. I will go, as straight as I can, to London and wait for my companions there. But, before I start for London, I must also see Rome. At half-past two, Wednesday Angust 6, I found myself again in the " Eternal City."

In many respects Rome is the most wonderful city of all the world and of all the ages. It is wonderful in its antiquity, wonderful in the influence it has exerted upon the nations of the earth, wonderful in

OLD ROME.

its treasures of architecture and art, wonderful in its ruins and wonderful in its associations and memories. Rome was founded, by a band of robber-shepherds, seven hundred and fifty-three years before the birth of Christ. It is therefore now 2643 years old.

The leaders of the men who built Rome were twins, named Romulus and Remus. If tradition is to be believed, they were cast out to perish, when infants, and were brought up by a she-wolf, in place of her cubs killed by hunters. Whether that story is true or not, the chief emblem of Rome has always been, and is to-day, a wolf nursing two little boys. Rome began on the Palatine Hill, on the left, or eastern, bank of the river Tiber, about fifteen miles above its mouth. Thence it spread until it covered six other hills and the intervening valleys, and was called the "Seven-hilled City." The seven hills of Rome are the Palatine, the Aventine, the Capitoline, the Esquiline, the Cœlian, the Quirinal and the the Viminal.

From the beginning Rome was engaged in almost constant war. She was a savage wolf, rending the nations in pieces and devouring their flesh, till she grew so large that, when she stretched herself out, she covered the whole world then known. Think of one city conquering and ruling all other cities, and all the nations of earth. That seeming miracle was wrought by ancient Rome. Her wars of conquest, with two brief intervals of peace, lasted nearly seven hundred years. Then, under the Emperor Augustus, the temple of Janus was shut and universal peace was proclaimed. In the midst of that peace, the doors of Heaven swung open on their golden hinges, and, while the angels sung : " Glory to God in the highest, and on earth peace, good will toward men," the Prince of Peace came down to earth, to establish his empire of love in the hearts of men. Soon the two empires, Rome and the Church, met in deadly combat Rome fought with sword and fagot The Church used no sword but the word of God, no fagot but the torch of divine truth. The Church was victorious. In the year 312 Constantine, the first Christian emperor, proclaimed Christianity the religion of the Roman Empire.

Ere long the splendor of the imperial city began to wane. The seat of government was removed to Constantinople. In 395 the empire was permanently divided into two parts. In 410 Rome was taken and plundered by northern barbarians. In 475 the Western Empire fell. Then Rome saw five hundred years of invasions, famines, pestilences and civil dissensions.

Meanwhile a new power had risen on the banks of the Tiber. In the place of the Emperors were the Popes. In place of the civil power was the spiritual power. Upon the ruins of the ancient Roman Empire there gradually arose a new empire, which soon became more powerful than the other, because it claimed control over the souls of men as well as their bodies, and extended its dominion beyond this life into eternity. For long centuries the Popes ruled the world; and temporal sovereigns rose or fell according to the will and nod of him whom they regarded as the successor of Peter and the vicegerent of the Almighty. In the latter part of the fifteenth century many of the nations declared themselves independent of the papal power. Since then the influence of the Popes in civil affairs has been constantly growing less and less. For centuries the Head of the Catholic Church was the absolute political ruler of the city of Rome and of the surrounding territory. But, in 1870, Victor Emmanuel came with his army and made Rome the capital of free and united Italy, and the Pope a private citizen under his regal government.

There are two Romes—the ancient and the modern. Ancient Rome lies on the eastern bank of the Tiber, and is the most interesting series of ruins on the globe. Modern Rome lies on both sides of the river, and is slowly creeping over the site of the ancient city. Since it became the capital of Victor Emmanuel's kingdom, Rome has enjoyed a rapid growth and has greatly improved in every respect. It is really a clean, beautiful, splendid city; and it is becoming more worthy of its illustrious name, every year. Its population is three hundred and forty five thousand souls.

After lunch I started out to see the wonders. The first object of special interest which I saw was the Column of Marcus Aurelius, rising in the center of a square of the same name. Marcus Aurelius was emperor from A. D. 161 to 169. He erected this column to commemorate his victories over the Marcomanni and other German tribes on the Danube. It is ninety-five feet high. A spiral band, ascending its cylindrical shaft, is covered with carvings of marching armies and fighting warriors. Three hundred years ago it was repaired by order of Pope Sixtus V. and a statue of St. Paul was placed upon its top.

I made a long pause in the Forum of Trajan. Here stands Trajan's Column, erected in the year

114. It is the most beautiful of all the historical columns, and the model for every similar structure. It is wholly of white marble, and is one hundred and thirty-two feet high. Around it runs a spiral band, three feet wide and six hundred feet long, covered with admirable bas-relief sculptures presenting a continuous history of Trajan's warlike achievements. No less than twenty-five hundred human figures are delineated, beside horses, fortresses and implements of siege. In the interior a staircase of 184 steps ascends to the top. Beneath this monument the body of Trajan was buried, and on the summit stood his statue. Many hundred years ago the image of the emperor was taken down, and a bronze statue of St. Peter, fifteen feet high, was put in its place.

As I stood looking, I said to myself: How comes it that the form of that high and mighty potentate, who reared this column, has disappeared, and the statue of an obscure and unlettered Galilean fisherman has taken its place? What power wrought that marvelous change? What has made Peter, the fisherman, so much greater than Trajan, the emperor? It was not the power of arms, or diplomacy, or money. It was the power of truth. It was the power of Christ. It was the power of God. God was in Christ. Christ was in Peter. Therefore, where there is one person who can tell you who Trajan was, there are a hundred persons who can tell you who Peter was. Trajan was on the losing side. Peter was on the winning side. I exhort you to get on Peter's side, which is Christ's side; for the time is coming when "at the name of Jesus every knee shall bow, of things in heaven, and things in earth, and things under the earth, and every tongue shall confess that Jesus Christ is Lord, to the glory of God the Father."

Passing on from Trajan's Forum and Column, I saw the ruins of a temple of the heathen goddess Minerva, built, it is probable, nineteen hundred years ago. Nothing remains but a portion of the front, in white marble, quite well preserved. I saw a doorway, and was about to enter, as I supposed, the place where once the goddess of wisdom was worshiped. But immediately I started back in disgust, with my hand at my nose. The place was the dwelling of a swarm of filthy Italians.

When this temple was built, the religion of Minerva and Mars and Apollo and Jupiter was universal and, seemingly, almighty. It was deeply rooted in the superstition of a hundred million worshipers, and was upheld by the power of the mightiest empire that ever stood on the earth. But there came a band of humble missionaries, preaching the new religion of a crucified Jew; and, lo, in a few years, the gods of Greece and Rome had gone to keep company with bats and owls, and every pagan temple had been demolished or transformed into a Christian church.

Standing in front of that ruined house of her who was fabled to have been born from the brain of the Father of Gods, I want to tell you that every false religion on the face of the earth is destined to give place to the only true religion, the religion of Jesus Christ. Christ is going to conquer this world. The best thing you can do is to surrender to him at once, and let him make your heart his spotless temple.

The next place which I visited was the Pantheon. Considering its age, we must pronounce this the best preserved building in ancient Rome. It was erected twenty-seven years before the birth of Christ, by Marcus Agrippa, the prime minister of the Emperor Augustus. Its walls are of brick, twenty feet thick, and were originally covered with marble.

Passing through a portico, seventy-two feet wide and fifty-four feet deep, supported by sixteen Corinthian columns of granite, we find ourselves in a circular room, one hundred and forty feet in diameter and two hundred and eighty feet high. That is more than eight times the height of this audience-room and nearly twice its greatest length. The surface of the wall is broken by seven large niches and many majestic columns. In the niches anciently stood statues of the gods of Rome, including Mars, Venus and Cæsar. The ceiling is dome-shaped, with a circular opening in the center, through which all the light enters which the room receives. When in its perfection, this was a marvelously grand and beautiful temple. The walls were covered with marble of many colors and of the highest polish. The floor was as rich as the walls. The ceiling was covered all over with gold. The outer walls were marble. The roof was tiled with gilded bronze.

More than half a century before the crucifixion of our Lord, the emperor and senators and generals and priests of old Rome dedicated this temple to every deity whose name they knew, and called it the "Pantheon," which means the house of all the gods. These very walls, this very ceiling, have re-echoed with the tread of sixty generations marching into eternity.

About fourteen hundred years ago the Pantheon became a Christian Church. It is now a church and a tomb. Here lie the mortal remains of Raphael, and

Victor Emmanuel, and many less distinguished men. Here they may sleep till the resurrection trumpet sounds through this vault, and the swarming millions of pagan and Christian Rome, with all mankind, stand before the great white throne of him who was nailed to a Roman cross. When that day comes, you will be present, my friend. Will you appear at the right hand of the Judge, or at his left? Will he say to you "Come thou blessed of my Father," or "depart thou cursed."

On the eastern slope of the Capitoline Hill I visited a little church, built over the old Mamertine Dungeon. The Mamertine Dungeon is very old. It probably dates back twenty-five hundred years. It is wholly underground. It is partly excavated in the solid rock, and partly built of masonry. It consists of two chambers, one below the other. A priest, with lighted taper, conducted us down a flight of stone steps, built in modern times, into a square stone chamber, very damp and cold and dismal. In the floor is a hole just large enough to admit a man's body, covered with an iron grating. That used to be the only entrance to the lower room; and through it the miserable prisoners were lowered with ropes, never expecting to be drawn out again. We went down a modern stairway. The lower room is shaped like a half-wheel, of which the straight side may be twenty-five feet long. On one side is a place where prisoners used to be strangled. There are two small holes in the wall running back into a narrow passage dug out in the rock. The victim was made to sit on the floor with his head against the wall. A rope was placed around his neck, and the ends were put through the holes. Then the executioner went around into the passage, drew the rope tight, tied the ends together, put a stick into the loop, and twisted the noose till the prisoner's face was black and his spirit had fled. On the other side begins a narrow passage, leading to an immense sewer, into which the dead body of the prisoner was thrust, as soon as life was extinct.

This horrible dungeon in which we stand is the place to which the historian Sallust refers when, in recording the execution of Catiline's confederates, he says : " In the prison is a chamber named the Tullianum, about twelve feet below the surface of the ground. This is surrounded by walls and covered by a vaulted stone roof ; but its appearance is repulsive and terrible on account of the neglect, darkness and smell." It is indeed repulsive and horrible. The chill and damp, and thoughts of the cruelties practiced here, send icy tremors through the visitor's body and soul. Here Jugurtha, king of Numidia, after adorning the triumph of Marius, perished by starvation. Here Vercingetorix, king of the Gauls, met his fate ; and many other noble captives, all along the centuries of relentless Roman tyranny.

But it was the memory of a more illustrious prisoner than any of these that brought me to the Mamertine Dungeon. Here, as we have good evidence for believing, Paul was confined just before his martyrdom. The Apostle to the Gentiles suffered two captivities at the capital of the world. The first was comparatively honorable and pleasant. For two whole years he dwelt in his own hired house, chained to a soldier who kept watch over him, and received visitors, and preached the gospel to multitudes in his rooms and before his door. After being released and having traveled and preached several years, he was seized again and cast into this noisome prison.

With what emotions thrilling my heart I stood within the walls which re-echoed the prayers and songs of Christ's greatest minister and where he wrote his last letter, to Timothy his spiritual son. Transport yourself in imagination, back through eighteen centuries, to Rome's oldest and most dreadful dungeon. The floor is bare and cold. The walls are covered with a slimy sweat almost as cold as ice. No light or fresh air ever penetrates the place, except when, now and then, the guards above remove the stone to save the prisoner from absolute suffocation. The sun never looked into this infernal pit. It is a horrible hole—a place for malaria, and fever, and asphyxia, and gloom, and despair, and madness and death. As we peer around, by the dim light of a sickly lamp, we see an old man sitting on the floor. On his knees lies a piece of parchment, which the guards have flung down to him and a little horn of ink, obtained in some way. He is writing. Slowly and painfully he forms the Greek letters, for the light is poor, his posture is cramped and his eyes are dim. You recognize Paul—the greatest man whom God ever gave to the Church or the world. Getting down on the floor behind him, and looking over his shoulder, you see that what he is writing is addressed to Timothy, the first Bishop of Ephesus. Can you read what he is writing this moment? Look sharp, and tell us what it is. "The cloak that I left at Troas with Carpus, when thou comest, bring with thee, and the books, but especially the parchments."

Paul expects a visit from Timothy, if he shall live so long. The cell is cold and damp. He wants his cloak. The hours are long and tedious. He wants his books to while away the time. He is soon to be tried for his life. The parchments are some documents which he needs to establish his innocence of the crimes laid to his charge.

While the priest, my guide, held his light, I took from my pocket my little Testament and read aloud the fourth chapter of Second Timothy, in the very spot where it was written. With special interest I dwelt on the words: "I am now ready to be offered, and the time of my departure is at hand. I have fought a good fight, I have finished my course, I have kept the faith: henceforth there is laid up for me a crown of righteousness, which the Lord, the righteous Judge, shall give me at that day; and not to me only, but unto all them also that love his appearing."

A few days after the writing of those words, one morning the jailers uncovered the round hole in the ceiling of the cell and shouted down: "You are wanted, old man!" Then they put ropes under his arms; and roughly hauled him up; and led him down the hill into the Forum, and past the spot where Cicero used to thunder against Catiline and Antony, and close by the heathen temples—which Paul knew would ere long be turned into Christian churches—, and under the shadow of the Palatine Hill and Nero's "golden house," and along the Ostian Way where hundreds of conquerors had marched—but none so great as he—and out through the gate, which afterwards took his name and bears it to-day. Then they led him to one side, out of the crowd which was coming and going, and, while he bent his neck and breathed a prayer for the forgiveness of his enemies, one of them, with his sword, struck off his head, and his liberated spirit flew up into the paradise of God.

That old Mamertine Prison suggested these thoughts to me ; and taught me a lesson, which I wish to repeat to you. It is the lesson of how to be happy. Paul, in spite of all his trials and tribulations, was a very happy man. The words, which I read to you a few minutes ago, prove that he was happy when expecting death, in that horrible dungeon. In one of his letters he wrote : "I am exceeding joyful in all my tribulations." What made Paul so happy? I think every one in this congregation can answer that question. His religion made him happy. The religion of Jesus Christ makes every one happy, who possesses it in all its fullness. The only way to be happy is to be a Christian. If you will give your heart wholly to God, he will take it and fill it with his joy. Everybody is in pursuit of happiness. O that everybody would seek happiness along the path which infinite Wisdom and Love have marked out for all human feet! Then would their happiness be real, sure, permanent, above the reach of circumstances. Then, perfectly satisfied with the service and companionship of Jesus, they could sing :

"Content with beholding his face,
  My all to his pleasure resigned,
No changes of season or place
  Can make any change in my mind ;
Whilst blest with a sense of his love,
  A palace a toy would appear ;
And prisons would palaces prove,
  If Jesus would dwell with me there."

On the floor of the place where Paul was confined,

the priest pointed out a hole in the floor where tradition says the Apostle Peter, when confined here, miraculously caused a spring to burst forth, that he might baptize his jailer, whom he had been instrumental in converting. My guide showed me on the wall near the stairs, under a protecting net-work of strong wire, the impress of St Peter's head and face, where he had leaned against the solid rock. I said the guide showed it to me. He tried to. But my imagination was too feeble to see the apostle's profile, and my faith was too weak to believe that such a miracle was ever wrought. The priest evidently took pleasure in believing his story, and I had no time to waste in trying to argue him out of it.

Leaving the prison, and the church which covered it, I looked down upon the Roman Forum, lying many feet below. It is, or was, an oblong level area, running eastward from the base of the Capitoline Hill bounded on the south by the Palatine and on the north by the Quirinal and Viminal hills. Along its sides were rows of magnificent temples and stately halls and courts of justice, while its surface was sprinkled over with monuments and statues. It was the centre of the political, religious, financial and social life of the ancient city. More than any other spot under the skies, it was the centre of the world. Here was a marble column sheathed in gilded bronze, called the "golden mile-stone," and inscribed with the names and distances of the chief towns of the Empire on the roads which radiated from the thirty-seven gates of Rome.

In the Forum all elections were held. In the Forum all laws were enacted. In the Forum all decrees were proclaimed. In the Forum all judicial trials took place. In the Forum all revolutions were consummated. Through the Forum all triumphal processions marched. In the Forum great Cæsar fell by the daggers of Brutus and his fellow conspirators. In the Forum the Republic died. In the Forum the Empire was born. In the Forum ancient Roman life was extinguished and buried. Next to the sacred places of Palestine, the Forum is the most interesting spot on earth.

For centuries the Forum was buried out of sight by rubbish and ruins, except as those degraded Italians dug down in places to make lime of its precious marbles. The miserable wretches called it the "Cow Field," and used it for every profane and ignoble purpose. Within the past century it has been unearthed and its priceless treasures exposed to the wondering gaze of scholars and tourists from every land.

I went down into the sacred place. I walked under the Triumphal Arch of Septimius Severus. I stood on the Rostrum, where Cicero used to pour out such torrents of eloquence. I walked along the Sacred Way, on the very stones over which the triumphal processions used to pass. I traversed and retraversed the pavement of the Basilica Julia. I looked up at the few remaining pillars of the temples of Peace, of Saturn and of Castor and Pollux. Farther east I saw the Basilica of Constantine, turned into a church, and the Temple of Romulus. I tried to print the scenes on my physical and mental eye, and, in a measure, succeeded.

As I walked among the sorrowful ruins of worldly glory, forever passed away, I thought of the eternal kingdom of Jesus Christ and felt like praising God that I had a right to call myself a citizen of that benign and perfect government.

At the eastern end of the Forum I passed under the arches of Constantine and Titus. The latter interested me most. It was built in the year 81 to commemorate the destruction of Jerusalem, by the armies of Rome under the general whose name it bears. It seems in a remarkable state of preservation, when we reflect that it is more than eighteen hundred years old. Under the arch, on one side, is a beautiful carving of Titus, crowned by Victory, riding in a four-horse chariot, driven by a female figure representing Rome. On the opposite side we see a stone picture which almost brings tears to our eyes. It is a band of captive Jews, marching in the triumphal procession of their conqueror, bearing on their shoulders the golden table of shew-bread, taken from their demolished Temple, and the seven-branched, golden candle-stick.

As I looked, I thought of the time when Jesus sat on the Mount of Olives, weeping over the approaching downfall of sinful Jerusalem, and saying : " The days shall come upon thee, that thine enemies shall cast a trench about thee, and compass thee round, and keep thee in on every side, and shall lay thee even with the ground, and thy children within thee ; and they shall not leave in thee one stone on another ; because thou knewest not the time of thy visitation." And I thought : this monument is a standing proof that Jesus of Nazareth was a true prophet, and that he was, what he claimed to be, the true Messiah, the son of the Most High God.

Near the Arch of Titus is the most celebrated ruin in Rome. It is the Colosseum, or, as it was originally called, the " Flavian Amphitheater." It was built by Titus, in the years 70 to 80, with the enforced labor of hundreds of thousands of unhappy Jews, who had outlived their city and nation. It is in the shape of an elipse. Its long diameter is 615 feet, and the shorter 510 feet. Its external circumference is nearly one-third of a mile. The arena measures 274 by 174 feet. On the outside it has four stories, and is 156 feet high. Within, above the arena, rise four ranges of tiers of seats, intersected by steps and passages. It has no roof; but, in ancient times, a huge canvas was stretched above it, on stout masts, to protect the spectators from sun and rain. It could seat 87,000 people. It is built of three different materials. On the outside it is composed of huge blocks of brown limestone, originally held together by iron clamps. On the inside it is brick laid in the most durable kind of cement. Between the limestone and brick is a volcanic sand-rock, called tufa. I brought away specimens of the tufa and brick.

I saw brick walls which have been exposed to the action of the weather for many centuries, in which the brick is as firmly held by the cement as though the masons had left it only a week before. The old Romans planned and built for the ages. Only about one-third of the structure remains. For many centuries it was a quarry, from which the lazy Italians dug materials for other buildings. The soft stones are full of holes where they bored in to extract the ore used in clamping them together.

The Colosseum has ever been a symbol of the greatness of Rome, and gave occasion for a prophetic saying:

"While stands the Colosseum, Rome shall stand,
When falls the Colosseum, Rome shall fall.
And when Rome falls, with it shall fall the world."

I was awed and charmed by this marvelous ruin. I slowly walked back and forth within the circuit of its solemn and majestic walls, examining its stones, and bricks, and arches, and stairways, and arena, and looking down into its two stories of dens and chambers, under the arena, where the wild beasts used to be kept. Then I climbed the stairs, and walked around the entire circumference, on the platform just above where the emperor and nobles used to sit at the shows and games.

My head and heart were hot with thoughts, during the hour which I spent in that marvelous ruin. I thought of the dedication, 1810 years ago, lasting one hundred days, during which five thousand wild beasts were slain; and hundreds and thousands of gladiators slaughtered each other, in the presence of Rome's best men and women; and the arena was flooded with water, and a great naval battle was fought, as though two hostile fleets were contending at sea. Then I thought of the wonderful and blessed change which Christianity has wrought in human society and human hearts, making such spectacles impossible now; and I thanked God that I was born in the nineteenth century in Christian America, rather than in the first century, in pagan Rome. If there is an honest, consistent and intelligent infidel in the world, he is very sorry that he was not born in time to be present at the dedication of the Roman Colosseum, before Christianity came to curse the world with its doctrines of peace, fraternity and love.

I had another thought. It took full possession of my soul. It blotted out the present, and carried me back seventeen hundred years. I want to seize every one of you and carry you back with me. Invisible to human eyes, we are standing in the arena of the Flavian Amphitheater.

It is a bright summer afternoon. The seats above, and all around us, are filled with a noisy and excited crowd. Eighty-seven thousand pairs of eyes are looking down on the sand where we are standing. Up there, in the front row, on an elevated seat, is the Emperor, the sovereign ruler of the civilized world. On his right and left are the senators and vestal virgins. Behind him are the knights and nobles. On the highest and most distant rows are the ruffians and blacklegs of Rome. Between are all classes and conditions of the better sort. Hark! what is that strange, muffled sound, which seems to come up through the solid earth, as though this arena were stretched over the mouth of hell, and the demons were screaming with pain. Why! do you not know? Those sounds are from the throats of hundreds of wild beasts, which have not tasted food for many days. Wild beasts! Wild beasts without souls under us! Wild beasts with souls possessed by the spirit of evil above and around us! Surely, if there is a hell on earth, this is it.

While we are thinking, suddenly a door is thrown open from under one of the arches, and a crowd of men, women, youths and maidens enter the arena, pushed forward by the spears of a cohort of soldiers. Standing in the center of the arena, around a gray-haired man, they begin to sing. We do not understand the words; but from the tones and faces of the singers, we know that it is a pean of joy and victory. They are Christians. The old man is their pastor. Eighty-seven thousand throats send up a yell of insult and hate; but we can hear the Christian song rising to heaven like incense from the golden altar in the Temple of Jehovah. This seems a section of Heaven let down into the mouth of hell.

Suddenly a trumpet sounds. Immediately, through a score of open places under the arches a hundred ferocious beasts spring upon the sand. For a moment they glare up at the crowded seats and forward at the singing martyrs. The song rises louder and more joyfully. With frantic yells the beasts spring upon their prey. At once the song becomes less in volume, but rises higher in sweetness and triumph. All is confusion before our eyes — clouds of dust with the mingled forms of bounding beasts and falling martyrs. The song grows softer and softer, but sweeter and sweeter.

The air grows clearer. We can see only one human form—a beautiful maiden, clad in snowy white, with clasped hands and upturned face, singing as mortal never sang before. For a moment, savage beasts and brutal men are awed into silence. Then men yell and clap their hands, and beasts yell and spring upon helpless innocence. Instantly the song ends in one triumphant note, and nothing remains but the beasts on the seats shouting with delight, and the beasts in the arena quarreling over a few white bones and blood-smeared rags.

That scene, enacted a thousand times in the old Roman Colosseum, means the victory of the martyrs —the victory of the truth. Truth cannot be destroyed. Truth will prevail. The history of eighteen centuries proves that Christianity cannot be destroyed ; that Christianity will prevail. Therefore Christianity is the truth.

The only wise and safe course for you, my friend,

is to embrace Christianity, by abandoning all your sins and giving yourself by faith into the hands of Jesus Christ, to be his in time and in eternity. The martyrs overcome by the blood of the Lamb and the word of their testimony. By faith in that blood, and by witnessing for Jesus, you shall overcome sin and death and reign with God forever and ever.

VIII.

MODERN ROME.

" Seest thou these great buildings ? "—Mark xiii. 2.

These words will serve merely as a motto, while I proceed to tell you more about the great buildings and wonderful sights of the most famous city in the world.

It was hard work to get away from the Colosseum. By its grandeur and its strange memories, it seemed to entrance me and to hold me in willing captivity.

At length I succeeded in tearing myself away, and, taking a carriage, drove about three-quarters of a mile in a south-east direction, almost to the city wall. The carriage stopped in front of the Basilica di San Giovanni in Laterano, which, being interpreted, is the Church of St. John Lateran. This is the oldest church in Rome. It outranks all others in the Catholic world. It is the Pope's church—the Cathedral of the Bishops of Rome. They call it the "Mother and Head of all the churches of the world." A Latin inscription on each side of the entrance so declares. The coronation of every pope must take place here. It has been so for many centuries, perhaps from the beginning of the papal power. Five Œcumenical Councils have been held within its walls. The only council ever held elsewhere, in Rome, was the so-called Vatican Council, which proclaimed the doctrine of papal infallibility, in St. Peter's Church, in the year 1870.

In ancient times a palace stood on this spot belonging to a man named Lateranus. Being implicated in a conspiracy against the government, under the reign of Nero, his estates were confiscated and became the property of the emperor. When Constantine the Great ascended the throne, he gave the palace to Pope Sylvester, and built a church on the palace grounds close by. The palace was the residence of the popes for nearly a thousand years.

The church has been their peculiar charge ever since the donation of Constantine. And yet the palace and church are not the same as at the beginning. Twice they have been destroyed by fire, and once by an earthquake. They have been rebuilt, enlarged, embellished and improved, times almost without number.

The front of the church looks toward the east. Going up a flight of steps you pass under a portico, thirty-three feet deep and one hundred and ninety-six feet long. There are five doors into the interior of the church. One, called the "Holy Gate," is walled up, and is opened only in the year of jubilee, for the entrance of the pope. The central entrance has two splendid bronze doors, adorned with garlands and other ornaments. To the left is an ancient statue of Constantine, found in his bath house.

As you walk up the nave—or main aisle, as we would call it,—four hundred and twenty-six feet long, you see twelve huge pillars, of many-colored marbles, each of which cost as much as this whole church. In the face of each pillar is a niche, wide and high and deep, and in each niche is a large white-marble statue of an Apostle. As you walk back and forth, and gaze at the stone images, they seem to be alive, and you almost fancy that the twelve most intimate friends of your Saviour have risen from the dead, in their glorified bodies. You distinguish them from each other by the peculiar emblems which they bear, as well as by their countenances. For example, Peter carries a bunch of keys, because Jesus said to him, or to the whole college of the apostles through him : " I will give unto thee the keys of the kingdom of heaven." Andrew bears an X-shaped cross, because tradition says that he was put to death by being nailed to such an instrument. Simon holds a saw, because, if we can believe reports, he was sawn asunder by the enemies of the truth. Thomas always lifts at a long pike, or spear, indicating that he was killed with that kind of a weapon, thrust through his body. The emblem of John is an eagle; of James the Greater, a pilgrim's staff ; of James the Less, a fuller's pole ; of Bartholomew, a knife ; of Philip, a long staff with a cross at the top; of Matthew, a hatchet ; of Jude, a club; of Matthias, a battle-axe.

While you are looking at those statues, I want to say something about the men whom they represent. Those twelve men have done more to reform and purify and civilize and bless the world than any other twelve men who ever lived, or ever will live. They founded the Christian Church. As St. Paul declared, "the household of God " is " built on the foundation of the apostles and prophets, Jesus Christ himself being the chief corner stone." They founded the Church, and founded it so well that it has withstood the storms of eighteen centuries, and is stronger and more beautiful to-day than ever before.

When we say that the Church is built on the apostles, one thing which we mean is that the whole Christian scheme depends on the doctrines which they taught and the facts of which they were witnesses. They declared to the world that they were intimately acquainted and associated with a man named Jesus, for the space of three years. They described his character and repeated his teachings. They affirmed that they had seen him perform hundreds of miracles in broad day light in the presence of thousands of spectators, such as curing the leprosy, opening the eyes of the blind, stilling the tempest, walking on the sea, turning water to wine, feeding crowds of hungry men with a handful of bread and raising the dead. They avowed that they saw him die; that they witnessed his burial; that after three days they saw him alive; that, during the space of forty days, he appeared to them and conversed with them many times; that they put their hands upon him; that he ate in their presence; and that, finally, having commissioned them to proclaim his doctrines to all mankind, he went up to heaven in their sight, in the day time, from a mountain on the east of Jerusalem.

Now there are three theories in regard to the apostles and their Master, one which we must accept. The first theory is that they were weak-minded men; that Jesus was a vile imposter, and that they were his dupes. We cannot, as rational men, accept that theory. Their subsequent lives, and the wonderful work which they accomplished, prove that they were not fools. It is impossible that twelve men, as clearheaded as we know them to have been, could be made to believe the story which they told if it was all a lie.

The second theory is that the Apostles were cunning knaves, who invented this story on purpose to deceive the world and make capital for themselves. What could they expect to gain by such a course? What did they gain by insisting that Jesus Christ was crucified for the sins of the world, and that he rose from the dead on the third day? They gained poverty, social ostracism, toil, hardship and persecutions of every kind. Did they gain anything else? Yes. Peter gained crucifixion with his head downward. James the Less gained the privilege of being beaten to death with a fuller's pole. Andrew gained death on a cross of a peculiar form, which ever since has borne his name. Bartholomew gained the satisfaction of having his skin stripped from his body while he was yet alive. James the Greater gained the honor of having his head hewed from his shoulders by King Herod's executioner. Thomas gained a spear through his body. Philip gained the hangman's rope around his neck. Matthias gained a shower of stones bruising his flesh, and an axe cutting off his head. Jude gained a shower of arrows through his heart. Simon gained the special distinction of being cut in two with a saw. Matthew gained martyrdom by sword or hatchet, in a distant corner of Africa. John was the only one of the Twelve who did not win a martyr's fiery crown. Do you believe that the Apostles invented the story of Jesus and his miraculous works for the sake of what they could make by deceiving the world? If you believe that, there is nothing which you could not believe.

Only one theory remains, a theory which every honest and intelligent person accepts: The Apostles told the truth. Jesus Christ is the eternal Son of

God. He laid down his life on the cross for the sins of the world. He rose from the dead and ascended into heaven. He is the Saviour of men. His religion is the only true religion. If you repent of your sins and believe in Christ, you will have everlasting life. It you reject Christ, you will everlastingly perish.

In the last chapter but one of this Holy Bible, I read that on the twelve precious stones which compose the foundations of the jasper walls of the Celestial City are graven the names of the Twelve Apostles of Jesus Christ. I understand that to mean, that none can ever enter Heaven who willfully rejects the testimony and teaching of these twelve men, whose marble statues I saw in the church of St. John the Baptist at Rome.

Moving up the nave we reach the center of the transept where, raised four steps above the richly inlaid floor, is the canopy, a beautiful work erected five hundred years ago. It covers numerous highly venerated relics, including, it is said, the heads of the saints Peter and Paul. Beneath it also is the high altar, believed to contain a wooden table used by St. Peter as a communion table. At this altar no one is ever permitted to say mass except the pope or some priest especially appointed by him.

Turning to the right, we leave the church through the door of the north transept. We are in the Piazza di San Giovanni in Laterano, or the Square of St. John Lateran. In front, in the center of the square, is the largest obelisk in existence. It was erected in front of the temple of the Sun at Thebes in Egypt, thirty-five hundred years ago, and brought to Rome by Constantine in the year 357. It is of red granite, weighs six hundred tons and, including the pedestal, is one hundred and thirty-five feet high. What a mass of stone that is, to be hewed out of the quarry in one block ! .

At our left is an old baptistery, where, according to Roman tradition, the Emperor Constantine was baptized, by Pope Sylvester, in the year 324. On our right, stretching far out, is the old Papal Palace, already mentioned. After His Holiness moved to the Vatican, it became an orphan asylum. Since 1843, it has been a museum for heathen and Christian antiquities. I did not go in.

Around in the rear of the palace was something which I was determined to see. And I did. It was the Scala Santa, or Holy Staircase. It is more generally known to tourists as " Pilate's Staircase." It is simply a flight of twenty-eight white marble steps, contained in a little chapel erected for the purpose. It is alleged, by the Romans, that this is the staircase which led up into Pilate's judgment hall at Jerusalem, and that these identical stones were pressed by the feet of Jesus four times, during his trial by the Roman governor and by Herod and after his condemnation to the cross. It is also asserted that it was carried by angels from Jerusalem to Rome. The fact seems to be that Helena, the mother of Constantine, brought it from Palestine in the year 326. But whether Christ or Pilate ever trod it, no one knows, and no one ought to care.

You are told that if you ascend that staircase on your knees, kissing each step as you go up, and then repeat a prayer at the top, you will receive a peculiar spiritual blessing. Millions have tried the experiment, until the stones are almost worn through by their knees and lips. A wooden covering has been placed upon them, and that is well-nigh worn away.

To me the chief interest attaching to Pilate's Staircase was the fact that Martin Luther undertook to climb it, three hundred and seventy years ago, but could not reach the top. For years he had been groaning under a crushing burden of conscious guilt. He had tried every way to obtain the forgiveness for his sins and the assurance of the love and favor of God. But the more he scourged and starved and tormented himself, the worse he felt. At last he came to Rome. Rome could do nothing for his sin-sick soul. One day, hoping for relief, he was crawling up this staircase. Suddenly, when about half way up, he heard a voice, seemingly as loud as thunder, shouting in the ears of his soul : " The just shall live by faith." As quick as a flash of lightning, he saw God's way of saving the soul. He saw, and laid hold, and felt that he was saved. Springing to his feet, he faced about, and walked down the stairs, and hurried home to Germany a new man, and began to preach the grand, old-fashioned, New Testament doctrine of justification by faith. He preached what Christ and the Apostles had preached : " That if thou shalt confess with thy mouth the Lord Jesus, and shalt believe in thine heart that God raised him from the dead, thou shalt be saved. For with the heart man believeth unto righteousness ; and with the mouth confession is made unto salvation." I turned away from the Holy Staircase, confirmed in that creed which says, in the words of Paul in his letter to the Romans : " Therefore we conclude that a man is justified by faith without the deeds of the law."

You may ascend the Holy Staircase, as many times

as you please. You may be baptized in the very place where Pope Sylvester baptized Constantine the Great. You may receive the Holy Communion at the high altar of the church which is styled the "Mother and Head of all the churches of the world." You may keep all the rules of the Church with perfect exactness. Still, if you have not saving faith in the Lord Jesus Christ, these things will profit you nothing. When Christ commissioned his ministers he said: "Go ye into all the world, and preach the gospel to every creature. He that believeth and is baptized shall be saved; but he that believeth not shall be damned;" and when the Philippian jailer said to Paul and Silas: "Sirs, what must I do to be saved?" their instant answer was: "Believe on the Lord Jesus Christ, and thou shalt be saved."

From St. John Lateran, I went to the Church of St. Peter in Chains. It derives its name from the fact that it was built to contain some chains which tradition says were worn by the Apostle Peter when he was a prisoner in the imperial city. There is nothing very remarkable about the church itself. But it contains something which is very remarkable. I do not refer to St. Peter's chains. I did not see them, or ask to see them, or care anything about them.

I went to the place simply and solely to see one of the most famous works of one of the greatest sculptors the world has ever known—the statue of Moses by Michael Angelo. It did not disappoint me. I gazed at it long and earnestly. It is the figure of a majestic old man, in white marble, with a long flowing beard, holding the tablets of the law in his hands, and looking as though he had just come down from forty days of communion with Jehovah on the summit of Mt. Sinai. There is a far-away expression on his face, as though he were looking into the unseen world, and into the face of God.

Moses was one of the greatest and most successful men that ever lived. He was great and successful chiefly because he lived in constant communion with the Almighty and drew his intellectual and spiritual life from him. If you would have your life a success, you must live in God, and God must live in you.

There is one very singular thing about this statue of Moses. He has small horns growing out of his head. He is always thus represented by mediæval artists, owing to an erroneous translation of the statement in Exodus that when he came down from the presence of God his face shone. The Hebrew word to shine is *karan.* Horn is *keren.* The men who translated the Bible into Latin mistook *karan* for *keren*, and made the Bible say that Moses had horns on his head, when he came down from the mountain.

Perhaps you will be dissatisfied unless you hear more about the chains of St. Peter. They are kept in a cabinet under the high altar, behind bronze doors, and are exhibited only once a year, namely, on the first day of August.

When I left the church it was almost night. So I went in pursuit of food and a bed. These I found on the Via Cavour, in a hotel near where I lay sick during those wretched days which I shall always remember with horror, yet with gratitude.

The next morning I visited, before breakfast, the neighboring church of Santa Maria Maggiore. Rome has about three hundred and sixty churches, eighty of which are dedicated to the Virgin Mother of Christ. Of the eighty, this is the largest ; hence its name, Maggiore. It is one of the oldest churches in Rome, and, indeed in Christendom. Its foundation dates back nearly fifteen hundred years. A legend says that the Virgin Mary appeared, at the same time, to the pope and to a devout layman, and commanded them to build her a church on a spot where they should find a deposit of snow the following morning—the fifth of August. Since first erected, it has many times been restored, enlarged and improved. It is a very grand and beautiful building ; but, for lack of time, I shall not attempt to describe it.

On the fifth of every August a special service is held here, to commemorate the miraculous snowstorm, by which the Virgin Mary indicated the place of her sanctuary so many centuries ago. One part of this special service is a fall of snow. An American lady who was present on one of these occasions told me what she saw. At a certain point in the ceremonies the officiating priest informed the assembled crowd that the time for the snowstorm had arrived. Immediately large flakes of snow began to fall upon the pavement, within a circular railing, from the dome. Down they came till the floor was white. The people were greatly excited. By and by the storm ceased. Then the priest permitted the people to go forward and help themselves to pinches of the snow, which they carried away to their houses, with every demonstration of joy. The American lady went up and got a handful of snow. What do you think it was ? It was the petals of white roses.

After breakfast, I secured a carriage and set out for St. Peter's and the Vatican, more than two miles distant. I had a very enjoyable ride through many streets of old and new Rome. Some of the streets were crooked ; some were straight ; some were narrow ; some were wide. All were clean. I saw uninhabited ruins, swarming hovels, mediæval palaces, modern mansions and all kinds of unfinished buildings rising from new foundations.

All the while I was looking out for Rome's famous river, the yellow Tiber. Soon it appeared, and yellow it was. It is always yellow, with the mud which it carries down to the sea from the lands through which it flows. I could not help contrasting it with another river, which flows through another city. This city, by a figure of speech, is called eternal. That city is eternal. No mortal has ever trodden its pavements of crystaline gold. But John saw it, and his angelic guide showed him "a pure river of water of life, clear as crystal, proceeding out of the throne of God and of the Lamb." I have had one of my most ardent earthly desires gratified in seeing the muddy river of Rome. Shall I ever see the pure River of Life, which flows through the City of God? May that be the most intense longing and steadfast purpose of every one who hears my voice to-night !

We crossed the Tiber by the Bridge of St. Angelo, right in front of the frowning castle of the same name, which used to be the Mausoleum of the Emperor Hadrian, and, turning to the left, were soon in the Square of St. Peter. I call it a square, although it is nearly round. The Italians call it a piazza. It is 780 feet in diameter from right to left. In its center is an obelisk brought from Egypt by Caligula, fourth Emperor of Rome. On either side of the obelisk is a beautiful fountain. The open space is nearly enclosed by two imposing colonnades, on the right and left. Each colonnade consists of four series of Doric columns. These covered passages, the central of which is wide enough for two carriages abreast, are formed by 284 columns and 88 buttresses. On the roofs are 162 statues. The cost of construction was $820,000. The pavement of the space which the colonnades enclose cost more than eighty thousand dollars. The effect is striking, and the piazza forms a fitting approach to the largest church in the world.

At the right of the church, and close to it, is the Vatican, with its gardens and grounds. The Vatican is the palace of the popes—the largest palace in the world. It is also the largest and richest art gallery that ever existed. According to the most trustworthy estimates, it contains more than ten thousand rooms ; and a catalogue of its paintings and statues by the most gifted artists, would fill many ponderous volumes.

Passing around through the right hand colonnade of the piazza, I came to the principal entrance of that world of artistic wonders, my heart bounding with a joyous expectation which had lain there, wide awake, ever since I decided to take this European trip. Suddenly I found myself confronted by two of the pope's guards, in fantastic mediæval uniforms, armed with muskets and bayonets, and was positively but politely informed that the Vatican was shut against all visitors, every afternoon, from the beginning of June to the end of September. My consternation and disappointment and grief were greater than I can describe. Had I come through so many toils and perils and leagues of expensive travel, to be driven back, by hostile steel, from the very gate of Art's own paradise? I tried every kind of persuasion which I could invent without effect. I have since thought of one other thing, which did not then come to my mind. Perhaps if I had shown the guards a few pieces of silver or gold, they would have relented and let me in. But I turned sadly away, and shall never cease to feel the pangs of that, the greatest single, disappointment of my life.

And yet there is rarely a great loss without some small gain. In that case the gain was a valuable spiritual lesson, which came with great weight to my mind and heart. I expect to get into Heaven, the palace of God, as much as I expected to get into the Vatican, the palace of the Pope. But I may be disappointed. By-and-by when I come up to the celestial gate, I may be repelled with the awful declaration that I can never enter, that I am everlastingly too late. According to the Bible, many will thus be disappointed.

I suppose everybody in this congregation expects in some way to get into heaven. My friend, on what do you base your expectation? Is it your church-membership? If that is all you have, you have nothing. The Church cannot save you. Is it the fact that you have been baptized and have partaken of the Holy Communion? Baptism and the Eucharist will do you no good, unless your heart is right toward God. Do you depend upon the good works which you have performed? St. Paul says: " Though I bestow all my goods to feed the poor, and though I give my body to be burned, and have not love, it profiteth me nothing." Do you rely upon the money which you have given for the support of the gospel?

Do not be so foolish as to imagine that you can buy your way into the golden City. Hear what Christ the great Bishop of souls has said : "Strive to enter in at the narrow gate : for many, I say unto you, will seek to enter in and shall not be able. When once the Master of the house is risen up, and hath shut to the door, and ye begin to stand without, and to knock at the door, saying, Lord, Lord, open unto us; and he shall answer and say unto you, I know you not whence ye are ; then shall ye begin to say, we have eaten and drunk in thy presence, and thou hast taught in our streets. But he shall say, I tell you, I know you not whence ye are : depart from me all ye workers of iniquity." Again the Saviour said : "Not every one that saith unto me, Lord, Lord, shall enter into the kingdom of Heaven ; but he that doeth the will of my Father which is in heaven. Many will say to me in that day, Lord, Lord, have we not prophesied in thy name? and in thy name cast out devils? and in thy name done many wonderful works? And then will I profess unto them, I never knew you : depart from me, ye that work iniquity." My great mistake at Rome was that I did not more carefully study the guide books, and find out at what hour the Vatican was open. In that case I should have gone to the palace in the forenoon instead of the afternoon, and should have gained admittance. The great mistake of millions now is that they do not with sufficient care study the great Guide Book which God has given them—the Holy Bible. If you will study this book for yourself, and follow the directions which it gives, you will certainly get into Heaven.

In Europe you rarely meet a tourist who has not a

guide book in his hand. Frequently I saw travelers reading in their guide books while they were walking along the streets. You ought to have the Bible in your hand every day, and meditate upon its precepts while you are busy with your secular work. You cannot read the Bible much without making this discovery : that, in order to gain admission to the palace of God, you must truly repent of all your sins ; you must believe on the Lord Jesus Christ ; you must be born again ; you must live a life of self-denial, honesty, virtue and purity.

Shut out of the Vatican, I went to the Basilica, or Church of St. Peter. This is the largest and most famous church in the world. Constantine the Great, in the early part of the fourth century, erected a church on this same spot, and gave it the same name. The site of both edifices had been occupied by Nero's circus, where it is known thousands of Christians suffered martyrdom. It is claimed that the Apostle Peter was among the number. Some were sewed up in the skins of wild beasts and torn in pieces by dogs. Some were crucified. Some were smeared with pitch and set on fire, to light up the place by night while a horse-race was in progress.

The present church was commenced about 'the year 1450, and dedicated in 1626. Several architects assisted in its construction, among whom were Raphael and Michael Angelo. The building covers an area of 162,000 square feet, and yet it is so symmetrical in its proportions that the tourist cannot comprehend its immensity till he has studied it many days. It covers nearly four acres. The ground which it occupies would hold thirty-two churches as large as the one in which we worship to-night.

Crossing the portico, which is 43 feet wide and 234 feet long, under a magnificently decorated ceiling 66 feet high, we enter the main portion of the edifice. The floor is made of different colored marbles, laid in beautiful patterns. Before us stretches the entire interior length of the church, 615 feet, or nearly one-eighth of a mile. On either side of this nave—or main aisle, as you would call it—which is 87 feet wide, are four enormous pillars, supporting the roof. The pillars are made of marble, in many colors, exquisitely polished. Each pillar has a large niche, fronting the nave, filled with marble statues. Huge marble arches span the spaces between the pillars. Passing under these arches to the right and to the left, we find ourselves in the aisles of the church, which are most elaborately and richly adorned with pillars, and arches, and mosiac pictures, and hundreds of statues, and monuments of deceased popes and other distinguished persons. Opening upon the aisles are numerous side chapels, each gorgeously furnished with an altar and other apparatus of Catholic worship.

The church contains twenty-nine altars, in addition to the high altar, 148 columns, and, nobody knows how many, hundreds of statues. It is a grand aggregation of splendid churches, chapels, tombs and works of art. If you look straight up, as you walk along the two aisles, you will discover that the soft light which casts a sort of celestial glory upon every object, comes down through sixteen large domes, all finished in mosaics. Coming back into the nave we look up at the gorgeously coffered and gilded vaulting of the ceiling. How high do you think it is? If you guess, you will not guess enough. It is one hundred and fifty feet.

Let us walk up the nave. Halt! Now we are three hundred feet from the door. We are opposite the fourth pair of columns. Do you see that bronze statue of a man sitting against the north column, on a throne of white marble, under a canopy, with two large candelabra in front? That represents St. Peter. He extends his right foot for you to kiss his great toe. Millions on millions have rendered that homage ; and, if you go nearer and look, you will see that the soft lips of the worshipers have worn away the hard metal till the Apostle's toe is almost gone. If you run a tape line around the pillar against which St. Peter sits, you will find that it is 234 feet in circumference. The circumference of the audience room of the Medina Methodist church is 250 feet. So you see that the base of St. Peter's pillar is nearly as large as the entire floor of the sanctuary where you worship. That pillar is one of four—all exactly alike—which support the great central dome.

Come and stand under the dome with me. It is 195 feet in diameter and 613 feet in circumference. Look straight up. From the pavement, where your feet are, to the summit of the lantern the height is 403 feet. Is it not grand, majestic, sublime? It is the greatest monument to the genius of Michael Angelo, by whom it was designed and partially completed. It is pictured all over, in mosaics, with figures of evangelists, apostles, the Virgin, the Saviour, and the Almighty Form looking down over all. Just think! That dome is so large that if it rested on the ground it would cover nearly half an acre. And yet the hand of Michael Angelo has tossed it up into the air so high that its base is two hundred feet above the earth.

Directly under the dome is the high altar, beneath a bronze canopy, where the pope alone reads mass on high festivals. Under the high altar is the tomb of St. Peter. To get to the tomb, I went down a flight of stone steps, into a large oval roofless apartment, which might be called a depression in the floor of the church. Around the edge, resting on the church floor, is a marble railing supporting a circle of eighty-nine ever burning lamps. A guide opened the tomb, and showed me a casket, in which, looking through a pane of glass set in its face, I saw what is said to be two old wooden coffins in which the remains of Peter and Paul were found many centuries ago. There rest the ashes of the two saints to-day, according to the guide, except their heads, which are exhibited in the church of St. John Lateran.

After several hours of sharpest inspection, I turned away, feeling that I had only begun to see the world's grandest temple, which had cost, at its dedication, fifty million dollars, and on whose maintenance thirty-seven thousand dollars are annually expended.

If an atheist were to ask me who planned and built St. Peter's Cathedral, I think I should reply, not intending to deceive him, but wishing to open his mind to receive the truth about God: No one built or planned it. It came by chance. Particles of dead matter, swirling about, happened to shape themselves into these walls, and domes, and columns, and statues, and frescoes and altars. If then he should stare at me and exclaim : " Impossible ! " I should take him in imagination, if I could, for a walk, through a forest, on a June morning. I should say : This is nature's cathedral. These over-arching trees, from the study of which man first learned to rear the

Gothic arch, are the columns. The woodland road is the nave. The verdant vistas are the aisles. The emerald leaves, flecked with golden sunlight, are the frescoes. Moss, and grass, and flowers make up the mosaic pavement, such as no mortal artist ever dreamed of making. Heaven's bending canopy is the dome. Yonder brook, tumbling over the rocks in ceaseless melody, is the organ. Countless forms of beast and bird and insect life compose the congregagation. This is a cathedral which far surpasses the grandest ever reared by human hands.

Can you believe that nature's temple came into existence by chance? "Every house is builded by some one; but he that built all things is God." A man who should say that the Basilica of St. Peter, at Rome, came into existence without human hands would be a fool. He is a greater fool who says that this world was not created by a person of infinite intelligence; who says: "There is no God."

IX.

FROM ROME TO LONDON.

"How long shall thy journey be?"—Nehemiah ii. 6.

When I was at Genzano, and the time drew near when it would be safe for me to resume my travels, this was the question which I put to myself : " How long shall thy journey be?" After long deliberation and prayerful weighing of probabilities, I decided to go from Rome to London, as straight as I could. To the question : " How long shall thy journey be?" I found an answer in a rail-way guide book ; " Eleven hundred and fourteen miles, and forty-three and a half hours."

At the close of last Sunday evening's discourse, we had just come out of St. Peter's Church. Using our imagination, we can say that we *have* just left St. Peter's. It is now about four o'clock. Our train does not leave until nine forty-five. We have three or four hours more, before dark, which we can spend in viewing Rome. We could well use four weeks, if we had so much time.

That was my feeling that afternoon. But I was determined to see and remember all I could. Getting into a carriage, I was driven over the Tiber, by the same bridge which I had crossed before. Turning to the left, and keeping near the river for a distance of nearly a mile, we reached the Piazza del Popolo.

Crossing that famous square—with its Egyptian obelisk, standing in the midst of four water-spouting lionesses—we passed through Rome's most northern gate, the Porto del Popolo, and soon were in the Borghese Villa.

The Borghese Villa is simply a surburban park of vast extent and extraordinary beauty. I have not the time, or ability, adequately to describe it. Beautiful lawns, majestic trees, magnificent vistas, perfect carriage drives, lovely statues, crystaline fountains, graceful temples and fascinating ruins make up its endless charms. It seemed to lack but one thing to make it a perfect earthly paradise. It was the dry season. No rain had fallen for many weeks; and every leaf and flower and blade of grass, except in the vicinity of the fountains, was crying for water. What would this physical world be without water? It would soon become a horrible desert of drifting sand, without one speck of animal or vegetable life.

What material water is to the physical world, the water of life, the pure religion of Jesus Christ, is to the moral and intellectual world. If Jesus, the Son of God, had not lived and died and risen again, there would not be on this globe, one particle of virtue, love and truth; all would be corruption, sin and spiritual death. Every good thing under the skies owes its existence, directly or indirectly, to "the glorious gospel of the blessed God." Nothing is needed to cure all the evil of this world, and to make it a paradise of moral beauty but a copious and protracted rain of gospel grace, falling on all nations and cities and families and hearts. O God! when will this dry season come to an end, and the spring time of universal and everlasting greenness and beauty begin?

From the park we drove back into the city, through the Porto del Popolo, and, turning to the left, ascending the Pincian Hill. This has never been counted among the hills of Rome. It stood partly within and partly without the ancient city. It was called the "Hill of Gardens." Here were once the famous gardens of Lucullus. It is covered with elegant mansions, and charming little parks, and groups of trees, and shaded walks, and statues of celebrated Italians. It is a fashionable drive in the evening, when the wealthy citizens frequently pay and receive visits in their carriages. The projecting terrace at the summit commands a magnificent view of the entire city. On the right, winding through the landscape from the farthest rear to the most distant front, is the river. Far away to the south, beyond the city walls, stretches and rolls the Campagna, the home of desolation, the summer resort of malaria and fever and death. Toward the south-east, just within the walls, is the Church of St. John Lateran, styled "the Mother and Head of all the churches of the world." Half a mile west, in nearly the same line, rises the Palatine Hill, covered with the ruins of the palaces of the Cæsars. Immediately in front of that, we catch a faint glimpse of the tops of some of the ruins in the Forum. Close to the Forum, at the left— I am not sure that your eyes are sharp enough to see it—is the Colosseum. The intervening space in front is filled in with the spires and domes of scores of immense churches and an indistinguishable mass of buildings of every kind and size and shape. Down here at our feet are the Piazza and Porto del Popolo, from which radiate three important streets. The middle one, nearly a mile in length, is the Corso, the great street of modern Rome, the center, every spring, of that eight-day revel, called the Carnival, which ushers in the gloom and blackness of Lent. Almost directly west are the Palace of the Vatican, covering more than twenty acres of ground, the Castle of St. Angelo and the Basilica of St. Peter. St. Peter's dome is the most conspicuous object within the circumference of our vision. From whatever direction the tourist may come, it signals his entrance into the Eternal City. Viewed from a distance, it seems suspended midway between earth and heaven. It is to Rome what Vesuvius is to Naples, only a greater wonder ; for the Almighty threw up the mountain, while a man, Michael Angelo, hung the dome.

Descending the Pincian Hill, I rode through the city in all directions. I cannot begin to name the interesting objects which I saw. One was a very odd-looking dwelling, where Rienzi, known to every school-boy through a reputed speech of his beginning : " I come not here to talk." used to live.

Another building, which greatly interested me, was St. Paul's Methodist Episcopal Church, a small but beautiful stone edifice, the first protestant house of worship ever erected in the Seven Hilled City. There a congregation of native Italians meet every Sabbath, under a pastor of their own nationality, and worship God with the same forms which we employ. Methodism is a feeble plant in Rome ; but is destined to grow, and fill all Italy with fragrance and beauty. Methodism was once a feeble plant in America. One hundred and twenty-five years ago there were only five Methodists in all this great country. To-day, beneath the "stars and stripes," there are nearly five million persons who are actual members of the Methodist church ; and five million more who belong to Methodist Sunday-schools, and regularly attend Methodist services. These figures prove that the Methodists are the largest Protestant body in this country ; and that, if they were to count their children, as our Catholic friends do theirs, they would be the most numerous of all the American churches. I have referred to the growth of Methodism in America, during the past century and a quarter, to give you an idea of what it may be in Italy during the coming one hundred and twenty-five years. There is reason to believe that, in the year 2015, there will be more Christians in Italy calling themselves by the name of Methodists than by any other denominational title.

After driving around in an aimless kind of a way for about an hour, we turned the horses' heads to the west and south and left the city by the gate of St. Paul. Passing the Pyramid of Cestius, and the Protestant Cemetery—where sleep the remains of Shelby and Keats and of many other distinguished pilgrims—we came, after riding about a mile, to the church of St. Paul beyond the walls.

This sacred edifice stands on the spot where tradition says the Apostle Paul was beheaded. It was founded in the year 388, but has been many times seriously damaged and extensively restored. Most of the present edifice is nearly new. It is one of the most beautiful churches in the world, so far as its interior embellishment is concerned. I have not the time to give you a minute description. I would like to have you notice a few of its chief attractions. Imagine yourself standing in the nave, near the front, or western entrance. Under your feet is an inlaid marble pavement, almost as smooth as glass. Seventy-five feet above you is a richly coffered ceiling. Running down each side, is a row of forty Corinthian columns, of Simplon granite. Each column is at least thirty feet high, was hewed from a single piece of stone, and is so perfectly polished that you could use it as a mirror in combing your hair or shaving your face. Above each column is a medallion portrait of a pope in mosaic, five feet in diameter. Between the windows, in the upper part of the nave, are pictures of scenes in the life of Paul, by distinguished artists. At the other end of the nave, about three hundred feet distant, you see a huge arch, nearly as wide and high as the nave itself. On either side of the arch, standing on a heavy pedestal, is a colossal statue. One represents Paul; the other Peter. Beyond the arch is the high altar, under a canopy supported by four yellowish columns of oriental alabaster, standing on pedestals of Russian malachite. They are incomparably the most beautiful columns I ever saw.

The whole interior of the church is rich, and brilliant, and gorgeous, and resplendent, beyond description. It was a great delight to me, because I was surprised by its exceeding beauty, not expecting to find such a magnificent temple in such an out-of-the-way place.

Tearing myself away from what might have employed my closest attention for a week, I climbed back into the carriage and was driven across the country eastward to the Appian Way.

This is the most celebrated of the Ancient Roman roads. It was constructed by Appius Claudius about 313 years before the birth of Christ. Originally it extended from Rome to Capua, 125 miles. Subsequently it was continued across the Italian peninsula to Brundusium. It was built in a very expensive manner, on a foundation of solid concrete ; and was paved with large blocks of the hardest stone, closely fitted and laid in cement. Those old Romans, if you do call them semi-barbarians, could not tolerate such wretched roads as we have in Orleans County. The old pavement still remains, in many places ; and I had the pleasure of riding over the identical stones which were scratched by the wheels of Pompey's chariots and pressed by the feet of Paul the Apostle.

For a long distance the road is lined with ancient Roman tombs, crumbling into dust. Back in the fields, I could see the ruined arches of old aqueducts built when Rome was the imperial mistress of the world. It was difficult to realize that it was the nineteenth century in which I was living. If there were wonders about me, there were greater wonders under my feet. I was riding above the catacombs. I passed near several churches built over the entrances to these subterranean dwellings and cemeteries of the early Christians. I had neither time nor strength to descend and explore.

The catacombs are chambers and passages, dug out in the soft rock underlying the soil of the Compagna. It is estimated that the total length of all their galleries amounts to 590 miles. In them, during the days of cruel persecution, when it was a capital crime to profess the Christian religion, the Christians lived, and worshiped, and died, and were buried. The number thus laid to rest, where the light of the sun has never penetrated, is estimated at six millions.

What a hard time Christians had in those days! What an easy time Christians have now! During the first two centuries, millions of men and women gladly lived in the catacombs and cheerfully died by the most horrible torture, that they might honor the name of Jesus Christ and spread his gospel through the world. Christianity was a mighty power then. Nothing could stay its triumphal march.

In these days we have a weak, emasculated, kid-gloved, white-slippered, silk and satin kind of Christianity, which whines and complains, if it is asked to suffer anything or do anything. Think of the catacombs and the wild beasts of the Colosseum, and then blush with shame at your weakness and cowardice. Those Roman Christians could face a hungry tiger, for the sake of Christ. You cannot go to church in the face of an April shower. They had courage to brave the wrath of an emperor with a hundred thousand soldiers at his back. You turn pale and dare not confess Christ at a prayer-meeting of fifty neighbors, his friends and yours. They exultingly surrendered every pleasure and honor and life itself, that they might please God. You think you make a tremendous sacrifice, if you pay ten dollars a year for a sitting in some elegant church. At the call of their Master, they waded through fire up to their chins. You think so little of your divine Lord that you cannot go to his sanctuary on his holy day, if the mercury drops to zero, or six inches of snow covers the ground. Their type of Christianity is represented by a maiden singing alone in the Colosseum, with eighty-seven thousand wild beasts, with souls, yelling on the seats and a hundred wild beasts, without souls, yelling on the arena Your type of Christianity is represented by an able-bodied man, in perfect health, sitting in front of a parlor grate, on a drizzly Sunday, reading his Sunday newspaper, while his pastor is in his pulpit, a block away, preaching to almost empty pews. When I say *"you,"* I do not mean all nineteenth century Christians; I mean a majority, or at least a large minority, of the kind of Christians which make up our American churches. If I have painted the portrait of any church member in this congregation, I hope he will look at it till he despises himself, and becomes a better representative of the Saviour who died to redeem him.

In the gathering twilight I rode back to Rome. A short distance south of the city I passed a little church on the right called the church of Domine Quo Vadis. It is so named from the legend that St. Peter, fleeing from the death of a martyr, here met his master and enquired of him: "Domine, quo vadis?" "Lord, whither art thou going?" to which he received the reply: "Venis iterum crucifigi," "I am going to be crucified a second time." Then the Apostle ashamed of his weakness returned. It is well for all Christians to understand that when they are guilty of a mean or cowardly act, "they crucify the Son of God afresh, and put him to an open shame." On we drove into the city by the Gate of St. Sebastian, beneath the Triumphal Arch of Drusus, under the eastern brow of the Palatine Hill, around the Colosseum and the Forum, and back to my hotel on the Viminal Hill.

At nine forty-five I bade good-by to the Eternal City and boarded a train, at a railway station not far from the old Prætorian Camp. Travel by rail in Europe is not quite the same as in America. The railroads over there do not differ from ours, except that, as a rule, they are more thoroughly built, are

straighter—running through hills by tunnels instead
of around them by sharp curves—and sometimes
have iron ties. But their rolling stock is very
peculiar. The locomotives are much smaller than
ours; their shape is very inartistic and odd; they
have no cab for the protection of the engineer and
fireman; and they are destitute of cow-catcher and
bell. The coaches over there are the queerest things.
I presume most of you know about them, and yet a
description will do no harm. They are much shorter
than ours, and some narrower and lower. Externally
they are shaped and painted so as to look as much
as possible like a lot of stage-coaches stuck together.
They have but four wheels apiece. They have no
doors, or windows, in the ends. Each car is cut up
into about five compartments, or rooms, by solid
partitions running across. Each compartment has
two seats facing each other, running across the car,
about two feet apart. Each compartment has also
two doors, one on each side of the car, opening outward, with a window on each side of each door. The
upper half of the door is also a window. The six
windows all slide up and down, by means of long
leather straps. There is no ventilation, execpt what
the windows afford. Into one of these compartments
you are securely locked, as though the railroad
officials were afraid you would jump out and run
away. You are liable to be one of ten passengers,
wedged in so that you cannot move, exposed to the
peril of filthy clothing, bad breaths, too much or too
little ventilation, contagious diseases and even rob-
bery and murder. There are some American palace
and sleeping cars in Europe; but I never rode on a
train which contained one of them. The British rail-

roads generally make better time than ours; the Continental not so good.

The night I left Rome, I had the good fortune to have clean and respectable traveling companions. They were an Italian family of three—father, mother and little boy—and a solitary Italian gentleman. As there were five of us, we had a little more than three feet apiece, in which to stretch ourselves out. As I am five feet and nine inches long, it was impossible for me to get myself into a horizontal position. Consequently I got but little sleep, and what I did get was very poor. The night was very long; and I was very glad when morning came.

I was busy with my thoughts nearly all the night. I thought how strange it is to be riding behind an iron horse, with heart of fire and breath of steam, at the rate of twenty-five miles an hour, where Etruscan, and Roman, and Carthaginian, and Gallic, and Gothic, and French, and Spanish armies used to drag themselves slowly along. It took Julius Cæsar many months, and even years, to get from Rome to England, with his army, through dense forests, and dismal swamps, and trackless wastes, and savage tribes; while I expect to make the distance in forty-three hours, through populous cities, and smiling gardens, and blushing vineyards and every evidence of the highest cultivation.

What, I asked myself, has wrought this wondrous change? I do not know how you would answer that question. But the only answer which I could find was: the religion of Jesus Christ has changed Europe from a wilderness to a garden, and has transformed its scattered tribes of filthy savages into dense populations of artists, poets, philosophers, merchants, bankers, and honest, peaceful, happy artizans and tillers of the soil. The people of Europe still suffer from many political and moral evils ; but every one of these would disappear, if all classes and individuals would receive the gospel of Christ, in all its fullness, into their hearts. Then I thought of my dear native land. Our ancestors, a few generations ago, were half-naked, beastly savages, roaming through the forests of northern Europe, till Christian missionaries came among them and told them of Jesus, who died to make all men happy and good. Because they embraced Christianity, we are what we are. There are many relics of barbarism and corruption from which Christian America still needs to be cleansed. But not one of them would exist, if every American were thoroughly imbued with the principles of the Christian religion.

At four forty Friday morning our train stopped in the city of Pisa. I regretted very much that I had not time to look through the city and see its wonders. But I do not know why I may not tell you something about the place. It is a very old town, of about fifty-four thousand inhabitants, situated on the River Arno, seven miles from the sea. It is surrounded by an extremely fertile and beautiful plain, the salubrity of whose climate draws invalids from all parts of the world. It has a cathedral eight hundred years old ; a noted art gallery ; a university, in which Galileo, the inventor of the clock, the microscope, the thermometer and the telescope, was a student three hundred years ago; a famous baptistery; a leaning tower ; and many other curious things. The Leaning Tower is its best-known attraction. It is 183 feet in height, fifty in diameter and leans out of the perpendicular thirteen feet. Whether it was built to lean, or has assumed that position since its erection, no one can tell.

At Pisa the solitary Italian gentleman left the compartment in which I was riding, and a priest, a large portly man, took his place. These priests attract the tourist's attention, wherever he goes on the continent of Europe. They are seen in great numbers, in all public places, especially in Italy. They are known by their dress. Unless they belong to some order of monks, they wear the same uniform —a long, black robe reaching to the feet, closely buttoned, and a rough, black, broad-brimmed, round-topped hat. The ministerial brother, who became my traveling companion, had a kindly, intelligent face, and, had his language and mine been the same, I think we should have fallen into conversation. He sat directly opposite to me, and, taking out his Latin breviary, or prayer-book, began to read. Soon he added another occupation—the taking of snuff. From that time on, for several hours, he took a good heavy pinch every fifteen or twenty minutes. I have been told that the Catholic clergy in Europe are forbidden, by ecclesiastical law, to smoke, or chew, tobacco, but are allowed to use it in the form of snuff.

It seems to me that, if a man feels compelled to use tobacco, snuffing it is the least objectionable mode, so far as the comfort of other people is concerned. If a gentleman smokes in the presence of ladies, there is the smoke to choke them. If he chews, there is the spittle to nauseate them. But if he puts the poisonous weed into his nose, he does not greatly injure any one but himself.

That clergyman on the cars, between Pisa and

Genoa, gave me a lesson to bring home to the tobacco-using gentlemen of Medina. It is this: When your health requires you to use tobacco on the street, or on the platform of a horse-car, or in the post-office or in a place of entertainment, remember that people who do not use tobacco have rights as well as yourself, and snuff your weed instead of smoking or chewing it. Imagine a gentleman, walking the street, puffing a cigar in the face of a wind which carries his smoke directly into the teeth of a lady walking behind. Can a gentleman do such a thing as that? Many, who are considered gentlemen, do. The Methodist Episcopal Church has advanced beyond the Catholic Church of Italy, and has made a law that no man shall be admitted to her ministry who will not take a vow to wholly abstain from the use of tobacco.

Nearly all the way from Pisa to Genoa the railroad runs along close to the sea, and for most of the distance is cut into, or through, the solid rocks which line the shore. More than half of the time we were in tunnels. We would run in total darkness for ten or fifteen minutes; then flash out into the light and see the beautiful blue Mediterranean, flecked with white-winged ships; and then plunge again into midnight blackness. It was a strange experience.

I said to myself: Such is our earthly life. It is made up, almost from the cradle to the grave, of alternate day and darkness, light and shadow. For a while everything goes well with us; the sun of worldly prosperity shines in a cloudless sky; the argosies of pleasure bring us every blessing over seas of liquid silver, rippled with burnished gold; we think we would like to live in such a world forever

Then, without a moment's warning, we are plunged into a black, smoking tunnel of disease, or poverty, or bereavement, and we cry out in an agony of terror, and wish we could die. But we hold on to life and to God, and ere long we are in the bright light again. Bright days come and go, till we begin to think they will continue to the end, when, suddenly, we are in the midst of another sorrow blacker, if possible, than the first. And so it will be till the day when we shall step off the train of divine providence in the City of eternal brightness and glory.

Why is this so? Why is our course through earth to heaven like the tourist's route from Pisa to Genoa? There are two reasons: first, it must be so; such is the nature of the country through which our journey lies. Second, God is an artist; each human life is a picture, which he is painting for our eternal enjoyment; and every picture necessarily consists of blended light and shade.

About the middle of the forenoon we reached Genoa, whence I had sailed for Naples three weeks before. At one o'clock in the afternoon we were in Turin, four hundred miles from Rome. There I had to change cars, and wait about an hour. I had a strong desire to see the city, but could not stop. Turin, called Torino by the Italians, is a beautiful city of two hundred thousand inhabitants. It contains many splendid churches; a magnificent palace, once the residence of Victor Emmanuel and his predecessors, the kings of Sardinia; numerous works of art; and many large manufacturing establishments. Without taking time to allude to any other, I will say that there is one factory which employs 450 laborers in producing nine million matches per day.

While waiting at the rail-way station in Turin, I picked up an Italian newspaper containing an illustrated account of the execution, by electricity, of Kemler, at Auburn, N. Y. I never studied Italian, but I could make out a good part of the article.

On leaving Turin, I fell in with a young English gentleman going to London, and found him a very pleasant companion all the rest of the way. Soon after starting we were among the mountains—the Italian Alps. They kept getting larger and grander, and we kept climbing higher and higher. By and by I could see peaks whose summits were streaked with snow. We passed numerous Alpine villages, and saw many peasants at work in the fields or driving cows or goats along the roads. We threaded numerous tunnels and thundered along the edge of awful precipices. At twenty-five minutes past five o'clock we plunged straight into the face of the mountain, and were in darkness just twenty-seven minutes. We were in the Mount Cenis Tunnel, which was begun in 1857 and finished in 1870, at a cost of fifteen million dollars. It is eight miles long. It is a marvel of engineering skill and perseverance. The passage was dark and disagreeable. It seemed long, and much longer than it was. But I had no doubt that it would end ; that there was light ahead ; that, having left the kingdom of Italy behind, I should soon be in the Republic of France. And so it was. Suddenly the darkness was past and I was in the midst of glorious day.

That tunnel seems to me to represent death. Some persons, infidels, say that death ends all ; that there is no life beyond the tomb ; that this black sooty tunnel, which runs into the mountain, never comes out. Faith says: "Beyond death is unending existence. This tunnel leads to the kingdom of eternal day." My friend, which statement seems the most probable? You see the tunnel of death right before you. You have seen hundreds of trains go in. Is it reasonable to suppose that not one of them has ever come out on the other side? I tell you nay. To the Christian, death is the gate to endless joy. If you will get on board the gospel train, you w'll be delivered from the fear of death. When the cars dash into the tunnel, there will be one short pang— and then the brightness, and glory, and bliss of heaven for ever and ever.

A few minutes after leaving the tunnel we were at the French town of Modena, and had to have our baggage examined by the custom-house officals. Ere long darkness came down upon us. There vere just four men of us in our compartment, and we 'nad room to lie at full length, so that I slept pretty well. When morning came, we were flying through the smiling fields of beautiful France, where everybody was busy gathering in the wheat. At five minutes past seven we were in Paris, 950 miles from Rome

After a little delay, and a change of cars, we started for Calais. Through a pleasant country, many villages and the city of Amiens, we rode 167 miles to that famous town. For more than two hundred years Calais belonged to the English. It was re-taken by the French during the reign of Queen Mary, who, when she heard of its capture, was so overcome with grief, that she declared that, if her heart should be examined after death, the name of her beautiful Calais would be found written thereon.

.Immediately we went on board a steamboat to cross

the Strait of Dover. We were two hours and twenty minutes in making the passage of twenty-one miles. The sea was rough, and the boat was small and mean. I might have been sea-sick, but for the fact that I stretched myself upon a couch in the cabin, and slept all the way over. In due time I was on the cars at Dover.

A pleasant run of seventy miles, through Chatham and Canterbury, and the intervening villages and country, brought me to London at fifteen minutes past seven, two hours late.

It was Saturday night. I was a total stranger in the largest city in the world. But I was in the land of my ancestors, where I could hear my mother-tongue, and so I felt perfectly at home. I thanked God, from the depths of my heart, that my long journey of eleven hundred and fourteen miles was at an end, and that I was where I could rest, free from all danger of the Italian fever.

Something like that, only infinitely more delightful, will be the emotions of the weary pilgrim, when the journey of this mortal life is over and his feet press the golden pavement of the capital of the universe. He will not feel like a stranger. The countless millions of angels and redeemed human spirits, whom he meets, will seem to him as familiar friends, because the language which they speak will be the language which he learned in the Church on earth. They will hail him: "Brother!" Through their shining ranks he will make his way to the Father's house, the palace of God; and Jesus, his adorable Lord, who bore his sins on the cross and cleansed him from all unrighteousness, will conduct him to the mansion which infinite wisdom and love have long been preparing as his everlasting habitation.

X.

LONDON.

"Now Nineveh was an exceeding great city of three days' journey."—Jonah iii, 3.

These words seem to mean that Nineveh was so large that it would take a man three days to walk around it. The same statement could be truthfully made of the city of London. London is an exceeding great city of three days' journey. In the area which it covers it is smaller than old Nineveh was, and still smaller than ancient Babylon. But, in population, it is probably the largest city on which the sun ever shone. When the last census was taken, in 1881, it had 3,814,571 inhabitants. Its present population is variously estimated at from five to seven millions. It is the political capital, and commercial and financial center, of Great Britain, and of an empire which covers more than eight million square miles of territory and includes two hundred and sixty millions of inhabitants.

London derives it greatness from England and the English. With all their faults and sins, England is a wonderful country, and the English are a wonderful people. England proper is a portion of a rock-bound island, only a little larger than the State of New York. And yet, beginning, six hundred years ago, with half the present population and a small fraction of the wealth of our Empire State, she has stretched her boundaries and extended her conquests and multiplied her power, till now she rules one-seventh of the entire territory and one-sixth of the population of the globe. In territory, in population, in commerce, in wealth and in military resources and prowess, England (I now use that word to include everything over which floats the English flag) is the mightiest empire that has ever existed.

We can hardly help asking the question: "What is the secret of England's greatness?" An African prince, many years ago, sent an embassy to the court of St. James, to put that question to Queen Victoria. The queen did not bring out her jewels, or display her ships and armies and munitions of war. But, handing the embassador a beautifully bound copy of the Bible, she said: "Tell you master that this is the secret of England's greatness." England is great chiefly because she is a Christian nation, and because her Christianity is of that type which permits, and commands, the reading of the Bible by the common people. There is a great deal of wickedness in England, and the English government, managed by wicked men, has committed many political crimes; but the masses of the English people are Christians, and their hearts are imbued with the principles of the gospel.

London is a great and wonderful city, because it is the capital of England and of the British Empire. London is situated on both sides of the River Thames, about sixty miles from its mouth. In its winding course through the city, the width of the river varies from seven hundred to twelve hundred feet. For a long distance, it is confined by embankments of solid masonry; and it is spanned by a great number of magnificent bridges, of which the most important are London Bridge, Waterloo, Westminster and Blackfriars. Several tunnels under the river connect the two banks. The oldest and largest of these is twelve hundred feet long, and has two arched passages, fourteen feet wide and sixteen high, separated by a brick wall four feet thick. By far the larger and better part of London is on the left, or northern, bank of the river.

Before the Romans conquered Britain, London was nothing but a collection of huts, on a dry spot in the midst of a marsh, surrounded by a ditch and a rampart of earth. The Romans built a stone wall around the place, inclosing a space one mile long and half a mile wide, and called it Londinium. Portions of that old wall are standing to-day, after the lapse of fifteen hundred years.

After the Romans came the Anglo-Saxon kingdom, and London, as its capital, grew in size and importance. Under William, the first of the Norman kings, it had a population of forty thousand souls. During the succeeding six hundred years, with many fires and famines and pestilences and riots, nevertheless, it enjoyed a large and substantial growth. In 1664 it was turned into a city of mourning and woe by the ravages of the Great Plague, by which it lost one hundred thousand citizens. Treading closely on the heels of the plague, came the Great Fire, which destroyed thirteen thousand houses, in September, 1666. But the fire was really a blessing; for it burned up the germs of the plague, and prepared the way for the re-building of the city in much better form and style.

It was not, however, till the reign of Queen Anne that London began to put on its present appearance. Since then, and from a population of seven hundred thousand, it has steadily and rapidly grown to its present enormous proportions and extraordinary splendor. Its populations has almost exactly doubled within the last forty years, and within the same period about two thousand miles of new streets have been constructed.

There are in London more Scotchmen than in Edinburgh, more Irish than in Dublin, more Jews than in Palestine, and more Roman Catholics than in Rome.

The people of London eat, every year, ten million bushels of wheat, four hundred thousand oxen, one and a half million sheep, quarter of a million swine, one hundred and thirty thousand calves and four hundred million pounds of fish, besides enormous quantities of other kinds of food, washing it all down with two hundred and nineteen million quarts of alcoholic liquors. The total value of the trade of this great metropolis of the world amounts to one thousand million dollars a year.

The principal streets of London are paved in the most perfect manner, and are kept clean by labor performed every minute in every day except Sunday, but are not yet furnished with electric lights. The public buildings are large and magnificent. The private edifices are less stately and beautiful than those of our largest American cities. The police is the best in the world.

London consists of ten independent boroughs, or corporations, each of which is a city by itself. They are the city proper—the old city presided over by the Lord Mayor—Chelsea, Finsbury, Greenwich, Hackney, Lambeth, Marylebone, Southwark, Tower Hamlets and Westminster.

I established myself in the old city, on Giltspur St., at the Queen's Hotel. It was a most excellent starting point from which to visit and view the places which I had come to see. Within half a mile of my bed and board were St. Paul's Cathedral, the Bank of London, the Mansion House, Guildhall, the General Post Office, Smithfield, Charterhouse, Temple Bar and Blackfriars Bridge.

I arrived in London Saturday night. Therefore the first place to which I went was the house of God. In the greatest of cities there are fourteen hundred churches, of which eight hundred are Episcopal. one hundred and fifty Methodists, one hundred and thirty Baptists, fifty Catholic and two hundred and seventy Congregational and Independent.

Of all the great preachers in London, the one whom I most wished to hear was the Rev. Charles H. Spurgeon. Accordingly, in company with an American gentleman whom I found at the hotel, I went directly south a little less than half a mile, crossed the Thames and went a mile south on the other side. That brought us to a part of the city called Newington Butts, where, near an inn named the "Elephant and Castle," we fell in with a dense crowd moving toward a large, plain, brick building. Entering, we found ourselves in the Tabernacle, the largest Baptist church in the world.

The auditorium is an immense and grand, but somewhat dingy, room, oval in shape, with vaulted ceiling supported by iron columns, and with two galleries running entirely around. The pulpit platform projects out into the room from the first gallery. The place is so perfect in its acoustic conditions that a voice in the pulpit can be distinctly heard in every pew. The guide book says that there are seats for six thousand persons. One of the ushers told me that there was room for seven thousand.

Although it was raining very hard, when we went in, there must have been five or six thousand people present. A seat was given us on the main floor, about one-third of the distance from the door to the pulpit. As I glanced around, I said to myself: This does not compare at all with the cathedrals which I have been visiting in Belgium and France and Italy. What St. Peter's at Rome cost would build two hundred churches like this. I see no polished marbles, no golden candelabra, no rich mosaics, no tombs of saints, no statues, no pictures, no altar, no organ. The place seemed bare and cold and dreary. But I soon became sure that God was there, as I had not felt his presence in any other house of worship since I left my native land, and I thought: What does the Almighty care for the place where we worship him, if only our hearts are honest and pure.

When we went in the great preacher was in his pulpit, where he had stood for thirty years, reading and expounding the third chapter of the Gospel of John. Next a hymn was sung, the minister standing to read the first stanza, and sitting to read each succeeding one separately. Then he prayed—a prayer of great simplicity and childlike faith, which lifted us all nearer to God. He prayed especially that no one might go out from that service unsaved. The second hymn followed the prayer. There was no choir and no instrument. A man stood on the platform with Mr. Spurgeon and acted as leader, and all the people sung. The singing was like the voice of many waters.

The sermon was based on John III : 33 : "He that hath received his testimony hath set to his seal that God is true," and was just fifty minutes long. It was simple, earnest, spiritual. It was full of the most pathetic appeals and warnings to sinners to repent and give their hearts to God. He did not confine himself to the text, but made much of the last verse of the chapter : "He that believeth on the Son hath everlasting life : and that he believeth not the Son shall not see life ; but the wrath of God abideth on him." Again and again he thundered out those solemn words : "The wrath of God abideth on him." He told his hearers plainly that if they did not believe in Christ they would go to hell and suffer there forever. That great preacher believes in hell as well as in heaven ; and when he means hell, he is not afraid to use that word. All the great preachers of the ages—all who have had eminent success in winning souls and building up truth and righteousness—have been firm believers in the doctrine of eternal punishment, and have boldly and constantly preached that doctrine.

Mr. Spurgeon's wonderful power and success lie in the fact that he can see men hanging on the crumbling edge of the "Lake of Fire," and his great loving heart, filled with the Divine Spirit, will not let him rest, or hold his peace, so long as there is one whom he can reach and save. In thirty years he has received twenty thousand persons into his church ; educated hundreds of ministers, in his training college ; built thirty-six chapels in different parts of London ; founded and endowed a large orphan asylum ; edited an influential religious paper; and written and published many valuable books, which have had a world-wide circulation.

Monday morning, August 11, with my American friend, I started for the Tower of London. The distance was about a mile and a half. We walked, going most of the way along the river bank, on the north side, down toward the mouth. On the way we passed through the Billingsgate Fish Market. On account of the vile language which the fish-women there used to employ, the word billingsgate has come to mean "foul or profane language." That is Webster's definition of the term. The talk of the fish-wives is not so rank as it was in the olden times; but I do not believe that the smell of the place has much improved.

In due time we were at the Tower. This is perhaps the most interesting and widely known of all the buildings of London. It consists of a bewildering mass of towers, forts, batteries, ramparts, barracks and store-houses, covering an area of thirteen acres. The oldest part of the building is the White Tower, built by William the Conqueror, eight hundred years ago. At first it was a royal residence; then it was a state prison; now it is an arsenal, a fortress and a museum. As a prison, it is identified with the most thrilling portions of English history. No one, who has read that history, can walk through its gloomy apartments without shuddering, as he recalls its dark and bloody memories. Here scores of the purest and noblest of England's sons and daughters have groaned away their lives in horrible captivity, or poured out their blood on the reeking scaffold. If dead matter could be endowed with sight and hearing and memory and speech, it seems to me that every separate stone and brick, in these grim and frowning walls, would utter a wail of sympathetic terror and agony which would be heard in every house in London.

We went in through the Lion's Gate. We saw the Traitor's Gate leading up from the Thames, through which persons accused of treason used to be conducted, having been brought thither by boat.

We saw the Bloody Tower. Every tower in this old pile is bloody; but this one deserves the name more than all its fellows. Do you know the story? Richard Plantagenet wanted to be king of England. His brother, Edward the Fourth, was king, and had two little sons, one of whom, by law, would be his successor. When Edward died Richard was made protector of the little princes, till the older one should be of age. Richard said to himself: "If these boys were out of the way, I should be king of England." So he had them shut up in the Tower, and one night, when the little innocents were soundly sleeping in their bed, locked in each other's arms, a heartless minion of their cruel uncle stole in and smothered them with pillows. Twenty years after, their bones were found, in an old chest, under the stairs of the White Tower, and were buried in Westminster Abbey. Ever since, the tower where they were murdered, by their uncle's orders, has been called the Bloody Tower.

Richard seized the coveted crown; but, after the murder of his nephews, he never had a night of peaceful sleep. He had horrid dreams which tormented him beyond endurance. He would frequently jump out of his bed in the dead of night, seize his sword which he always kept near his pillow, and run round the room, striking at imaginary ghosts and devils and howling in an agony of terror. That was remorse. That infamous king was having a foretaste of the torments of hell, into which he entered, about two years after he began his usurped reign, from the battle field of Bosworth, where he lost his life. Conscience is a stern judge and a relentless executioner.

We went through the White Tower. Here, on the first floor, Sir Walter Raleigh was confined thirteen years, for no crime at all, and here he wrote his History of the World. Going up the stairs we were in the Chapel of St. John, built in the old Norman style, where pretended followers of the gentle Jesus used to come to worship God, with murder in their hearts and their fingers dripping with innocent blood.

Beyond the chapel we entered the Banqueting Hall, once the scene of royal feasting, now the resting place of old cannon, its walls and ceiling adorned with trophies of arms, skillfully arranged in the form of stars, flowers, shields and other similar figures. On the third floor is the old Council Chamber, where many a dark and bloody deed has been contrived, now converted into an armory, or museum of arms.

Imagine to yourselves a room, about fifty feet wide and one hundred feet long. The floor, the walls, the ceiling all are stone. Here is displayed almost every kind of deadly weapon ever used in ancient, mediæval or modern times. Down through the middle runs a broad aisle, bounded by two fences in which the pickets are swords and the rails are chains of pistols. Beyond the fences are glass cases filled with various small objects of interest. Between the cases are stands of arms and instruments of torture and execution. Among these we saw a block, on which they used to chop off human heads, and, leaning against it, a beheading axe. On the block we could see the marks of the axe and stains of blood.

Beyond each row of cases is another fence of swords and pistols ; and, beyond the second fence, along either wall, is a row of wooden horses, which look just like horses of flesh and blood. On each horse is the image of a man clad in complete armor. Each suit of armor represents some particular period in the history of the art of human butchery. Each martial figure represents the king, or knight, who wore that particular suit in battle or tournament or parade. Most of the armor is of the most perfect finish. Some suits are plated all over with shining silver ; others are inlaid with rich enamel and burnished gold. Interspersed among the horsemen are mail-clad footmen, bearing aloft in their gauntleted hands, spears and pole-axes and halberts. The scene looks like reality. It seems as though we were about to be crushed between two opposing lines of charging warriors.

We do not care to linger long in such a place. I left the Tower Armory with a horrible realization of the fact that man's chief occupation for six thousand years has been the shedding of human blood. Who, I asked myself, have been the great men of history? I am compelled to answer : chiefly those who have surpassed their fellows in their skill to inflict torture and death on their fellow men. All history, down to recent times, is a sickening recital of carnage, massacre and rapine. I do not understand how any man can read history and say : "I do not believe in the the doctrine of human depravity." I left that chamber of death hating war, as I never had before, thanking God that more peaceful times have dawned upon the nations, and earnestly praying for the coming of those days, so long foretold, when "nation shall not lift up sword against nation, neither shall they learn war any more."

Crossing an open space to the west, we entered Beauchamp Tower, where the victims of royal hate and cruelty used to be confined before they were brought to the block. The interior walls are adorned with inscriptions, in which the unhappy and hopeless prisoners poured out their longings and their despair. Here is one over the fire-place : " The more suffering for Christ in this world, the more glory with Christ in the next." The man who carved that was imprisoned and beheaded for wishing to marry a certain lady, when Queen Elizabeth wished him to marry another lady, or not to marry at all. In the north-west corner is the single word " Jane," repeated in the window. It represents the gentle and accomplished young Lady Jane Gray, whose head was hacked off by command of Queen Mary, because one of the political parties had sought to make her queen after the death of Mary's predecessor.

In the open court, a little north of Beauchamp Tower, a stone in the pavement marks the spot where executions used to take place. Here Anne Boleyn, the wife and queen of Henry VIII., stood on the scaffold with bowed head while the executioner of Calais divided her slender neck with one blow of his heavy sword. Catharine, the fifth wife of the same old monster of cruelty, met her fate in the same manner.

Everywhere I went in England, in every palace and gallery and museum, I saw the portrait of that combination of hog, hyena and tiger, Henry VIII. I was righteously angry whenever I saw it. If ever the British people are wholly cured of their national brutality, they will tear those pictures down.

Henry's first wife was Catharine of Aragon. Growing tired of her, because she was not handsome and was older than himself, and falling in love with another woman, he applied to the pope for a divorce. Being refused he seceded from the Catholic Church, compelled his subjects to do the same, organized the Church of England, made himself the Pope of England, granted himself a divorce and married Anne Boleyn. He soon tired of her, and had her executed on a charge of adultery and treason.

On the nineteenth of May, 1533, Anne Boleyn went to the Tower, as England's queen, in a barge on the river Thames, surrounded by fifty other barges, all blazing with gold and banners; and on the nineteenth of May, 1536, in the same Tower, she lost her head. The next day the happy widower married his new love, Jane Seymour, who escaped the axe by dying in her bed one year after her wedding. Henry's fourth wife was Anne of Cleves. He got sick of her the first day. Not daring to cut off her head, because she was the daughter of a foreign prince, he divorced her six months after the marriage. The same year he married Catharine Howard. He let her live five years. Then he snapped his fingers, and off flew her head. His sixth and last wife was Catharine Parr, who had the unspeakable happiness of attending the funeral of the royal brute whom she had been compelled to call husband.

I was very anxious to see the interior of St. Peter's Church which stands within the inclosure of the

Tower, just north of the old beheading place. So I aprroached one of the fantastically uniformed guards, called " Beef-eaters," and asked him if I could go in. He answered " No." He assured me in the most positive terms that no visitor was ever allowed there. I turned away, but soon returned with the same request, at the same time showing a shining English shilling. Immediately his stern countenance relaxed, and, with the greatest suavity, he led me into St. Peter's and explained everything that I wished to see. In the land of our forefathers money has wonderful power.

St. Peter's contains the tombs of thirty-five victims of royal cruelty, who died by axe or poison or exhausting imprisonment. Of the place Lord Macauley says in his History of England : " Thither have been carried through successive ages, by the rude hands of gaolers, without one mourner following, the bleeding relics of men who have been the captains of armies, the leaders of parties, the oracles of senates and the ornaments of courts. In truth, there is no sadder spot on earth than this little cemetery."

As I stood among those graves, I said to myself : How could human beings be so cruel? I want to tell you something, which perhaps you do not know. Our ancestors were terribly brutal. Our Anglo-Saxon race has many good qualities ; but, unrestrained by the humanizing influences of the Christian religion, it is coarse and beastly and cruel. Naturally it is strongly inclined to drunkenness and selfish ambition and ruthless cruelty. It is far less mild and gentle than some of the races which we deem inferior. We see frequent outbursts of these ingrained qualities, even in this age and this land. If you ask what I mean, I point you to our treatment of the Indians, the Negroes and the Chinese, and to the criminal records of our public journals. To keep down and cast out this Anglo-Saxon devil, which has made English history so awfully bloody, we need, as a nation and as individuals, the mighty sanctifying power of the gospel of Jesus Christ.

I fear you have not enjoyed our visit to the Tower of London, with the blood-curdling memories which it has awakened. Come with me and I will show you something beautiful, before we leave the dismal old fortress-prison. Near bloody Tower, in Wakefield Tower, in a glass, under a double iron cage, are the splendid objects which compose the Regalia of England, or the Crown Jewels, as they are generally called. They consist of crowns, scepters, and other things worn or carried at the coronation ceremony; sacred vessels used in Westminster Abbey on the same occasion; the gold table plate used at the coronation banquet; and a set of the insignia of the various British Orders of Knighthood.

The crown of Queen Victoria occupies the highest place in the case. It was used at her coronation in 1838. It is gorgeous and magnificent in the extreme. It weighs three pounds and a half. The circlet consists of a gold band, surrounding a crimson velvet cap bordered with ermine. The band supports four golden branches, which, meeting in the center, form two arches, from which rises a mound of diamonds, over which is the cross, also composed of diamonds, with a magnificent sapphire in the center. Round the band or circlet, and alternating with the springing of the arches, rise four *fleurs-de-lis*, composed of brilliants. The arches rise from four crosses, each of which is completely covered with diamonds and other precious stones. The circlet, or band, which forms the base of the crown, is edged above and below with pearls. I cannot describe this most perfect specimen of the jeweler's art. I will merely add that it contains five rubies, eleven emeralds, seventeen sapphires, 277 pearls, and 2,783 diamonds.

As I stood gazing at that crown, almost paralyzed with wonder, I remembered the words of Jesus to me and to every disciple : " Be thou faithful unto death, and I will give thee a crown of life ; " and I said to myself : If I am true to my divine Master, and hold out to the end, after the toil and care of this life are over, God will place on my head a crown as much more glorious than that as the unclouded noonday sun is brighter than the tiniest glow-worm's spark. A crown of gold and precious stones is nothing compared with a crown of eternal life. Be thou faithful unto death, and, Christ will give thee a crown of life.

Besides the crown which I have so poorly described, the Regalia of England contains the Prince of Wales' Crown ; the Queen Consort's Crown ; the Queen's Crown ; St. Edward's Crown ; St. Edward's staff (which contains ninety pounds of gold) ; the Royal Sceptre ; the Sceptre of the Dove; Queen Victoria's Sceptre ; the Ivory Sceptre ; the Sceptre of Queen Mary ; the Orbs of the King and Queen ; the pointless Sword of Mercy ; the Swords of Justice ; the Coronation Bracelets ; the Royal Spurs ; the Coronation Oil Vessel in the form of an eagle ; the Anointing Spoon ; the Salt Cellar of State, in the form of a model of the White Tower ; the Baptismal Font for the royal children ; the Wine

Fountain; and the Insignia of the Orders of the Bath, Garter, Thistle, St. Michael and St. George and Star of India. All these are made of the most costly materials and the finest workmanship. The total value of the Regalia is estimated at fifteen million dollars.

From the Tower we went down to the river and took a steam-boat for Chelsea, a portion of the city five or six miles up the stream. If you will take your stand with me on the deck of the boat, I will point out some of the objects of interest. The general course is west. On our right is the north. Now we are passing under London Bridge. Down to one century ago this was the only bridge across the Thames. It is nine hundred and twenty eight feet long. It is borne by five granite arches, of which the central one has a span of one hundred and fifty-two feet. It is estimated that 15,000 vehicles and 100,000 pedestrians cross it every day. It cost ten million dollars.

Now we are under Southwark Bridge. It consists of three iron arches, on stone piers. It cost four million dollars. Over there, quarter of a mile up from the Bank, is St. Paul's Cathedral, the grandest building in London, dedicated one hundred and eighty years ago. I hope we can visit it before we leave the city.

Now we are right under the Blackfriars Bridge. It is built of iron and is 1,272 feet long. It derives its name from an ancient monastry of the Black Friars, or Monks, which used to stand here on the river's bank. Straight down there, south, two miles, is Spurgeon's Tabernacle. That huge building standing right on the bank of the river is a law-school, called the Temple. This building, standing almost at the water's edge, is an old palace, called Somerset House. It is now full of government offices employing nine hundred officials. The building contains 3,600 windows.

This is Waterloo Bridge, one of the finest structures of the kind in the world. It consists of nine arches, is 1,380 feet long and cost five million dollars.

Now we are under Charing Cross Rail-Way and Foot Bridge.

Another Bridge ! It is Westminster Bridge. Like all the others, it is substantial and elegant. We are between two immense buildings, which seem to rise right out of the water. Each presents a front of about one thousand feet. The one on the left, or south, side is St. Thomas' Hospital. The other is the Houses of Parliament. Just over beyond rise the towers of Westminster Abbey.

Now we are gliding under Lambeth Bridge. Right here is Lambeth Palace, the city residence of the Archbishop of Canterbury. This large six-sided building is Millbank Penitentiary. Just beyond is Vauxhall Bridge. Now it is over our heads.

For about a mile there is nothing worth looking at, on either bank. Now, at almost the same instant we glide under the Victoria Railway Bridge and the elegant Chelsea Suspension Bridge, and are at Chelsea. Here we will get off.

My chief object in going to Chelsea was to hear a grand concert, given by four military bands combined—those of the Grenadier Guards, the Household Brigade, the Cold Stream Guards and the Scott Guards—led by the celebrated Dan Godfrey, the

Gilmore of England. There were about two hundred musicians. The music was grand, overpowering, unequaled by anything of the kind that I ever heard before.

An exposition was being held at Chelsea, called "The Royal Military Exhibition." It included everything pertaining to the military life and history of Great Britain. I saw every kind of warlike implement, ever used by Englishmen; every style of uniform, ever used in the British army; pictures of battles; portraits of distinguished English generals; and war relics, of various kinds, too numerous to be mentioned. I was not greatly interested in these things. Since I landed on European soil I had seen so many soldiers (every European city swarms with them), so many military monuments, so many pictures of battles, so many instruments of death, that I was heartily sick of the very thought of war.

But I saw one collection of relics which did interest me, and which suggested a lesson which I wish to repeat to you. It was the portrait, saddle, sword and pistol of the unfortunate Prince Imperial, the son of the late Emperor Napoleon III., killed in Zulu Land, in 1879.

The lesson which these relics taught was the danger of procrastination. They were a powerful comment on the text: " Behold, now is the accepted time; behold, now is the day of salvation." The young prince to whom they belonged had joined the English army fighting the Zulus. One day he was with a squad, riding outside the camp. It was a dangerous situation. One of the company said: " Let us return. If we do not hasten, we may fall into the hands of the enemy." " Oh," said the prince, "let us stay here ten minutes and drink our coffee." Before the ten minutes had passed, a company of Zulus came upon them, and, in the skirmish, the prince was killed. When his mother was informed of the facts, in her anguish, she said : "That was his great mistake from babyhood. He never wanted to go to bed at night in time, nor to arise in the morning. He was always pleading for ten minutes. When two sleepy to speak, he would lift up his two little hands and spread out his ten fingers, indicating that he wanted ten minutes more. On that account I sometimes called him Mr. Ten-Minutes."

The habit of procrastination caused the death of that young prince. There is great danger that the same habit will cause the eternal death of some of you. For years you have intended, at some time, to give your heart to God and become a Christian. But all the time you have been saying : " Not now." When God has said : " Now is the acceptable time ; now is the day of salvation," you have said : " Not now. Some other time." Thus the habit of procrastination has firmly fastened upon you It is growing stronger and stronger every day. It is almost second nature to you to say : " Not now ; not now." The longer you defer the work of repenting and seeking God, the harder it will be. Now is the best time you will ever have to commence a Christian life. O settle the great question of your soul's salvation to-night. To-morrow may be too late. " Now is the accepted time ; now is the day of salvation." Do not close your eyes in sleep till you know you are saved. If you do not seek the Lord now, to-night, he may cut you off before you have another chance.

In the presence of these sad relics of a promising young man, who lost his life through the habit of saying: "Not now; wait ten minutes," I want to shout in your ears the words of God: "Behold, now is the accepted time; behold, now is the day of salvation."

XI.

MORE ABOUT LONDON.

"What city is like unto this great city?"—Revelation xviii, 18.

I am well aware that, when the inspired prisoner of Patmos penned these words, his mind was not on the city about which I am to talk to you to-night. And yet I venture to take them as my text, because they exactly express the feeling which filled my mind all the time I was in the metropolis of the British Empire. "What city is like unto this great city?"

London is so great that I could talk to you every Sabbath evening for two months, about its wonders, without any fear that you would lose your interest in my theme. To give but one evening to the greatest city in the world would almost seem a sin. To give more than two or three at this season would not be wise. Therefore, you will have nothing but London to-night, and not much about London after to-night.

In the immediate vicinity of my hotel were several points of minor interest, at which we will briefly glance. About five minutes' walk to the north was Smithfield. In old times Smithfield was an open common, just outside the city walls, where tournaments and fairs were held, and where executions took place. Subsequently, during a long period, it was London's only cattle-market. Now it is occupied, on its north side, by the Central London Meat Market, covering three and one-half acres, and by a market for poultry and provisions and fruit and vegetables, covering two acres more. It is worth the cost and time of a long journey to walk through these markets and see the enormous quantities of provisions which are exposed for sale. I had never seen anything of the kind which would bear a moment's comparison with this. Beneath the meat market is an extensive depot of the Great Western Railroad, to which the meat is brought in cars, and from which it is lifted up into the market by means of elevators.

But I did not go to Smithfield to see the beef and pork and poultry and vegetables. In front of the market is a large open space, in the center of which is a small circular garden, with a handsome fountain. Right where the fountain stands, martyrs used to be burned at the stake, in the days of bloody Mary. On the opposite side of the park from the market, on the wall of St. Bartholomew's Hospital is a tablet bearing the inscription: "Within a few feet of this spot John Rogers, John Bradford, John Philpot and other servants of God suffered death by fire for Christ's sake in the years 1555, 1556 and 1557."

I read that inscription with very great interest. John Rogers was one of the most learned and pious men that England ever produced. He was arrested and condemned to be roasted alive, simply because he declared that Christ was the only head of the Church. On the fourth of February, 1555, early in the morning, in Newgate Prison (three minutes' walk from my hotel toward the south) where he was confined with thieves and murderers, he was awakened out of a sound sleep, and commanded to prepare for the fire. He begged that he might speak a few

words with his wife before burning ; but this was
refused. He was immediately conveyed to Smithfield. On the way he sang a psalm, and the people
were astonished at his constancy and firmness. His
wife and ten children—one an infant at the breast—
met him on the way to the stake. It was a piteous
spectacle. His heart was wrung with anguish at the
thought of leaving his darlings to the cruelty of a
cold and heartless world. But when his persecutors
offered him life and liberty if he would recant, he
said : "Go on ; I will not recant." And so they
burned him. As he was burning, he bathed his
hands in the flame, and thus, after lingering agony,
rendered up his life in defense of the gospel of
Christ.

At Smithfield I got a better idea than I ever had
before of the cost of the religious liberty which we
Americans enjoy. God help us to maintain what our
English forefathers purchased with their lives.

A short distance east of Smithfield I visited St.
Giles' Church. Beneath the chancel lie the remains
of John Milton, one of four or five men—the greatest poets who ever lived. In another part of the
church is a tablet on the wall bearing the inscription:
"John Milton, Author of Paradise Lost. Born Dec.,
1608, died Nov., 1671. His father died March, 1641.
They are both interred in this church." Many other
distinguished men lie buried here, among whom I
notice Martin Frobisher the discoverer, and the
author of " Foxe's Book of Martyrs." Oliver Cromwell was married in this same place.

From St. Giles' Church I went north a few rods to
the Charterhouse, where John Wesley and many
others of England's greatest men, were fitted for the

University. The building was first a monastery; then a palace; then, by the purchase and endowment of Thomas Sutton, a school for forty poor boys and a refuge for eighty poor men. In 1872 the school was removed; but the refuge remains. I was shown the park around which Wesley used to walk three times every morning before breakfast.

Returning past my hotel and going a little distance to the south, I was at the corner of Newgate street and Old Bailey, where stands Newgate prison. Within its walls all executions for the city take place. When a man commits murder in England, he is immediately put on trial, if he can be caught, and is speedily brought to punishment. Whether he is a beggar or a Lord, a pauper or a millionaire, he soon swings by the neck. In this country it usually takes from one to three years to convict and execute a murderer, and, if the guilty party has plenty of money, he snaps his fingers at justice and goes scot-free. Crimes of violence are alarmingly on the increase in the United States. The chief cause is the tardiness and uncertainty with which American justice pursues the guilty. Crime, among us, is lynx-eyed, and travels by lightning-express; while Justice is blind, or near-sighted, and travels by stage-coach or canal-boat. Because wicked men, who have no fear of God, have little fear of human vengeance, they hesitate not to shed the blood of their fellow men. If there were a reasonable certainty that death would speedily overtake the manslayer, there would not be one murder where now there are three. To make a bad matter worse, a strong effort is being made, all over the land, by people of sickly sentimentality, to abolish capital punishment.

I believe in capital punishment, for many reasons, chiefly because the Bible says : " Whoso sheddeth man's blood, by man shall his blood be shed : for in the image of God made he man." I would not ordain any cruel or barbarous mode of execution ; but, in some form, death should speedily be visited on every one who intentionally and maliciously takes a human life. It will not do to say that the divine statute which I quoted has been repealed. It is not a Jewish ordinance, which Christianity has supplanted. It was enacted long before the Jewish dispensation, in the infancy of human history, and will be in force as long as the world endures.

Diagonally across the street from Newgate Prison, stands St. Sepulcher's Church, from whose square tower a knell is tolled whenever an execution takes place at Newgate. In old times, when Tyburn was the place of execution, every criminal, on his way to death, was presented with a nosegay at the door of this church. I wonder if that was the origin of the American custom for ladies to fill the cells of condemned malefactors with costly bouquets, especially if the hapless victims of murderous rage happened to belong to their own sex?

I went into St. Sepulcher's and reverently stood above the grave of the gallant Captain John Smith, whose life was saved, in Virginia, by Pocahontas, the Indian maid. The first line of the now nearly illegible epitaph runs thus : " Here lies one conquered that hath conquered kings."

From St. Sepulcher's it is only a short walk to St. Paul's. This is the grandest building in London. It was designed by Sir Christopher Wren, and was begun in 675 and completed in 1710. It is an interesting fact that the whole edifice was erected by one architect and one master mason, under one bishop. The cost of construction—nearly four million dollars—was defrayed by a tax levied on the coal brought into London during the period of its erection. The ground plan of this cathedral is a Roman cross. It is five hundred feet long and one hundred and eighteen broad, and the transept is two hundred and fifty feet long. The dome, from the pavement to the top of the cross, is three hundred and sixty-five feet high. Its circumference is three hundred and fifty-two feet.

St. Paul's is the fourth largest church in Christendom, being surpassed only by St. Peter's at Rome, the Cathedral of Saville, in Spain, and the Cathedral of Milan. St. Paul's resembles St. Peter's, with this difference, however, that Rome's cathedral covers twice as much ground as London's, is seventy feet higher, has a much larger dome and cost more than twelve times as much. I ought to add that the interior decorations of St. Peter's are as much richer and more beautiful than those of St. Paul's as you could imagine. There is no comparison whatever between the two, in this respect.

We approach the front of St. Paul's from the west. Here is a semi-circular, paved court, with a row of forty large stone posts running around it. Just within the court, surrounded by a high fence of iron pickets, is a marble statue of Queen Anne. Around the base of the lofty pedestal on which she stands, sit four emblematic figures, representing, respectively, England, France, Ireland and America.

Now look at the church. Its material is white marble. But two hundred years of London smoke and fog have covered most of it with a coat of paint almost as black as ink. There is enough of the white stone in sight to enable you to imagine how beautiful the building must have been when it was new. The front—or façade, as the architects call it,—presents a double portico, consisting of twelve Corinthian pillars below and eight composite pillars above, a pediment and two campanile towers, each two hundred and twenty-two feet in height. The tower on our left has a fine peal of twelve bells. The other tower contains the largest bell in Great Britain, called "Great Paul," weighing more than sixteen tons. When that bell speaks, all London is compelled to listen.

Look up at the pediment—you would call it the gable—between the towers. It is filled with statues, or figures in very high relief. You see a group of horsemen. The animals are rearing and plunging, so that the riders can hardly keep their saddles. One, in the middle of the group, has fallen to the ground, under a blaze of glory which is flashing down from the parted heavens. That represents the conversion of Paul. You are familiar with the story. The name of the man was called Saul at the first. He was a Jew. He was a man of gigantic intellect, of prodigious learning, of unconquerable will, of tireless energy. In short, of the legions of great men whom the Jewish race has given to the world, he was the greatest. He was a Jew. He was not a Christian. He hated Christianity. He honestly believed that Jesus of Nazareth was an impostor and that his religion was a tissue of impositions and lies. His mistake was that he had not carefully and prayerfully investigated the subject without rancor or prejudice. But, believing that Christianity was a fraud, he was determined to destroy it, branches and root. So he organized a persecution, which began with the martyrdom of Stephen,. in whose murder he had a hand. From that he went on, making havoc of the Church and casting both men and women into prison. "Breathing out threatenings and slaughter against the disciples of the Lord," "and being exceedingly mad against them," he started for Damascus, with a company of armed men, clothed with authority to arrest and bind, and bring to Jerusalem for trial, any Christian whom he might find in that foreign city. Just as the cavalcade had reached the top of a hill overlooking Damascus, at the hour of noon, when the sun was shining, in that Syrian sky, with a dazzling brilliancy such as it never wears in this humid climate, suddenly a light from heaven shone round about them so intensely bright that the sun turned pale like the moon, and every horseman was hurled to the ground. With the light, came a voice, speaking in the Hebrew language: "Saul, Saul, why persecutest thou me?" The disarmed and blinded persecutor answered: "Who art thou, Lord?" The answer came: "I am Jesus, whom thou persecutest." Looking up through the parted heavens, Saul saw Jesus sitting on the right hand of God the Father. He saw his mistake. He saw that the Christians were right. He saw that Jesus was the Messiah foretold in the Old Testament Scriptures. Like an honest man, he acknowledged his error and humbly asked: "Lord, what wilt thou have me to do?"

I have not time to continue the story. You know that Saul became a Christian; that he was called Paul; that he did more to build up the Church of Jesus Christ than any other man who ever lived; that he showed the sincerity of his conversion by sacrificing every worldly advantage and by laying down his life for the sake of the truth, as his great intellect and heart saw and felt the truth. The conversion of such a man as Paul, and his subsequent life, prove that the Christian religion is true. I believe that every man who honestly, carefully, persistently and prayerfully seeks to know the truth, will come to the conclusion that Jesus is the Son of God and the Saviour of the world.

Look up at the Cathedral again. On the apex of pediment you see a statue. It is fifteen feet tall. It is St. Paul. On his right is St. Peter; on his left St. James. At the bases of the towers are the four Evangelists—two on the north tower and two on the south. Look still higher. You see the dome rising, from the junction of the arms of the cross, three hundred feet back from the front. Do you see the ball and cross surmounting the lantern at the top of the dome? Together the ball and cross weigh 8,960 pounds. The ball is hollow, and will hold twelve men at once.

Let us go in. We must ascend a flight of twenty-two marble steps. Passing under the portico and through one of the doors, we find the interior imposing from the vastness of its proportions; but it strikes us as being bare and dark. It is thickly lined with statues and monuments of England's great men, many of whom are buried here.

I went down into the crypt. Directly under the dome is the sarcophagus of Lord Nelson, Britain's greatest sea-fighter. Near by, with lights always burning around it, is a larger and more beautiful sarcophagus of the Duke of Wellington. Wellington and Nelson, two little men (I mean physically) conquered Napoleon, who was physically a little man, at Waterloo and Trafalgar. Those three little men shook the earth and the sea, proving that it does not take a great mass of flesh and bones to make a great man.

Among those sleeping under the great church I noticed the name of one American—Benjamin West, formerly President of the Royal Academy of Painting and Sculpture, born in the state of Pennsylvania.

Every stone in the floor of that great subterranean chamber covers the remains, and bears the name, of some distinguished person. I must not fail to mention the architect of the Cathedral, Sir Christopher Wren, who here reposes, with his wife by his side. A memorial tablet up stairs, over the entrance of the north transept, has his name, and age at death—ninety years—with the Latin inscription: " Lector, is monumentum requiris, circumspice," " Reader, if you seek his monument, look around you." I left St. Paul's saying to myself: If I had not been to Milan and Rome I should call this a most magnificent church.

Wednesday morning, August 13, between nine and ten o'clock, I started for Westminster Abbey. I rode on top of a bus as far as Charing Cross and Trafalgar Square. A part of the route lay along the Strand, one of the busiest and most celebrated of London's streets. Charing Cross is the place where the bier of Queen Eleanor, the wife of Edward I., was set down for the last time on its way to Westminster Abbey. On the spot now stands an equestrian statue of King Charles I.

Immediately north of this is Trafalgar Square, one

of the finest open places in the world. It is dedicated to Lord Nelson, and commemorates his glorious victory at the battle of Trafalgar, gained by the English fleet over the combined armaments of France and Spain. This victory saved England from invasion by the armies of Napoleon and gave Nelson the title of Saviour of his country. In the center of the square rises a massive granite Corinthian column, one hundred and forty-five feet high, crowned with a statue of Nelson, seventeen feet in height. The pedestal is adorned with reliefs in bronze, cast from cannon captured from the French. On the north face is a scene from the battle of Aboukir, representing Nelson wounded in the head, declining to be assisted out of his turn by a surgeon who has been dressing the wounds of a common sailor. On the east side is the battle of Copenhagen. On the west side is the battle of St. Vincent. On the south side is the death of Nelson at Trafalgar.

On the morning of that battle the great admiral displayed from the mast of his flag-ship a signal, on which every sailor, in every one of his thirty-five men-of-war, read the inspiring words: " England expects every man to do his duty." In the hour of victory Nelson was mortally wounded by a musket-ball from the rigging of a French ship ; but his last message to his men, inscribed on his monument in Trafalgar Square, will be remembered to the end of time.

That would be a good motto for us, who profess to be Christians, only putting God in place of England. " *God* expects every man to do his duty." Because every man in the English fleet did his duty at Trafalgar, England won a glorious victory. If every member of the Church, in any place, would do his duty, that church would be grandly successful in every department of effort. But the trouble, in all churches, is that there are so many dead-heads, who expect some one else to do their work and pay their bills. My brother, God expects every man to do his duty; he expects you to do your duty. Will you do your duty like a man, or will you shirk like a craven and a coward?

At the base of the Nelson Monument are four colossal bronze lions, modeled by Sir Edwin Landseer, crouching upon pedestals running out from the column in the form of a cross. The monument was erected in 1843 by voluntary contributions, at a cost of two hundred and twenty-five thousand dollars. North of the monument are two fountains and several statues.

North of the square is the National Gallery of Fine Arts. Noble buildings surround it on the east and west. From the south side runs Whitehall, a broad street, named from a palace which used to stand there. Walking down Whitehall, you pass a variety of uninteresting buildings. On the left, over beyond a short distance, out of sight, flows the river, in an opposite direction to that which you are taking. On the right you pass the Horse Guards, the headquarters of the British Army ; the Treasury Building ; the head of Downing Street ; and the Public Offices, a large pile of buildings, which cost two millions and a half of dollars. Over back of the Horse Guards is St. James' Park, full of beauty, covering fifty-nine acres On the north of St. James' Park is St. James' Palace. On the west is Buckingham Palace. The latter is the Queen's city residence, and the place where she holds her drawing-rooms. The former is used only for levées. The difference between a levée and a drawing-room is that, at the former, gentlemen only are presented to the sovereign, while at the latter it is almost entirely ladies who are introduced.

You and I could not get into either of these palaces, into the presence of the Sovereign of the British Empire. If we should try to enter, armed guards would push us back with the points of their bayonets. But hear what the Sovereign of the Universe has said: "Thus saith the high and lofty One that inhabiteth eternity, whose name is Holy, I dwell in the high and holy place, with him also that is of a contrite and humble spirit, to revive the spirit of the humble, and to revive the heart of the contrite ones." The Queen of England will not let you come into her house. The King of Heaven will come into your home and your heart.

If you should go through St. James' Park and past Buckingham Palace, you would find yourself in Green Park, which covers sixty acres. Just beyond that, to the west, is Hyde Park, which covers four hundred acres. While I am on the subject of parks, I might as well tell you that London has three other large parks—Victoria, Regents' and Kensington Gardens —which cover nearly a thousand acres, besides a great number of smaller ones. All these are right in London's heart. Surely we may well exclaim: "What city is like unto this great city?"

But I was on the way to Westminster Abbey, and was almost there, when I stopped to tell you about the palaces and the parks. However, we will not go into the Abbey to-night. If we do, we shall stay too long, and unduly protract this service; or we shall not be able to remain long enough to get any satisfaction.

We will go across the street, eastward, to the Houses of Parliament, or Palace of Westminster—as it is sometimes called. It is an immense building, in the late Gothic style of architecture, covering eight acres and costing fifteen million dollars. Its imposing river front is nine hundred and forty feet long, and is adorned with statues of all the English monarchs from William the conqueror down to Queen Victoria. It has three towers—St. Stephen's, Middle and Victoria—whose respective altitudes are 318, 300 and 340 feet. In St. Stephen's Tower is a clock with four dials, each twenty feet in diameter. It takes five hours to wind up the striking parts of this clock.

This enormous building, with its eleven courts, one hundred stair cases and eleven hundred rooms, does not excite one's admiration, when viewed from the outside, as much as our Capitol at Washington. It stands too low to show what it really is. I walked through the Queen's Robing Room, the Royal Gallery, the Prince's Chamber, the Central Hall, the House of Peers, the House of Commons and Westminster Hall, beside many smaller apartments. Each one of these, with its pictures and statues and costly furnishings, deserves half an hour of description.

The last named—Westmister Hall—is seven times as large as this audience room, and about three times as high, and has no columns to support its ceiling and roof. It has been the scene of many memorable events. Here Charles I., was tried and condemned; also Walace Bruce, Sir Thomas More, Guy Fawkes and scores of other noted historical characters. Here Warren Hastings was acquitted, after a trial running through seven years. Here Oliver Cromwell, wearing the royal purple lined with ermine, and holding a golden sceptre in one hand and a Bible in the other, was saluted as Lord Protector. Eight years afterward the Protector's body was dragged from its resting place in Westminster Abbey and thrust into a pit at Tyburn, while his head was exposed on one of the pinnacles of this same Westminster Hall, where it remained thirty years. What a commentary on the fickleness of fortune and the barbarity of those times!

I visited the Royal Mews (so called), in the rear of Buckingham Palace, where the Queen's horses and carriages are kept. There are one hundred and ten horses in that place. They were all bred and raised there, and none are ever sold. The attendants showed me an immense array of harness and trappings, heavy with gold, used by the present monarch and by her predecessors. I saw the Queen's carriages. I saw one, seldom used, which cost 38,000 dollars, and weighs four tons. It is a real work of art, built in 1762. I was also shown eight beautiful cream-colored horses, just alike, with long silvery tails sweeping the floor, which are never used except when the Queen rides from Buckingham Palace to Westminster, to open Parliament.

The Queen's equipage—I said to myself—is nothing compared with God's horses and chariot of fire, which took Elijah to heaven, and which will come to get the soul of the poorest and most despised Christian pauper, when the hour of his departure shall have arrived. This Book declares that "the chariots of God are twenty thousand, even thousands upon thousands: the Lord is among them, as in Sinai, in the sanctuary."

I wish I had time to tell you all about the South Kensington Museum and the National Gallery. But I should need a whole evening for each, and then my subject would only be begun. In the latter place, I lingered longest in the Turner Room. It contains sixty of the best pictures of England's greatest painter. Most of them are large. I did not like them at first—they are so peculiar. But they grew upon me rapidly. I consider his favorite, "*The Fighting Temeraire Towed to her Last Berth*" the best. After I had seen that, I could hardly look at any other. My eyes kept going to it, in whatever part of the room I might be. It seemed to have a magnetic power which it was almost impossible to resist.

So, I thought, it will be with the face and glorified form of our Saviour in heaven. There will be ten thousand things to attract our attention there—the angels, the prophets, the apostles, the martyrs, our friends whom we knew on earth. But when once we have looked in the face of him who died for our redemption, all other things will seem nothing in comparison, and so through eternity; our eyes will follow him whithersoever he or we shall move. To him whose vision has been clarified by the regenerating power of the Holy Ghost, Jesus is, and always will be, "the chiefest among ten thousand" and the one "altogether lovely."

To a student, the greatest thing in London is the British Museum. It is the greatest institution of the kind in the world. I spent an entire day there, and part of an afternoon some days later. The building covers seven acres of ground, and has thirty acres of floors. It is filled with antiquities, for many of which fabulous prices have been paid, the whole forming a

collection which all the wealth of the world could not
buy. It is visited, every year, by nearly half a
million persons. It is a world of wonders. I went
through the whole, but spent most of my time in the
"Elgin," "Ephesus," "Mausoleum," "Assyrian" and
"Egyptian" rooms. In the first named are the
"Elgin" marbles—nearly all the sculptures of the
Parthenon at Athens, full of fascinating interest to
every Greek student. The "Ephesus" room contains
remains, not very extensive, of the Temple of Diana
at Ephesus, one of the "Seven Wonders of the
World." The "Mausoleum" room contains very
extensive remains of the Mausoleum of Coria, which
was built twenty-two hundred years ago, and was
counted among the "Seven Wonders." With what
interest and reverence did I gaze upon the colossal
statue of the old king which once crowned the summit of that famous monument! It must be about
fifteen feet tall. One of the chariot horses remains,
in two pieces. It is of white marble, about as large
as a good sized elephant. It once stood on the summit of a marble building one hundred and eighty feet
high. That marvelous tomb, of which these are the
shattered fragments, was built by a woman to express
her love for a noble husband, snatched away by cruel
death. The strongest human love is that which
binds together the hearts of husband and wife, truly
wedded, according to the original plan and purpose
of God. Fraternal, filial, paternal and even maternal
affection are far less strong than the purest conjugal
love.

Among millions of articles in the British Museum
one of the most highly prized and eagerly visited, is
the Portland Vase. It is made of blue glass covered

with an enamel of white glass, and cut in cameo so as to show a finely artistic group of the wedding of Thetis and Peleus. It once held the ashes of a relation of the Emperor Alexander Severus, perhaps his mother, or those of the Emperor himself. That was over sixteen hundred years ago. Twelve hundred years after it came from the potter's hands, it was found in a tomb in Rome. In 1810 it became the property of the Duke of Portland. Although it is only ten inches high, it is one of the most valued relics of antiquity. Millions of money would not buy it. Mr. Wedgwood, one of the most distinguished manufacturers of ceramics, spent twenty thousand dollars in trying to make a vase like it, and confessed that he could not. In 1845 the Portland Vase was wantonly broken by a madman, named Lloyd; and the world sent up a cry of agony. But the numerous pieces have been so carefully reunited that you would hardly notice that it had ever been broken.

It was my fixed purpose, when I went to London, to see the Portland Vase; and yet I did not. The first time I went to the Museum, I thought I had plenty of time and would look it up at the next visit. The day before I bade good-bye to London, I went to the Museum for the second and last time. It usually closes at five o'clock. That day I saw a notice posted at the door that it would not close till six. I supposed that the whole museum would be open till six, and thought to myself: I will go to the "Gold Room" and see the Portland Vase between five and six. So I lingered in other apartments two or three hours, and when I came to the Gold Room at about fifteen minutes past five it was locked for the day. As I was to leave London, with the party, for Scotland, before that door would again swing on its hinges, I must go back to America with the shameful confession that I had not seen the Portland Vase.

That was a lesson for me. The lesson was: *Never put off till the next day or the next hour what ought to be done now.* I ought to have made sure of seeing the British Museum's choicest, single treasure the first hour I was there.

You can easily make a spiritual application of this thought. You intend at some time, to attend to religion and the salvation of your soul. But you think it will be just as well, if not better, to defer it to some future period, perhaps the evening of life. You think : " The last thing, just before death, I will repent and give my heart to God, and so enter heaven." But I want to tell you that when you are ready God may say: " Too late. You cannot enter now." Therefore, I close this sermon as I did the last : " Behold, now is the accepted time ; behold, now is the day of salvation."

XII.

WESTMINSTER ABBEY AND WINDSOR CASTLE.

" The two houses, the house of the Lord and the king's house."—I Kings ix. 10.

The two houses referred to in this text were built by Solomon, and were a temple, or church, in which the people assembled to worship God, and a palace, or castle, in which the king and royal family resided. I am to speak to you to-night about two houses— "the house of the Lord and the king's house." The house of the Lord, which I have in mind, is a church, Westminster Abbey; the house of the king is Windsor Castle, the chief residence of England's monarch.

Westminster Abbey is a church and a mausoleum, a place of worship and a place of burial, a house of God and a house of death. It stands, facing the west, with its back about eight hundred feet from the River Thames, between which and itself rise the walls and the towers of the Houses of Parliament. Its official name is the Collegiate Church of St. Peter. Its foundation dates back more than twelve hundred years. It has been several times demolished, rebuilt and improved. The present edifice, or the greater part of it, is six hundred years old. Its external appearance is grand and imposing, although age has greatly marred its beauty—the walls in many places being perfectly black. In front it shows two massive towers, just alike, each two hundred and twenty-five feet in height. The total length of the edifice from west to east, is five hundred and thirteen feet. The length of the transept, from north to south, is two hundred feet. The width of the nave and aisles is seventy-five feet ; of the transept, eighty feet. The entire area covered by the church is a little less than one-third of that of St. Peter's at Rome, and nearly ten times that of the building in which we are now assembled.

With its royal burial vaults and long rows of monuments to celebrated men, Westminster Abbey is regarded by the English as their national Temple of Fame ; and interment within its walls is considered the last and greatest honor which the nation can bestow on her most deserving children. " Victory or Westminster Abbey ! " was the cry of Lord Nelson, on the eve of the battle of Cape St. Vincent. " Victory *and* Westminster Abbey ! " has been the inspiration and hope of thousands of Englishmen in fighting against the difficulties which stand in the way of worldly success.

The shape of Westminster Abbey, on the ground, is that of a Roman cross. The lower part of the cross, if you imagine it to stand erect, is the nave and aisles. The cross piece is the transept. The upper part, above the horizontal beam, is filled in with nine chapels, named after kings and saints and lined with splendid tombs.

I entered the place through the door of the north transept. I found a religious service in progress. The clergyman and singers occupied the choir— which extends down into the nave, from the junction of the arms of the cross—and the congregation were sitting in the north transept. I sat down among the living and the dead—the former less numerous by far than the latter—and drank in the spirit of the songs and prayers and Scripture lessons. It was an hour of rare, strange and fascinating enjoyment

When the service was over, I arose, and for about five hours, wandered through that grand, old historic place, which, since, in early childhood, I read Irving's Sketch Book, I had longed to see. For five hours the nineteenth century was in the future, and I lived in the distant past. I seemed a ghost walking, unterrified, among the giant spirits of the generations gone.

With the help of your imagination and mine, I want to take you by the arm and conduct you through this temple of earthly fame and grandeur. We are now standing with our backs to the door of the north transept. We look south to the end of the other transept, two hundred feet away. The transept has a broad aisle, and two side aisles, with rows of columns between, supporting the roof. The ceiling is one hundred and two feet above our heads. Against the columns and walls of the transept stand statues and tombs of illustrious men. The statues all look like life. Some of the monumental tombs are rare and rich and costly; others are cheaper and more simple and plain. Most of the great names commemorated in this north transept belong to statesmen and warriors. A few, out of scores, I will point out.

Here, on our right, is a large monument to William Pitt, Lord Chatham, built of snowy marble. Above, in a niche, Chatham is represented in the attitude of an orator, with his right hand outstretched. At his feet sit two female figures Wisdom and Courage. In the center is Britannia with a trident. To the right and left are Earth and Sea. As an American I was interested in this monument of Pitt, because our city of Pittsburgh was named after him, and because, when the English aristocracy undertook to rob and enslave our fathers, he took our part, and, when the war of the Revolution came on, though sinking under the infirmities of age, he rallied all the great powers of his eloquence to oppose the cruel and oppressive measures which were put in practice to crush us. Pitt came up from among the people. Therefore he was our friend. We should never forget that, while the aristocracy of England have always been our enemies, and wish us all manner of evil now, the English people are, and always have been, our friends.

Over there, on the left, is the statue of Lord Beaconsfield, whose real name was Disraeli, the great Hebrew scholar, writer and statesman, who became prime-minister of England and virtual ruler of two hundred and sixty millions of people.

Nearly opposite Disraeli is another British Premier, Lord Palmerston.

Still farther down, on the same side, are the monuments, statues and graves of two rival statesmen and bitter political enemies—Charles James Fox and the younger William Pitt. They were both men of extraordinary genius, consummate eloquence and commanding influence. But Fox was an inveterate gambler, a hard drinker, an unprincipled profligate and the greatest spendthrift of his day ; while Pitt, though possessed of many virtues, selfishly kept England in a needless war, of twenty years duration, which cost rivers of blood and mountains of money.

While we stand by the graves of these inveterate enemies, we recall the well-known lines of Scott:

> "Drop upon Fox's grave a tear,
> 'Twill trickle to his rival's bier,"

and we feel like saying : since we are all going to lie down together in the grave, we cannot afford to be enemies ; let us all be friends ; let us do each other all the good we can ; let us never speak into each other's faces, or behind each other's backs, an unkind word which we shall regret on a dying bed or before the judgment throne.

But we must not linger longer in this transept. Let us turn the corner to the right and walk down the north aisle of the church. We are between two long rows of tombs. Those on the right are against the wall, while those on the left are against the columns which divide the aisle from the nave. Nearly every tomb, or monument, is adorned with one or more statues. Above, on the walls and columns, are memorial tablets. Still higher up, the pictured windows are filled with names and mottoes, reminding us of men who became great in war, or statesmanship, or art, or science, or law, or philanthropy. The south aisle is like the north. The nave is as full of tombs and tablets and statues as either aisle. The very stones on which we tread cover the ashes, and bear the names, of departed greatness.

I have not time to describe one hundredth part of all that this most wonderful of mausoleums contains. We will merely glance at a few of the tombs and statues and names. Here in the north aisle, sitting on his sarcophagus, is the statue of William Wilberforce, the Christian statesman, who distinguished himself by his self-denying efforts for the dissemination of the Scriptures, the christianizing of India, the granting of their rights to the American Colonies and the abolition of slavery. For the last of these, the abolition of African slavery in the British colonies, he introduced a bill in Parliament, one hundred years ago, and stood almost alone in its defense. Defeated at first, he renewed his efforts and persisted, till, after a struggle of twenty years, he had the joy of seeing the emancipation bill pass both houses.

Out in the nave, in front of the choir, is the monument and tomb of Sir Isaac Newton. The half-recumbent figure of the great philosopher reposes on a black marble sarcophagus, beside which are two small cherubs unfolding a scroll. Below is a bass relief illustrating the labors of the deceased. Above is an allegorical figure of astronomy upon a large globe. Newton was one of the greatest scientist that ever lived. He discovered the principle of the attraction of gravitation, and demonstrated the laws by which it operates on earth and among the stars. He was the father of the science of optics, and was the first to show to the world that the white light of the sun consists of seven colors blended together. He found out more of nature's great secrets than almost any other man who ever lived. And yet he was a meek and humble follower of the lowly Jesus. He laid down his heart, and all the riches of his gigantic intellect, at the pierced, bleeding feet of the man of Calvary. He, the prince of philosophers, used to say : " We account the Bible— the Scriptures of God—to be the most sublime philosophy."

There are some ignorant and weak-minded persons,

who think that the scholarship and intellect of the world are arrayed against Christianity. Standing in Westminster Abbey, in front of the mausoleum of Sir Isaac Newton, I want to tell you that that statement is the farthest from being the truth. The truth is that most of the great scientists and sages, the brainiest men in the world, have been and are Christians, at least in theory and belief.

Copernicus, the father of the modern science of astronomy and the discoverer of the true motion of the sun and earth, was a minister of the gospel. Galileo, the inventor of the clock, the thermometer, the microscope and the telescope, and the discoverer of the moons of Jupiter, was a member of the Church. Kepler, who wrought out the stupendous problem of the planetary movements, was a Protestant Christian. Sir Humphry Davy, a physician, chemist and discoverer of marvelous ability, was an earnest Christian. Faraday, the greatest of English chemists, declared himself a firm believer in the Christian religion. Humboldt, the famous German naturalist and geographer, used, admired, praised and believed the Bible. Hugh Miller, a prince among geologists, was a member of the Presbyterian Church. Morse, the inventor of the electric telegraph, was the son of a Congregational minister, and himself a Christian. Mitchel, the greatest of American astronomers, was an ardent believer in, and defender of, the Christian faith. Lieut. Maury, the greatest of geographers and meteorologist that America ever produced, was a Christian scientist, and once declared that the study of the Bible was a great help to him in his scientific researches. Agassiz, whose fame has filled the world, was the son of a Protestant clergyman of Switzerland, and a champion, on scientific principles, of the doctrines of a personal God, as set forth in the Holy Scriptures.

He once formed one of a small circle of literary guests at a private dinner. The conversation turned upon the subject of religion, which was treated with derision and railery. Each one had his own jest, except Agassiz. He was silent and thoughtful. At last there was a lull, and all seemed waiting for him to speak. With most impressive seriousness of expression, he said: "Gentlemen, I once thought and spoke as you do now; but I have read the Bible, and I know that it is true. If you ask me how I know that it is true, perhaps the best reason I can give is (laying his hand upon his breast), I feel that it is true."

"And what shall I more say? for the time would fail me to tell of" Dante, and Tasso, and Milton, and Shakespeare, and Cowper, and Bryant, and Tennyson, and Longfellow, and Herschel, and Guizot, and Prescott, and Carlyle, and Washington, and Adams, and Lincoln, and Grant, and Garfield, who believing in the Gospel, wrote poems, composed histories, originated philosophies, framed constitutions, governed nations and emancipated races. Surely he who affirms that the brains of the world are against the Bible and Christ, has small brains himself, or has little regard for the truth.

Some distance in front of Newton's tomb, not far from the center of the nave, is a large stone in the floor covering the remains, and covered with the epitaph, of David Livingstone, the great explorer and heroic Christian missionary, who penetrated the heart of Africa long before the world ever heard of Stanley and Emin Pasha.

Over in the south aisle are scores of beautiful and interesting monuments, statues and tablets. As a Christian and a Methodist, I was greatly interested in the memorial of John and Charles Wesley. It consists of a large marble slab against the wall, with a medallion of the two brothers in the upper section, and a bass-relief of John preaching on his father's grave, in the lower. Above the medallion are the names of the brothers, with the date of the birth and death of each. Under the medallion are John's dying words : " The best of all is, God is with us." Under the bass-relief is the motto which he took for himself when he was denied the privilege of preaching in the churches : " The world is my parish."

The Wesleys came to the front when religion in England was almost dead. When they began to preach, religion began to live. But the bats and owls, who made their vile nests under the shadow of the tomb of a dead Christianity, did not like to be disturbed and at once stirred up a bitter persecution against the evangelists. Although they were both ordained ministers of the Church of England, every place of worship was shut against them, and they were compelled to preach in the fields and streets. In the face of curses and yells of hate and stones and rotten eggs, they persevered, till now their spiritual children are counted by many millions and their faces, carved in enduring stone, are deemed worthy of a niche in England's grandest temple of fame. Charles Wesley was the greatest sacred poet since King David ; and John was the greatest gospel minister since the Apostle Paul. The doctrines which they preached and sung were chiefly these : Everybody can be saved if he will ; everybody must be born again ; everybody may know that his sins are forgiven ; everybody can be cleansed from all unrighteousness and made holy in heart and life. These are the doctrines which Methodism is proclaiming throughout the world. I proclaim them to you to-night. Every one of you may be saved, and be saved to-night. Every one in this house, who has not already been, must be born again. Every one of you may know, beyond the shadow of a doubt, that your sins are all forgiven and your name written in the book of life. Every one of you can be saved through and through—saved from the least and last remains of sin.

Passing up the south aisle, and around the corner into the south transept, we find ourselves in the Poets' Corner. It contains monuments and memorials of Chaucer, Shakespeare, Milton, Ben Johnson, Spencer, Goldsmith, Addison, Dickens, Thackery, our loved Longfellow and hundreds of others who have enriched the world with the treasures of their genius. The Shakespeare monument is a full length statue of the poet, with one elbow resting on a pile of books the other hand holding a scroll on which is carved a quotation from " The Tempest : "

> " The cloud-capped towers, the gorgeous palaces,
> The solemn temples, the great globe itself,
> Yea, all which it inherit, shall dissolve,
> And like this unsubstantial pageant faded,
> Leave not a rock behind. We are such stuff
> As dreams are made of ; and our little life
> Is rounded with a sleep."

The Longfellow memorial is a beautiful marble bust of the poet, as white as snow, with the inscription : " This bust was placed amongst the memorials of the poets of England by the admirers of an American poet."

Perhaps the most interesting portion of the Abbey is that which the nine chapels occupy. Within them are buried thirteen kings, fourteen queens and scores and scores of princes, dukes, lords, bishops and men and women of lower rank.

The largest and most beautiful of all the chapels is that which was built by King Henry VII., and bears his name. You enter it by ascending a flight of twelve black marble steps, and passing through a deep, gloomy but magnificent arch, where gates of brass swing heavily upon their ponderous hinges to receive you. You notice that the gates are adorned with roses, in allusion to the fact that the marriage of Henry VII. with Elizabeth, daughter of Edward IV., united the houses of York and Lancaster and put an end to the Wars of the Roses.

The architectural beauties of this place cannot be adequately described. It is a superb structure. It consists of a nave and aisles, with five small chapels at the east end. The chapel contains about one hundred statues and figures. On each side are carved choir-stalls in dark oak most beautifully designed and executed. Each stall is appropriated to a Knight of the Order of the Bath. Each seat bears the armorial bearings of its occupants in brass, and above each are a sword and banner. This is the place where the knights are installed, or initiated. Among the banners I saw that of the unfortunate Dom Pedro, the banished emperor of Brazil.

It will interest our Presbyterian friends to know that their church creed, which they are now trying to revise and amend, was drawn up in this chapel, by the Westminster Assembly, in 1643.

The most conspicuous object in this marvelous

chamber is the tomb of Henry VII. and his wife Elizabeth of York. It occupies the center of the eastern part of the chapel, and is surrounded by an elegant lattice-work of brass. On the double sarcophagus lie, on their backs, the figures of the royal pair in their robes.

Other royal personages, buried here, are Edward VI., James I., Charles II., William III., the two Marys, Anne, Elizabeth, Mary of Scotland, and the two little princes who were murdered in the tower. I was struck with the fact that those two royal dames, who in life hated each other so intensely, Elizabeth of England and Mary of Scotland, here sleep, but a few feet apart, in tombs almost exactly alike. How they will stare at each other when they wake up on the morning of the resurrection, and walk, side by side, to the judgment throne of God! There they will stand just like common sinners, Mary to answer for the murder of her husband and Elizabeth to answer for the murder of Mary. I was greatly pleased to learn that Westminster Abbey was not polluted with the ashes of the infamous Henry VIII.

The second largest chapel is that of St. Edward the Confessor, immediately back of the high altar. I have not time to describe it. It contains the tombs of six English kings, and three queens. In this same chapel is kept the old Coronation Chair, made by Edward I. six hundred years ago. I gazed at it with rapt attention and reverential wonder. It is a clumsy looking affair, of carved oak, with high arms and Gothic back. It stands on four lions. The seat is double and contains, plainly revealed, a large mass of sandstone, called the Stone of Scone. On that stone, believed to have been used as a pillow, by

Jacob, at Bethel, the Kings of Scotland, through long centuries, sat to be crowned. King Edward stole it, brought it to London and had this chair made to contain it.

Only think! in this chair, standing out in yonder choir, in front of the altar, and covered with gold brocade, twenty-six English sovereigns have sat to be anointed and crowned. It is the grandest throne on this earth, the throne of the monarch who rules one-seventh of the territory, and one-sixth of the population, of our globe.

What would be your feelings if you knew that some day, in England's great temple of fame, surrounded by the pride and pomp and power of earth's mightiest empire, you would sit on that throne in royal purple, anointed, crowned and sceptered, with princes, dukes, lords, statesmen, generals and bishops kneeling at your feet? I want to tell you that, if you are a Christian, an infinitely higher honor than that is in store for you. In the book of Revelation, I read the words of Jesus Christ, the Eternal Son of God, who says to every one of you: "Behold, I stand at the door and knock: if any man hear my voice and open the door, I will come in to him, and will sup with him, and he with me." All that is in this world. Jesus is now knocking at the door of your heart, unless you have already admitted him. If you will open the door he will come in, and cleanse and beautify your soul, and spread a feast more sumptuous than any earthly monarch ever saw, and be your abiding guest, and fill you with "joy unspeakable and full of glory."

Now hear what he has promised for the life to come "To him that overcometh will I grant to sit with me in my throne, even as I also overcame, and am set down with my father, in his throne." The simple meaning of this is that, if you become a true disciple of Jesus Christ, and hold out faithful to the end, in heaven you will be exalted to a seat with Jesus Christ on the throne of the universe—a throne as much higher and more glorious than England's throne as Mt. Blanc overtops and outshines the little ant-hill at its base.

Built up against the south-west corner of the Abbey is the Jerusalem Chamber. It is so called because its wood work of cedar and its stained glass windows were brought from Jerusalem, also because it contains tapestries depicting the history of that city. Henry IV. died in this chamber in 1413. Here all the work of King James' translation of the Bible, and of the recent revision, was performed. Hither are brought the crown jewels from the Tower on the day preceding the coronations, and on all public occasions. Here many other important events have taken place, which I have not time to mention.

We must immediately leave this "house of the Lord" and hurry away to "the king's house." We must leave Westminster and London and go to Windsor and its castle. In Westminster Abbey twenty-seven kings and queens are buried. In Windsor Castle many kings and queens have lived. Wednesday, August 13, I spent in Westminster Abbey. Thursday, August 14, I took a train on the South Western Railroad, at Waterloo station, and rode twenty-five miles, west, to Windsor. The route lay through as fine a rural landscape as can be imagined. Windsor is a beautiful town of twenty thousand inhabitants on the south side of the Thames. The

Castle—the chief residence of Queen Victoria, stands on a hill, surrounded by a thick and high ivy-draped wall, inclosing perhaps twenty-five or thirty acres. Its erection began under William the Conqueror, eight hundred years ago, and more. It was enlarged and improved by succeeding monarchs, till the present one, who has expended, to make it one of the most magnificent royal residences in the world, the sum of four and a half million dollars.

I first visited, within the castle wall, St. George's Chapel, begun in 1474. It looks quite fresh and new. In it are buried the Queen's father; Henry VIII; Jane Seymour, Henry's third wife; Charles I; George III; George IV; William IV; and other royal personages. It contains splendid monuments of persons whose graves are elsewhere, among whom are the Prince Imperial of France, the son of Napoleon III. The choir contains the stalls of the Knights of the Garter, with their coats of arms and banners. Here they are installed.

This order, founded by Edward III., in 1344, is the highest in Great Britain. Its membership includes the reigning sovereign, other members of the royal family, the principal foreign rulers and English peers. Its principal emblem is the garter, worn on the left leg just below the knee. It is made of dark blue velvet, edged with gold, fastened with a buckle, from which is suspended a pendant, both of gold On the velvet is the motto of the Order in gold letters. The origin of the order is said to be this. At a grand ball the Countess of Salisbury, who was dancing with King Edward, lost her garter. The Lords and ladies, seeing it lying on the floor, began to look at each other with indecent glances and laughter.

Seeing this, the king picked up the garter and holding it aloft exclamed : Honi soit qui mal y pense!" which means : "Shame to him who evil thinks!" On the spot he instituted the "Most Noble Order of the Garter," and gave it for a motto, the words which he had just uttered.

Next I visited the Albert Chapel, smaller than St. George's, but richer and more beautiful. It is a magnificent monument of the Queen's love for her deceased husband. In its interior, it is one of the most beautiful buildings I have ever seen. It is as beautiful as marble of every variety, and sculpture, and carving, and gilding can make it. Its size is sixty-eight feet by twenty eight, and its height sixty feet. It contains a most exquisite cenotaph of the Prince Consort, whose body lies at Frogmore, a mile or two away.

Next I ascended the Round Tower. It stands on an eminence forty-two feet above the court yard of the Castle, and rises eighty feet above that, commanding a fine view of a perfect English landscape covering twelve counties. From the top of the main tower rises a smaller one, thirty or forty feet higher.

There was a great crowd on the lower tower with me. We all noticed a company of fifteen or twenty persons on the higher tower, and wished to join them. But a policeman forbade us, saying that they had obtained a special permit. I asked him who they were. He said they were Americans. Then he asked me if I was not from America. I said, yes. "Well then," he added, "if you will wait till the crowd gets away, I will let you go up." I waited, and went up. So it seems to be everywhere in England. To say : " I am an American " is a passport into many places which an Englishman cannot enter.

The view from that elevation—some two hundred feet above the city and surrounding country—is very delightful. Come and stand with me and see what I see. Running your eyes around the horizon, you take in parts of twelve counties. Here at the west, among the trees, is the city of Windsor. Through the picture, from west to east, runs the silver river. Just across on the northern bank is Eaton College, one of the most famous of English schools, founded by Henry VI. in 1440. It has about one thousand students, who wear a uniform of short jackets, broad collars and tall hats. Far away beyond Eaton above the trees you see a church spire. That is Stoke Poges, the scene of Gray's famous " Elegy written in a Country Churchyard." Down at our feet, at the northeast and east, lies the Home Park, about four miles in circumference, surrounded, on three sides, by the winding river. Through the trees to the southeast we see Frogmore Lodge, and the magnificent mausoleum erected by the Queen to her husband, Prince Albert. To the south lies the Great Park, of eighteen hundred acres, stocked with several thousand deer. Right down here, from George IV.'s Gateway, into Great Park, runs the Long Walk, an avenue of majestic elms, three miles long.

Miles away beyond the park we see a little plain bordered with forest. That is the far-famed Runnimede, where, in 1215, King John signed the Magna Charta—the foundation and beginning of the political liberties of all English-speaking communities.

West of Great Park lies the famous Windsor Forest, fifty-six miles in circumference. Its trees are of magnificent growth and great age. It is full of game. Here roamed, in the days of yore, the Saxon and the Dane; these glades have echoed to the shouts and horns of royal hunting parties, for eight hundred years ; hither came Shakespeare to gather material for his Merry Wives of Windsor ; and here Queen Victoria, when living at the castle, takes her morning rides.

Description of such a scene is impossible. I can see it now with the eyes of memory, but cannot picture it in words. You must cross the ocean and see it yourself.

From the Round Tower I was conducted through the State Apartments of the Castle. I cannot begin to describe what I saw. It was splendor, splendor, splendor—magnificent rooms, sumptuous furniture, precious relics, and paintings by the most eminent artists. Chief among the rooms are the Guard Room, its walls hung with suits of old armor ; St. George's Hall, two hundred feet long and thirty-four wide ; the Grand Reception Room, hung with tapestry representing the story of Jason and Medea ; the Queen's Audience and Presence Chambers, adorned with tapestry representing the story of Esther and Mordecai ; the Old Ball Room, filled with portraits by Vandyke ; the Rubens Room, containing eleven pictures by that illustrious artist ; and the Throne Room, flashing with silver and gold. The Private Apartments, which the public are not permitted to see, are still more gorgeous and magnificent.

As I roamed through the magnificent halls, where the successive monarchs of earth's mightiest empire have dwelt for centuries, I said to myself : What do all this splendor and wealth and power amount to, to their possessor, if she has not "the pearl of greatest price !" Then the words of the Great Teacher came to my mind : "What shall it profit a man, if he shall gain the whole world, and lose his own soul ?" Very few persons have ever come as near gaining the whole world as Queen Victoria. We believe that she has also gained a title to a heavenly inheritance. But if that were not the case, what would all her possessions profit her? What would Windsor Castle profit her, if when she leaves it—as she must very soon—she should be compelled to remove into the gloomy regions of eternal darkness and despair.

As I close, I want to leave this question with every one of you: "What shall it profit a man, if he shall gain the whole world and lose his own soul?" There are men in this house to-night who are striving to gain the whole world, or as much of it as they can, and are giving no attention to the salvation of their souls. I want to ask them, in all seriousness and candor, if they think such an investment will pay. They are throwing away every chance for eternal happiness and running every risk of eternal misery, for the sake of collecting a few earthly treasures, which they know they must soon drop at the door of the tomb. In pursuing such a course, do they act like clear-headed business men?

My friend, in a few years, at the farthest, you will be in your coffin—that is, your body will be. Your coffin will be lowered into the dark earth, and the sods will be piled above your grave. The spot will be marked with a stone, bearing your name. You will not be there to see whether your grave monument cost ten dollars, or ten thousand. You—your immortal part, your soul—will be far below the grave, in eternal darkness, or far above, in eternal light and glory and bliss. These are facts which you cannot dispute. In view of them, I ask you once more: "What shall it profit *you* if *you* shall gain the whole world, and lose *your* own soul."

XIII.

OXFORD AND STRATFORD.

"*Let us go into the next towns.*"—Mark i., 38.

At the close of last Sunday evening's discourse we were in the town of Windsor. The next towns to Windsor, which are of any special interest to the tourist, are Oxford and Stratford. So when I say: "Let us go into the next towns," I mean: let us go to Oxford, the seat of England's greatest university, and Stratford, the place where England's greatest poet was born and died.

Oxford is forty-two miles north-west from Windsor, at the junction of the Thames and Chernell. I arrived there at five o'clock on the afternoon of August 14. Leaving the railway station without delay, I hurried in what I supposed to be the direction to the college buildings, knowing that after six o'clock every door would be closed. By accident I soon found myself in front of Christ Church College, the most extensive and magnificent establishment in the city, founded by Cardinal Wolsey in 1525, and refounded by Henry VIII., in 1532.

I passed through the lofty and massive tower, under "Great Tom," the thirty-first largest bell in the world—which, for more than two hundred years, has closed every college gate in Oxford, at five minutes past nine at night, by striking one hundred and one strokes—and found myself in the great quadrangle.

Every college in Oxford has its quadrangle—or "quad," as it is called for short,—which is simply a plat of grass or gravel, of greater or less extent, adorned with flowers and fountain, or unadorned, surrounded by the buildings of the institution. Christ Church quad (264 feet by 261) is the largest and noblest of all. Let us stand here in the center near this fountain, which, like the students, is enjoying a vacation, and look about us. Right at our feet is a large, granite-bordered pool, which catches the returning water, when the fountain is at play. Now it is as motionless and glossy as the most perfect mirror, reflecting our forms and features, and supporting around its center a circle of leaves and blossoms of the water lily. From the pool radiate graveled walks, in all directions, cutting, into many parts, what looks like a carpet of exquisite green velvet, but which in reality is English turf, an article as much superior to our best American turf as the best brussels carpeting is superior to the poorest ingrain.

Completely surrounding the square, is a long line of massive, old, gray, stone buildings, with battlemented roofs, and clustered chimneys. and many doors and windows, large and small. Here are suites of apartments for the President and faculty of the college, and rooms for lectures and other college exercises. Facing westward, you see the great tower, with its arched gateway through which we entered. I must tell you more about the great bell up there, of which I briefly spoke a few minutes ago. I gave you its name — "Great Tom." It weighs 17,640 pounds. It is three hundred and sixty years old. It was melted down and recast, to cure a crack, in 1680. For more than two hundred years it has never once failed to strike one hundred and one strokes every night, at five minutes past nine o'clock. It strikes one hundred and one times because that was the number of students belonging to the college when it received its charter.

Like that bell all Christians ought to be ; and some are. Great Tom is a perfect pattern of Christian fidelity. First, he is always in his place, day and night, summer and winter, in sunshine and storm, year in and year out. The faithful Christian is always in his place, unless circumstances, absolutely beyond his control, positively forbid. He is in his place at the Sunday service and the week-evening prayer meeting. He does not stay away because the weather is bad, or because he has company, or because he got so tired on Saturday, or because a collection is going to be taken. If his place in the house of God ever is empty, everybody at once concludes that he must be seriously sick. He never gets off the hooks because the minister does not call upon him often enough, or because he hears something from the pulpit which he cannot fully endorse. You always know where to find him, in his religious experience. Every day in the year, he is up in God's belfry, above the smut and dust of worldliness and sin, and his voice is always clear and strong for Christ and for the truth. Everybody likes to hear him speak, because there is perfect agreement between his profession and his life.

There are some church-members who are not so. You never know where to find them. You cannot depend upon them anywhere. They come to church when the weather is perfect, and they have nothing else to do, and they happen to feel just like it. They are continually flying off the handle, on account of something which the minister, or somebody else, has done, or failed to do. There is no stability in their religious experience. To-day they are up in the top of the highest bell-tower, making as much noise as ten good, honest, gospel bells ought to make. To-morrow you will find them down in the back alley of sinful association, with the word "hypocrite" chalked upon them by the honest judgment of the world. On the third day they will be found in some underground receptacle for old iron and brass, sending out, when struck, a voice which reminds you of the old hymn: "Hark! from the tombs a doleful sound." Nobody has any confidence in their piety, and unbelievers say: "If that is Christianity, I never want to be a Christian; I am mean enough already."

Again Great Tom at Oxford knows when to speak and when to be silent. He is not ringing all the time, like the bell on a switch engine in a railroad yard. But when the clock hands, on the dial, mark nine five, past meridian, he speaks out one hundred and one notes, so loud and clear that everybody in Oxford can hear. He has not failed to do this once in two hundred and six years.

So it is with the faithful Christian. He knows how to hold his tongue, and when to hold his tongue. There is no brag, or bluster, or slander, or tattling, or vituperation in his mouth. But when it is the time and place to speak, he always speaks for God, and Christ, and virtue, and righteousness, in tones which cannot well be misunderstood; and everybody listens with profit and delight.

One thing more about Great Tom. When he was

worn out by a century and a quarter of faithful work, he was melted down and recast into a new and better bell. So it will be with the faithful Christian. When he has served his generation on earth, and has worn himself out in his Master's cause, the Great Artisan who created the universe will melt him down in the crucible of the grave, and recast him in the glory of the resurrection morning, and place him in Heaven's highest tower, with an innumerable multitude of other bells, to ring out the praises of redeeming love through all eternity.

My brother, will you not make up your mind to be a faithful Christian, from this night forward—always in your place, speaking for God at the right time, filling the sphere in which Providence has placed you with the sweet melody of a consistent religious life? You may not be able to accomplish any great thing. But you can be faithful; and, if you would dwell among the redeemed in heaven, you must be faithful. The life which some church-members are living, if persisted in, will land them in some other place than the city with jasper walls and golden streets.

Without a guide, and aiming at nothing in particular, I crossed the quad and entered the college chapel, a grand old Church, the Cathedral of the diocese of Oxford. A service was in progress, and I sat and tried to worship with a little company led by a fine choir and an intoning priest. After the service I roamed around the grand, solemn, six-hundred-year-old Church, examining the mortuary tablets and the tombs, and trying to realize where I was and what changes had taken place since those stones were laid. One of the most beautiful objects in Christ Church Cathedral is the Bishop's chair, of carved walnut-wood, which cost five thousand dollars

Leaving the Cathedral, I passed through a massive gateway out upon Christ Church Meadow, the pride of Oxford, and the delight of all tourists. It includes fifty acres of luxuriant grass, surrounded by a shady walk a mile and a quarter in extent. Skirting the meadow on the western side, I reached the Thames, here called the Isis, at the point where the students have their floating club-houses, their boats and their water-arena for practice for the races, paid an old boatman a penny to ferry me over.

I returned, by the way of Folly Bridge, to the street which had led me from the station to the college, and found lodging in a humble inn bearing the sign "Temperance Hotel." The landlady (the chief hotel managers and bartenders in England—so far as I saw—are ladies) asked me what I would have for supper. I did not know. What could I have? She suggested mutton chop, saying that the mutton of Oxford was celebrated for its goodness all over England. So I took mutton chop, with other things, and found that what the old lady had said was worthy of belief, if the word toughness were only substituted for goodness.

The next morning, as early as I supposed the college gates would be open, I set out to do up Oxford. I went back to Christ Church College, passed under Great Tom, crossed the great quadrangle and ascended to the hall, or dining-room.

While we are going up the broad oak staircase, I will answer some questions which are in your mind, at the risk of telling you many things which you already know. How large a place is Oxford? It is a city of nearly fifty thousand inhabitants, without manufactures, living by trade with the surrounding farming country, with members of the University and with others whom the University draws to the place. The University is a collection of twenty-four colleges. It has its officers and governing boards, conducts examinations and confers degrees, but gives no instruction.

The colleges, two of which, however, are called halls, (a hall is a college without incorporation or endowment), were founded all the way down from 1264 to 1887. The government of each college is vested in a presiding officer—called head, dean, master, or otherwise—and several persons called fellows. The undergraduate members of the college live within college walls; pay for and furnish their own rooms; eat dinner together, at twenty-five cents apiece, in the college refectory; have their other meals from the college kitchen in their rooms, paying for what they order; wear gowns and mortar-board caps; attend chapel and lectures; take, and pay for, private instruction from self-appointed tutors, called "coaches;" and pass the University examinations and get their degrees, if they can.

I could not discover that the colleges of Oxford are much else than boarding-houses or dormitories. There are other students, belonging to no college, who live in the city and study for University examinations and degrees. The membership of the colleges ranges from two hundred and fifty students at Christ Church down to twenty-five at some of the less popular institutions. I was told that the entire number of students during the past academic year was three thousand. Every college has—and seemingly must have—these three things : a chapel, a hall and a library.

While we have been talking we have been walking, and now are at the door of the hall of Christ Church College, which we will take as a sample of all the "halls," only it is the largest and grandest of the twenty-four. It was built in 1529. It measures one hundred and fifteen feet by forty, and is fifty feet high from floor to carved and decorated ceiling. The walls are adorned, and well-nigh covered, with the portraits of distinguished graduates and patrons of the college. Among the latter I noticed Henry VIII. (full length, wearing the "garter" around his left knee), Queen Elizabeth and Cardinal Wolsey ; among the former, John Locke, the present Prince of Wales and Gladstone. The portrait of King Henry was painted in 1520. Many pictures of graduates are nearly as old. Here the students eat their dinners, sitting at long tables, running lengthwise through the room ; while the fellows eat on a platform, which crosses the hall at its upper end.

As I was leaving the place, I had the delightful surprise of meeting an old friend from the state of New York, with a large party whom he was conducting through Great Britain and the Continent. By invitation, I kept with them till I returned to London three days later.

During that Friday I visited eleven colleges, and saw the outside of all the others. The ones whose interior I inspected were Merton (the oldest), Baliol, Exeter, Oriel, New (more than five hundred years *old*), Lincoln, All Souls, Magdalen, Brasenose, Corpus Christi, and the one already described. I also passed through the Bodleian Library, with its

400,000 volumes, and saw, externally, the University Museum, the Sheldonian Theatre (where the degrees are conferred), and an immense modern building where the university examinations are held.

Each of these colleges has some one or more things in its buildings, grounds or history, to make it famous. Merton has apartments in which King Charles I. and his wife once resided. Baliol, founded by John Baliol, King of Scotland, to purchase exemption from public scourging at priestly hands, stands first in literary distinction. Exeter is famed for its beautiful chapel, like La Sainte Chapelle in Paris. Lincoln is dear to all Methodists because John Wesley, a graduate of Christ Church, was once numbered among its fellows. Magdalen is prominent for its massive and beautiful tower, and for a delightful walk along the river Cherwell, in its garden, known as Addison's walk. Brasenose is remembered for a huge brass human, or inhuman, nasal organ, which projects from over its chief portal.

A cross in the pavement in front of Baliol College marks the spot where the Christian martyrs, Latimer, Ridley and Cranmer, were burned at the stake in 1555 and 1556. In St. Giles Street, not far away, a beautiful triangular Gothic monument, seventy-five feet high and costing twenty-five thousand dollars, holding aloft the statues of the three men, commemorates the event.

Latimer and Ridley were burned in 1555. They were Bishops of the Church of England, the former of Worcester, the latter of London. When Bloody Mary, the daughter of Henry VIII. and Catharine of Aragon, came to the throne, she had these prelates arrested and sent to Oxford for trial. Their crime was that they differed from the queen in their religious opinions. The issue of the trial was determined beforehand. Of course they were found guilty and were condemned to be roasted alive. They might have saved their lives by recanting their opinions. This they would not do.

The evening before the execution, some of Ridley's friends were permitted to visit him in his prison cell. One of them offered to sit up with him all night. But he refused, saying: "I mean to go to bed, and, by God's will, to sleep as quietly as ever I did in my life." The next morning, as he was being led to the place of suffering, he saw his fellow martyr Latimer approaching. He ran to meet him, and, embracing him, exclaimed: "Be of good cheer, brother, for God will either assuage the fury of the flames, or else give us strength to endure them!" Reaching the stake, they both kissed it, and prayed earnestly. When they were bound to the stake, and the flames were devouring their flesh, Latimer said: "Be of good comfort, Master Ridley, and play the man. We shall this day light such a candle, by God's grace, in England, as I trust shall never be put out." And so their heroic souls went up to heaven.

Thomas Cranmer was Archbishop of Canterbury, the highest dignitary in the English Church. He was arrested at the same time as Latimer and Ridley, and for the same crime. But his execution did not take place till five months after theirs. When threatened with death by fire, he weakly yielded and signed a recantation of the doctrines which he firmly believed. The night following his recantation, he suffered the tortures of the stake ten times multiplied. In his prison cell he writhed in the flames of a remorseful conscience, almost as bad as hell itself.

The next day he was led into the church of St. Mary Magdalene, which was filled with people who had come to hear his public recantation. But, to their amazement, he recanted his recantation and firmly protested his allegiance to Jesus Christ, as the only Head of the Church. Immediately the enemies of the truth dragged him to the stake, filling his ears, on the way, with insults, jeers and imprecations. On the very spot where Latimer and Ridley had died, they chained him to the stake, and piled the dry fagots up to his waist. But he felt no fear. The mighty power of God filled his soul. When the flames were dancing and hissing around him, he stretched out his right hand, which had signed the recantation, and, without flinching, held it in the hottest fire till it was burned to a cinder and fell from his arm, repeatedly saying as he did so : " This hand hath offended —this unworthy right hand." Thus he died, sustained by the omnipotent power of the Holy Ghost.

What, think you? were my feelings as I stood on the very spot where those hideous acts of cruelty were perpetrated, and as I looked up at the statues of those heroic men of God? I felt like praying that the spirit of Latimer, and Ridley, and Cranmer might come on me, and on my dear people in America, and on the entire American Church. Brethren, if we had that spirit, there would be no complaining among us of heavy church burdens, and hard work for Christ, and too much money to be raised for the support of the gospel. If we had that spirit, revival flames would sweep through our congregation and through our village.

Before we leave Oxford I want to remind you that it is the birth-place of Methodism. Methodism, as a life, as a principle, as a doctrine, is as old as Christianity. As an organism, it came into being in the city of Oxford, in the year 1728. At that time John Wesley, who was a Fellow, or Professor, in Lincoln College and a Priest of the Church of England; his brother Charles, a student in Christ Church College; George Whitefield, a student in Pembroke College; and about twenty others—students and teachers—formed themselves into a society to read the Bible in the original languages, and to aid each other in mutual spiritual improvement. They received the Lord's Supper weekly and fasted twice a week; they spent much time in prayer and self-examination; they scrupulously attended public worship and all the ordinances of the Church; they visited the inmates of prisons and alms houses; they labored for the salvation of their fellow students; they strove to live holy lives and to do all the good they could. Their fellows in the University ridiculed their piety and called them "Bible-Bigots," the "Godly Club" and the "Holy Club." Because of the methodical way in which they did everything, they were also nicknamed "Methodists."

That was the humble origin of an organization which has been so blessed of God that it has grown, and expanded, till now there are nearly six million Methodists in the world, and the Methodist spirit and fire have largely permeated all the other Churches. The Methodists are sometime charged with being an ignorant people. That is a slander. The Methodist Church was born in the University of Oxford, and it has always been the friend and patroness of the broadest literary culture. If you ask what Methodism is, I answer, *it is cultured intellect, set on fire from heaven.*

The tourist company of which, for the time, I was one, arrived at Stratford-on-Avon at about noon, Saturday, August 16. On the way from the station to the hotel, we passed, after a brief pause before it, the exquisite fountain and clock-spire erected, at the junction of several streets, by George W. Childs of Philadelphia, as a tribute from America to the memory of the Bard of Avon.

One hotel was the Shakespeare House, a quaint building, part old, part new, the oldest portion, including the dining-room being a well preserved relic of the fourteenth century. The guest rooms are named from the titles of Shakespeare's plays. I, with two other masculine members of the party, was assigned to a spacious and very comfortable apartment, bearing over its door the words "Two Gentlemen of Verona." It at once became a very momentous question with all, which of us three were gentlemen, and who was the esquire, valet or what else. That question has not been answered, and probably never will be.

After a good lunch (dinner rarely comes in Europe till the close of the day) we started out to see the wonders. Of course, the first place was the "Shakespeare House." This is the place where the poet's parents lived, where his father carried on the wool business, and where he was born. The building, an elegant one probably for the time in which it was erected, exists in substantially its original condition. A few timbers and stones have been put in here and there to preserve the structure, and much of the plastering has been renewed. It is national property, and is preserved and guarded with the utmost care. To prevent destruction by combustion, no fire or light is ever permitted within its walls.

A sixpence purchased us admission to all the rooms. With something very nearly approaching awe, we stood uncovered in the chamber where, April 23, 1564, the world's greatest literary genius first saw the light. We were assured that, excepting the window sash and glass, and iron straps fastened to the ceiling to keep the plastering from falling off, the room was in the same condition as three hundred and twenty-six years ago. The panes of glass in the windows are scratched all over with autographs by the diamond rings of visitors, among which that of Sir Walter Scott is conspicuous.

One of the rooms is a museum, filled with Shakespearean relics, too numerous even to be named. We gazed long and closely at a portrait, said to have been painted directly from the bard. We saw the jug from which he used to drink water, or something stronger. We were permitted to sit half a second in a chair, which he used to occupy as president of a literary and social club. With all gravity and simplicity, the guide showed us an old tobacco pipe, which he said Shakespeare would have used had he been a smoker. On the wall, in a frame, under a glass, we saw a sheet of letter paper on which Washington Irving had written, in the birth room, these lines:

"Of mighty Shakespeare's birth the room we see;
That where he died in vain to find we try.
Useless the search; for all *Immortal* he;
And those who are *Immortal* never die.
W. I., Second Visit, October, 1821."

As we leave the "Shakespeare House" perhaps you would like to take a look at its exterior. It is built of brick. You cannot see the bricks, however, as the walls are plastered all over, and paneled with wood, painted black. It has three dormer-windows, three doors and a projecting porch on the side toward the street. Adjoining the house is a garden, in which are carefully cultivated the flowers mentioned in Shakespeare's plays.

You see that the world's greatest literary giant was not born in a palace. When the great All-Father comes into the world, bringing a soul of transcendent genius, which is destined to shine for ages as a star of the first magnitude, he usually puts it into the arms of a poor woman in a humble dwelling. His own Son, equal to himself, when made in the likeness of sinful flesh, first appeared to human eyes in a manger-cradle, in a stable, among the cattle and sheep, in the village of Bethlehem.

This ought to teach us not to despise the poor. The Holy Book says: "Hath not God chosen the poor of this world, rich in faith, and heirs of the kingdom which he hath promised to them that love him?" The men and women who are to hold the places of power and mold society, twenty-five years hence, are now children in poor families. You see then how suicidal, as well as unchristian and wicked, it is for a Church to despise and neglect the poor. The Church which does the most for the poor to-day will hold the most commanding place in the community to-morrow.

From the "Shakespeare House" we struck across several streets, and out into the country, where, after following the narrow path which "Will" used to take when he went courting, we came, at the end of a mile, to Shottery and to the Anne Hathaway cottage.

The house stands embowered in green, thatched with straw, presenting a very old-time appearance.

It is occupied by an old lady, who holds a life lease, and her son and family, and a younger lady who acts as guide to visitors. The old lady, seventy-seven years old, has lived here seventy years, during which period she has but once been on a railway train, and then only for a very short journey. She is a great grand-daughter of a niece of Shakespeare's wife. She showed us an old Bible, handed down through her father, printed in 1776.

We saw by the chimney-side the "courting bench" so called, the very same on which Will and Anne used to sit, more than three hundred years ago. We sat upon it by turns ; as also in a chair in the huge old-fashioned fire-place, where we could look up through the sooty flue and see the blue sky. Since the young lovers ended their courting, hundreds of thousands of visitors, like ourselves, have sat on that rude, unpainted settee. The number amounts to more than twenty thousand every year.

Up stairs, in Anne's room, we saw a curiously carved bed-stead, four hundred years old, which Anne used before and after she became Mrs. Shakespeare, and the very same sheets and pillow-cases—we were assured—on which she slept.

We looked out through the window where Anne used to hang out the signal for her Will, when the coast was clear.

You must know that Anne's parents considered themselves the social superiors of the Shakespeares, and were determined that their daughter should not marry, or keep company, with such a low-born fellow as the son of a wool-comber. So Will was forbidden to step foot on Squire Hathaway's premises. But he was lying around in the hedge nearly all the time, day and night; and whenever the old folks were gone, Anne would hang out the signal, and he would enter and enjoy the delights of Paradise. I doubt not that the young people found their courting all the sweeter because of the difficulties which they had to overcome to enjoy it. How absurd it seems now that a man should object to becoming the father in-law of William Shakespeare.

Do you suppose that young man found the distance long which divided his home from the cottage at Shottery? Do you suppose that the rain and mud, or cold and frost, ever hindered him from keeping his engagements with Anne? Do you imagine that he found the hours long which he spent, lying under the hedge, watching his sweetheart's window? "*No*, NO, NO!" everybody exclaims. Why? One word answers that question—love. Love makes all distances short, all hardships easy, all burdens light.

Hear that, Christian! If you loved your Saviour as you ought, and as you profess, long distances and bad weather would not keep you from his sanctuary, on his holy day; you would not complain of heavy burdens, borne in the support of his Church; your constant question would be: "What more can I do for him who has done so much for me?"

Returning to Stratford, we went to " New Place," where the poet spent his last days, and where he died, April 23, 1616. The house has disappeared, having been demolished in 1759 by its owner, a churlish clergyman, to rid himself of paying taxes on so old and poor a building. He had previously cut down "Shakespeare's mulberry tree," to save himself annoyance from the multitude of pilgrims who came to pluck its leaves. The name of that man—Gastrell—

has become a by-word and an execration. But the tree has shot up again; and the foundations of the house remain, covered with wire gauze.

We ate fruit from the tree, drank from the poet's well, and stood opposite where a bay window had been, just within which the bard wrote his last play: "As You Like It," and died.

Sunday morning, August 17, dawned clear and bright. A more delightful place to spend a beautiful Sabbath I never saw. We attended service at the Church of the Holy Trinity, where Shakespeare is buried. The sacred edifice is beautifully situated in a beautiful cemetery, on the banks of the lovely Avon, approached through the most charming avenue, four or five hundred feet long, over-arched by a double row of ancient linden trees. Unable to gain admission, at that time, to a sight of Shakespeare's grave, we returned at four o'clock. Then the great object of our visit to Stratford-on-Avon was realized, when, standing reverently at the spot in the choir where it is certain Shakespeare was buried, we read, on a slab in the floor, this strange inscription.

> "Good friend for Jesus sake forbeare
> To digg the dust encloased heree.
> Blese be the man that spares these stones,
> And curst be he that moves my bones."

That epitaph, written by the man himself, proves that mighty Shakespeare believed in the immortality of the soul and the resurrection of the body; for, surely, no sound-minded man would care a copper what might become of his body, if he really believed that death ends all. Shakespeare believed the old Bible doctrine as it is taught in the Old Testament and the New, that there shall be a resurrection of the dead both of the just and the unjust. Job said : " I know that my Redeemer liveth, and that he shall stand at the latter day on the earth ; and though, after my skins, worms destroy this body, yet in my flesh shall I see God, and mine eyes shall behold, and not another." And Jesus said : "The hour is coming, in the which all that are in their graves whall hear *my* voice, and shall come forth ; they that have done good unto the resurrection of life ; and they that have done evil, unto the resurrection of damnation."

The time is not very far distant when the awful blast of the resurrection trumpet shall reverberate through the solemn arches of Westminster Abbey, and Avon's ancient church, and every burial vault, and every cemetery, and every battle-field, and every ocean cavern ; and every human being who has ever lived will stand, in the same body that died, before the great white throne. Some will stand on the right and some on the left. " Then the King shall say unto them on his right hand, Come ye blessed of my Father, inherit the kingdom prepared for you from the foundation of the world. Then shall he say also unto them on the left hand, Depart, ye cursed, into everlasting fire, prepared for the devil and his angels. And these shall go away into everlasting punishment ; but the righteous into life eternal."

XIV.

WARWICK AND KENILWORTH.

"*In the forests he built castles.*"--II Chronicles xxvii, 4.

It was Jotham, King of Judah, who built castles in the forests. The same statement might be made concerning many of the early kings of England. "In the forests they built castles."

In the days of the Romans, of the Saxons, of the Danes and of the Normans, England was a vast area of forest and marsh, with here and there an infant city surrounded by a patch of cultivated ground. Through the forests roamed savage beasts and bands of marauding men, still more savage. As places of protection and as rallying points against these enemies, the kings, and nobles, and great men built castles in the forests. They could once be counted by hundreds, scattered all over the kingdom. The great majority of these buildings have entirely disappeared, so that not even their sites are known. A few remain. Of these, most are in ruins; here and there one, by frequent repairs and improvements, has been preserved in more than its original symmetry and beauty.

England is still a land of magnificent forests, preserved from ancient times, to beautify the landscapes, and to shelter game for the amusement of royalty and aristocracy in the noble sport of hunting. You remember Windsor Forest, fifty-six miles in circumference. Most of the castles of England, like that at Windsor, are surrounded by wide stretches of land from which the trees have never been cut, thus illustrating the text: "In the forests he built castles."

From boyhood, I had longed to see a castle. As there are two famous castles in the vicinity of Stratford. I resolved that I would not return to London till I had seen them. Monday morning, August 18, in the tourist company of my Syracuse friend, I started for Warwick and Kenilworth castles, eight and thirteen miles distant.

We rode, under a bright sky, in two carriages, through a beautiful section of country and along a perfect road. O those English roads! You can hardly imagine what they are. I wish you could see one of them. It would make you ashamed of the so-called roads of your native land, and almost of your native land itself. Why! the poorest back-country road in Great Britain is almost, if not quite, as good as our best asphalt pavement—without a stone, or a rut, or an uneven place, or a pool of water, or a spoonful of mud—smooth, solid, hard. Your carriage glides along with hardly a vibration, or a sound, and, seemingly, with no effort on the part of your plump and glossy steeds.

In this country, when you take a ride, it is one continuous jar, and jolt, and quiver, and quake, and plunge, and lunge, and rattle, and roar, while your garments are coated with dust or spattered with mud, the breathless horses are covered with foam and sweat. Usually the chief pleasure of a drive in the country, in America, is the getting to the end of your journey. How long will our intelligent farmers endure to drag their produce to market, over our wretched apologies for roads, when a slight increase of taxation would secure scientific road-building and enable them to haul double loads with half the cost of time and wear and tear?

We often speak of the Christian life as a road—a road to Heaven. The Bible does also. It says in one place: "An highway shall be there, and a way, and it shall be called the way of holiness; the unclean shall not pass over it; but it shall be for those: the wayfaring men, though fools, shall not err therein." The process of building this road is described in another place in these words: "Prepare ye the way of the people; cast up, cast up the highway; gather out the stones." These comparisons and similes lose nearly all their meaning to those who have never seen anything better than the ordinary American highway; but, to one who has traveled in the rural parts of England, they are very full of force and beauty.

Many persons think that the Christian life is terribly hard and difficult and painful. They think that it is like an American highway, full of ruts and stones and mud. They are grievously mistaken. The true Christian life is like an English road. If you will once get into it, and walk in the middle, as far from sin and the world as you can, you will find that the author of the Book of Proverbs told the truth when he said of pure religion: "Her ways are ways of pleasantness, and all her paths are peace."

On the way from Stratford to Warwick, about four miles from the former place, we passed, on the left, a large and elegant estate, called Charlecote. Back from the road, peeping through the trees, we could see the mansion, built more than three hundred years ago. Farther along, bordered by the highway, we saw an immense meadow, or park, dotted over with groves, and clusters of majestic oaks, among which were droves of red deer, numbering many hundreds, feeding as quietly and fearlessly as though they had been cows or sheep. It was a beautiful sight.

This Charlecote estate is forever linked with the name of Shakespeare. In those old days the place belonged to Sir Thomas Lucy, a knight and justice of the peace. William Shakespeare was arrested for killing deer in Sir Thomas' forest. The accuser was also the judge, and imposed on the offender a heavy fine. The young poacher paid the fine, and then, to get even with his persecutor, wrote a stinging lampoon in rhyme and nailed it to Sir Thomas' gate post. For this the enraged knight made Stratford too hot to hold the saucy poet, who was obliged to flee to London. But he had his revenge by holding Sir Thomas Lucy up to everlasting ridicule and contempt, under the name of Justice Shallow, in the play which bears the title of the "Merry Wives of Windsor." The descendants of Justice Shallow still reside at Charlecote.

The crime which young Shakespeare committed is still common in England. It grows out of the wretched and cruel land system which has always been in vogue in that poor, rich country. I call England a poor, rich country because, with immense aggregate wealth in the hands of a few lords and aristocrats, the masses of the people are miserably poor. The soil, of which every man ought to have a portion, is held by a few selfish lords-of-the-land ;

and immense areas which ought to give bread to the toiling millions, are kept as forests, stocked with game, for the amusement of kings, and queens, and princes, and dukes, and earls, and counts, and knights, and so called gentlemen and ladies of the realm. To preserve their game from capture by the starving people, the ruling class have been obliged to enact and enforce the most barbarous laws.

Poaching used to be a capital crime. A case is on record like this: a poor man, who could not find employment, going home to his starving family along a forest road, saw a rabbit bounding across his path. He caught up a stone and killed the animal. For that he was put to death by hanging. To-day if a man kills a rabbit in England, after dark, the penalty, for the first offense, is imprisonment at hard labor for three months; for the second, six months; and for the third, seven years. If he kills a deer, of course the punishment is correspondingly more severe. If the nourishing bosom of old Mother Earth could be divided up among her children, as it ought, England would become, what she has long been falsely called, "Merry England."

The best land-system ever invented is that which God gave to the Israelites, through Moses, more than three thousand years ago. When Canaan was divided among the sons of Jacob, every man received an equal share of the soil. What God gave him he could never sell. He might pawn it, for a money consideration; but it came back free in the next jubilee year. These thoughts came to me, as we rode past the mansion and deer-parks of beautiful Charlecote.

Ere long we were at Warwick. It is a fine old

borough, of twelve thousand inhabitants, the capital of the county of Warwick, situated on the river Avon. We drove directly to the church of St. Mary, where we saw, besides many other interesting sights, the tomb of Robert Dudley, Earl of Leicester, who figures so prominently in Scott's novel called "Kenilworth." On the earl's sarcophagus lies his sculptured form in white marble. They say that the face very closely resembles the face of the real, living man. I carefully eyed the marble, and thought of the man who disowned his beautiful and faithful wife, Amy Robsart, in the vain hope of becoming the husband of Queen Elizabeth, and virtual king of England. His love of power brought anguish and death to Amy, and shame and misery to himself. We did not spend much time in the church. We had come to, Warwick to see its famous old castle, which the son-in-law of King Alfred the Great built, in the forest, nearly a thousand years ago. It is in a perfect state of preservation, and is the home of George Guy Greville, Earl of Warwick. It is regarded as the most magnificent of the ancient feudal mansions of the English nobility still used as a residence.

The castle and its grounds are beautiful beyond description. I wish I could put into words the picture which now rises before my mental vision. Up from the right, or western bank of the Avon, rises an enormous rock. Its sides are precipitous or overhanging. Its top is a nearly level area of perhaps twenty-five acres. Surrounding this area, and running around the edge of the rock, is the castle's outer wall—thick, high, old, gray, gracefully irregular, hung with creeping ivy, crowned with battlements and pierced with embrasures. Of the space thus enclosed, a part is occupied by the inner walls and towers and various buildings of the castle, while other portions are devoted to lawns, and shaded walks, and gardens of exquisite delight, and little groves of venerable trees, and a variety of structures deemed essential to the comfort of an English lord. The whole is a paradise of beauty, cut off from the noise, and smut, and hurry, and worry of the toiling, groaning world, where you would almost be willing to spend your life in pleasure and rest.

We approached the castle through an embattled gateway called the Porter's Lodge. Immediately we found ourselves in a broad, ascending road, three hundred feet long, deeply cut through the solid rock, lined with clinging moss and creeping ivy, and overarched with the dense foliage of a double row of noble trees springing from the top of the ledge. At the end of the road, we stood on an arch of stone, spanning the unused moat, where once a draw bridge rose to shut out enemies and fall to let in friends. To the right and left stretched a stupendous line of fortifications, firmly rooted to its rocky foundations, and bidding defiance to the all-subduing power of time. On the left was the venerable Cæsar's Tower, said to be as old as the Norman conquest. Although it has braved the ravages of time and the depredations of man for more than eight hundred years, it still stands as firm as the everlasting rock, from which it lifts its hoary head one hundred and forty-seven feet toward the sky. Away at the right is Guy's Tower, with walls of solid masonry ten feet thick, one hundred and twenty-eight feet in height.

Directly in our front was an enormous arched gateway, flanked with towers, and succeeded by a second gateway, with towers and battlements rising far above the first. These were formerly defended by two portcullises—huge gates of timber and iron, sliding up and down in grooves cut in the stone.

Passing the double gateway, where ten brave men could withstand ten thousand of their equals, we find ourselves in the inner court. The spacious area is covered with a carpet of the richest green. On the left stands the grand, irregular, castellated mansion of the feudal barons of Warwick. In front is the mount or keep, clothed from base to summit with trees and shrubs. On the right appears the Bear Tower and another unfinished tower. The whole range of towers and buildings is joined by ramparts and embattled walls of amazing thickness, mantled with that luxuriant ivy which no country but England can grow in its perfection. Open flights of steps and broad walks on the top of the walls form a means of communication throughout the whole fortress.

The scene is so grand, and so perfectly fascinating, that the imagination could suggest no possible improvement. We were conducted through the public rooms of the castle, entering first a broad hall, through a massive door, where is displayed the ancient emblem of the Earls of Warwick—a black bear standing erect, grasping a ragged staff.

The rooms, which we visited, are elegant in their construction, magnificent in their furnishings and rich in their relics and works of art. I will mention a few of the rooms, and one in five hundred of the objects of interest. In the Great Hall they showed us the sword, shield, helmet, breastplate, walking-stick and tilting pole of Guy, Earl of Warwick, who flourished a thousand years ago, if he ever lived at all. The sword is a huge affair which an ordinary man could hardly lift. The other articles named correspond in size with the sword. We also saw Guy's "porridge pot," about as large as the largest wash-tub of a modern house-wife. Standing in the Great Hall, and looking west, we could see, at a glance, a grand suite of state rooms extending in a straight line three hundred and thirty-three feet. Far away at the other end, we seemed to see a man on horseback riding down upon us. Going forward to meet him, we found that it was an equestrian portrait of King Charles I., by the greatest of all portrait-painters Vandyke. The illusion was perfect. It did not look like a picture. From every position, near and remote, it looked like a real man, on a real horse. Vandyke has about twenty pictures in Warwick Castle.

In the Red Drawing Room are many paintings by such artists as Vandyke, Rubens and Raphael, and much exquisite furniture. The Cedar Drawing Room is filled with mirrors and vases and paintings and statues. Chief among the last I noticed, with pleasure and pride, an exquisite bust of Proserpine by Hiram Powers, the great American Sculptor, who carved the famous Greek slave.

The Great Dining Room is a magnificent apartment where any monarch might be proud to banquet. Its wall and ceiling flash with gold. Among the many works of art which it contains, are two tawny lions, created by the brush of the immortal Rubens, which seem about to spring upon you from the canvas, where they have been crouching for more than two centuries. What a wonderful artist he was who gave such life to these painted brutes, transforming coarse cloth and earthy pigments into bristling hair and vibrating tails, and throbbing chests, and fire-flashing eyes! Rubens was a most busy and prolific worker, as well as a most transcendent genius. When he died, he left behind him eighteen hundred pictures—most of them very large—embracing almost every conceivable subject.

The Boudoir is a lovely little room, forming the western extremity of the suite of rooms. The prospects from the windows are extremely fine, and the walls are studded with rare paintings. There were two which made a very deep impression upon my mind. They were portraits by Vandyke. One was a beautiful innocent boy, who looked the very personification of gentleness, purity and love. It would do your soul good to look at such a face; it would awaken all the good influences which might be slumbering in your heart. The other picture was a coarse, corpulent, brutal, cruel man. In his face you could see a little of the man with much of the hog, the hyena and the tiger. It was a most repulsive face, from which you would quickly turn away in horror and disgust. What was my amazement when I learned that the two were one. They were both portraits of King Henry VIII. They were Henry Tudor, as a boy and as a man. What a contrast! what a transformation! What was it that changed the beautiful boy into the beastly man; the gentle prince into the cruel tyrant; the angel into the devil? It is the unanimous verdict of the most reliable historians that Henry was a most amiable and promising boy, and a most unprincipled and infamous man. What was it that wrought such a marvelous change? I think you can all answer that question. It was sin. Sin changed the bright, pure, angelic child into the ugly, wicked, devilish man. Sin will work a similar change in your character, if you give yourself up to its cruel domination. It will blast, and blacken, and destroy your immortal soul. It will obliterate the image of God, and, through all eternity, transform you more and more into the likeness of the prince of devils. The supreme need of every human soul is deliverance from the guilt and power and pollution of sin?

Denied admission to the private rooms of the Earl and Countess of Warwick, we roamed through the extensive lawns and gardens, which are bounded by the outer castle walls. In the conservatory we saw the largest vase in the world. A man was there to tell us all about it in the broadest English brogue. He called vase "*vaws.*" He had it over and over again "*vaws,*" "*vaws,*" "*vaws.*" This vase is one of the greatest wonders, of the kind, in the world. It was found at the bottom of a lake at Hadrian's Villa, near Trivoli, in Italy, by Sir William Hamilton, then ambassador at the court of Naples, and by him presented to the Earl of Warwick, who placed it in its present position. It is circular in shape and is capable of holding four barrels. It has two large handles formed of interwoven vine branches, from which the tendrils, leaves and clustering grapes spread around the vessel's brim. The middle of the swelling body is enfolded in the skin of a panther, with the head and claws perfectly finished. Above these are the heads of satyrs, bound with garlands of ivy. The whole rests upon vine leaves, which climb high up its sides. All that I have described is carved as delicately as any vase on a lady's drawing-room table. And the greatest wonder is that the whole is cut out of one piece of snow-white marble. It is a vessel of honor, gazed at, in admiration, by tens of thousands of visitors every year. It reminds me of St. Paul's words to Timothy : " In a great house "—that is in a castle like that at Warwick—" there are not only vessels of gold and of silver, but also of wood and of earth ; and some to honor and some to dishonor. If a man therefore purge himself from these "—that is from the sins which the Apostle has been enumerating—" he shall be a vessel unto honor, sanctified and meet for the master's use, and prepared unto every good work." It ought to be the ambition of every Christian to be such a vessel, in God's castle, the Church,—I mean in spiritual dimensions, and beauty, and perfection—as the Hamilton Vase is in the castle of the Earl of Warwick. My brother, why should you be willing to remain a little shallow basin, as you were at your conversion, when, by the grace of God, and by watching, and prayer, and earnest work, you might grow up into the largeness, and beauty, and usefulness of a vessel of honor, " meet for the master's use and prepared unto every good work" ?

We descended into the deep, dark, dismal dungeons of the castle, under Cæsar's Tower, and thought of the wretched victims of tyranny who had there dragged out their lives, hidden from friends and the light of day. Many rude drawings, traced on the walls, sent a pang through my heart, as I imagined the poor wretches thus trying to amuse themselves and to while away the long days and years of an almost hopeless captivity. I thanked God that the world has grown better, and is growing better, under the purifying influences of Christ's religion of gentleness and love.

Then I thought of another dungeon, deeper and blacker and viler than the dungeon of Warwick Castle. In it is confined every drunkard, and every gambler, and every profane swearer, and every libertine, and every impenitent sinner. The name of that prison is sin. The jailer is Satan. The chains with which he binds his captives are evil habits. Their condition is wretched in the extreme; but, as long as life lasts, they are prisoners of hope. Jesus Christ has ransomed them, every one. He died to make them free. If they will assert their right to be free, and cry to him for deliverance, he will come and set them free. As his messenger, I come to the prison to-day, and, putting my mouth close to the only loophole through which any light or sound can penetrate, I shout down to them :

"Ye slaves of sin and hell,
 Your liberty receive,
And safe in Jesus dwell,
 And blest in Jesus live;
The year of Jubilee is come!
Return, ye ransomed sinners, home."

From Warwick we drove to Kenilworth. On the way we passed Blacklow Hill, on whose summit, through the trees, we saw a white monument, marking the spot where Piers Gaveston, Earl of Cornwall, the unprincipled favorite of Edward II., was beheaded, five hundred and eighty years ago, by the Earl of Warwick, who hated Gaveston for having fixed on him the epithet of "The Black Hound of Arden." Lust, and avarice, and selfish ambition, and revenge were the motives which impelled almost everybody in those old bloody times. That we are less wicked than our forefathers, is because the principles of the gospel of Christ have a wider and deeper influence now than they had then.

From Warwick to Kenilworth the distance is five miles. We dined in the village, at "The King's Arms Hotel," where we saw, unchanged, the room in which Scott planned, and partly wrote, his "Kenilworth." Then we drove about a mile to the castle. Although it is in ruins, it is surpassingly beautiful. It is full of interest to the student of history. Founded among the forests, nearly a thousand years ago, and restored and improved times almost without number, it has witnessed princely and royal pageants, rung with the songs and shouts of bridals and banquets, smothered the shrieks and groans of illustrious prisoners, resounded with the tramp of embattled warriors, and hurled defiance and death at besieging armies.

Kenilworth's most lasting fame comes from the story of Lord Leicester and Amy Robsart. Leicester, whose real name was Robert Dudley, was the favorite of Queen Elizabeth. She gave him Kenilworth Castle and made him Earl of Leicester; and gave the world and him reason to believe that she intended to ask him to share her throne. Meanwhile he had decoyed from her home, and married, Amy Robsart, the beautiful daughter of a country squire, whom he kept in concealment in Cumnor Castle, near Oxford. Love prompted him to acknowledge her as his wife; ambition, and his servant Varney, prompted him to hide, or kill her, that be might be free to marry the queen.

Leicester entertained Elizabeth and her court at Kenilworth, many days, with more than royal splendor. Amy went to the castle in disguise during the festivities. In the garden, one morning, she met the queen and implored her protection against Varney, who, to screen his master, claimed to be her husband. Amy denied this relationship, but dared not tell the whole truth, lest she should displease and endanger her lord. The queen was enraged at Leicester, who, by his silence, had assented to Varney's lie, and threatened to cut off his head; but was appeased with the story that Amy was insane.

Varney, without Leicester's knowledge, hurried Amy back to Cumnor Castle, and confined her in a chamber, at the summit of a tower. Between the chamber door and the top of the stairs was a section of flooring hung on hinges over a chasm which went down, perhaps, a hundred feet to the castle's vaults. Varney left the door unlocked, telling Amy that her husband, Lord Leicester, would soon come to see her. Leicester had a peculiar whistle with which he was accustomed to signal his approach. Dropping the drawbridge and hiding near, Varney whistled like Leicester. With a cry of joy, the loving woman threw open the door and bounded out, to cast herself into her husband's arms. It was not a loving husband, but grim death, whose embrace she felt. There was a rushing sound—a heavy fall— a faint scream—and all was over.

I had seen Amy's grave in the Church of St Mary, at Oxford. Now I was at the gate of the ruined castle, over which, in its splendor, she ought to have presided, as its lawful mistress. Above the gate I read the initials "R. D."—Robert Dudley. Within, covering an area of seven acres, I saw the most beautiful desolation. There were long lines of crumbling walls, half-demolished towers, scattered columns and huge masses of shapeless stones. And then Nature, as if ashamed of the nakedness of ruined art, had hung every turret, and buttress and wall with a luxuriant growth of the most beautiful ivy.

Against one wide expanse of masonry, I saw a mantle of green which must have been seventy-five feet high and fifty feet broad, growing from a stem as large around as the body of a man.

On the right we saw Cæsar's Tower—a perfect example of ruined grandeur. Further on was the kitchen, now represented only by two or three arches and parts of foundations. Still beyond, we climbed what remains of Mervyn's Tower. We stood in the chamber where poor Amy Robsart was concealed during the festivities, and, looking through a narrow window, down upon the ground where Leicester had his Garden of Eden, saw the place where she threw herself upon her knees, imploring the protection of the queen.

Adjoining Mervyn's Tower, on the south, we saw the Great Banqueting Hall where Leicester feasted Elizabeth and her court so many days. It must have been a noble room. The floor is gone, although a row of huge pillars on which it rested remains. The lofty windows are there, filled with tracery; the paneled spaces between; and the richly ornamented fire-places on both sides. Where are the hundreds and thousands who used to roam over these grounds, and feast in this banqueting hall, and lodge in these ruined chambers—kings, queens, lords, ladies, knights and men at arms? Gone, gone, forever gone! Gone to answer, at the judgment bar of God, for the deeds done here in the body. We are part of an endless procession, following them into the dim realm of shades. Let us live as those who realize that we must answer before the Eternal Judge for every act and word, and thought. Thoughts too big for utterance filled my soul, as I left Kenilworth that evening, and rode back to London behind the iron horse.

Speaking of the castles of Old England, I am reminded that God has a castle. It is larger, and grander, and stronger, and more beautiful than any that man can build. In the forests, kings and barons, long since dead, built the castles of England. The ever-living God built his castle in the midst of the forest of sin. You call this world beautiful, and, physically, it is. But, in a moral and spiritual sense, it is overgrown with a dense forest of the upas trees of sin. There are many large and small clearings of cultivated fields; but the forests are much larger than the vineyards and gardens. Through the forest swarm vast numbers of ravenous beasts, among which is one of gigantic size and marvelous cunning and power, named the Devil, that " as a roaring lion walketh about seeking whom he may devour."

In this forest of sin we were all born, and here we must perish, had not a God of infinite love and power provided us a place of refuge and defense. On the rock of eternal truth he has builded a castle, into which we are invited and entreated to flee. Its walls are righteousness. Its towers are salvation. Its encircling moat is the River of Life. Its only gate is Christ. Its drawbridge is repentance. Its portcullis is faith. The banner which floats above its highest turret is emblazoned with the blood-red cross of universal redemption. Within its walls, which all earth and hell cannot batter down, or scale, or pierce, or undermine, or shake, every soul may find salvation from the guilt, and power, and pollution, and consequences of sin ; from the dread of death ; from every tormenting fear ; from every gnawing care ; from every form and shape of real, essential evil. Abiding there, you will be as safe, as though you were actually within the jasper walls of Heaven itself.

I am sent out to invite you to come into the castle of God to-night. Leave all behind. Abandon the dark forest of sin. Throw down the burdens of self and the world which you are trying to carry. Plant your feet firmly on the drawbridge of evangelical repentance. Pass under the portcullis of faith. Enter the gate—Christ ; and be at rest. Behind you are the wild-beasts and robbers of lust and temptation. You have not a moment to lose. Hell is barking at your heels. Fly for your life. Fly ! fly ! fly !

XV.

EDINBURGH AND SCOTLAND.

"A city that is set on a hill cannot be hid."—Matthew v., 14.

That this statement applies to Edinburgh, the capital of Scotland, you must believe on my testimony, till I can get you there and let you see for yourself.

I returned to London, from Kenilworth, Monday evening, August 18. The next day the tourist company, which had left me at Rome twenty-five days before, arrived from Holland. The sight-seeing of the succeeding five days I have already given in my second discourse upon London.

Sunday morning, August 24, my ministerial traveling companion and myself went to City Road Chapel, the mother of all the Methodist churches of the world. There were Methodist churches before this; but it took the place of the first one ever erected, it was the acknowledged center of the work which John Wesley carried on, and it is the oldest existing Methodist house of worship. It was erected in 1778, under the direct supervision of Mr. Wesley himself. It is a large, plain, stone building, without spire or tower, with galleries on two sides and one end. Back of the pulpit is a curved recess, divided into an upper and lower section. In the upper section are three pictured windows of stained glass. In the one at the left hand is Paul preaching before Agrippa.

You remember the story. Paul preached with such earnestness and divine power that the king cried out: "Almost thou persuadest me to be a Christian!" Paul's reply was: "I would to God, that not only thou, but also all that hear me this day were both almost, and altogether such as I am, except these bonds." On the right hand window is Elijah going up to heaven in a chariot of fire, while his mantle is falling upon Elisha in the person of our Bishop Simpson. This window was erected by the contributions of many American Methodists. In the center is John Wesley preaching to representatives of all the nations of the world. On the right of the recess are memorial tablets—Charles Wesley, the poet of Methodism; Adam Clarke, its greatest commentator; and Thomas Coke, the first American Bishop. At the left are similar tablets—John Wesley, at the top; John Fletcher, in the middle; and Joseph Benson at the bottom. The walls, nearly all around the room, are lined with memorial tablets. The service was conducted by an old supply minster, who read the Church of England service very feelingly and preached a good spiritual sermon.

After service we introduced ourselves to the preacher, and were led into the vestry, where we were invited to sit by turns in a chair which Wesley used to own and use. In the rear, and on either side, of the church is an old cemetery. Next to the street is a monument to the mother of the Wesleys, one of the most gifted women who ever lived. Her body rests in another place. John Wesley is buried in the rear of the church.

With emotions of the deepest reverence and gratitude, I, a Methodist of the fourth generation, stood at the grave of the founder of Methodism and my spiritual ancestor. There sleeps the mortal part of a man, who, during the fifty years of his itinerant ministry, traveled two hundred and twenty-five thousand miles, preached more than forty thousand sermons and wrote and published books enough to fill the shelves of a good-sized library. Looking at his traveling, we wonder how he found time to write. Looking at his books, we wonder how he found time to preach.

Of course, we Methodists call Wesley a great man. Lord Macauley, the great historian, who was not a Methodist, says of Wesley : " He was a man whose eloquence and logical acuteness might have rendered him eminent in literature ; whose genius for government was not inferior to that of Richelieu ; and who devoted all his powers, in defiance of obloquy and derision, to what he sincerely considered the highest good of his species." Henry Thomas Buckle, the distinguished author of the " History of Civilization in England" styled him "the first of theological statesmen."

Just south of the church and cemetery is the old parsonage, which was Wesley's home when in London and is now the home of the pastor of City Road Chapel. We were not permitted to go in ; because the day was the Sabbath. So we had to content ourselves with looking at the outside of the house where John Wesley peacefully drew his last breath, at 10 o'clock in the morning, March 2, 1791, in the eighty-eighth year of his age. His' very last word was " farewell." Just before he expired he repeatedly said : " The best of all is, God is with us."

Directly across the street from City Road Chapel

is Bunhill Fields Burial Ground, where we stood by the graves of John Bunyan, Isaac Watts, Susannah Wesley (the mother of John and Charles) and Daniel Defoe. Over Bunyan's grave is a large block of stone, on which lies his image in stone. On one side of the base is a pilgrim, bearing a heavy bundle ; on the other side is the same pilgrim losing his burden at the cross. Defoe's monument was erected by the contributions of seventeen thousand boys and girls of England, who had read his " Robinson Crusoe."

The next day we took our journey to Scotland. A ride of nine hours and twenty minutes, and three hundred and fifty-seven miles, brought us to Melrose, whose celebrated Abbey we stopped to visit. This edifice was erected in 1156. While standing in its original splendor, it was the finest structure in Scotland. It has been twice destroyed by fire, and twice rebuilt. Its final demolition was effected by the hands of the Reformers, under John Knox. It is now regarded as the most beautiful ruin in the world. Of course, you understand that its demolition is not complete. Enough remains to give you an idea of the matchless beauty of the perfected building ; and enough is wanting to make you blame the mistaken zeal of the stern old Presbyterians, who destroyed what they could not admire. The place holds many tombs, among which is that of Walter Scott's " Last Minstrel."

From Melrose, we drove two miles and a half, through a most beautiful section of country, to Drysburgh, another ruined Abbey, on the other side of the river Tweed. There we saw the tomb of Scott. Thence we drove back, across the Tweed, four miles and a half, to Abbottsford, the famous mansion built by Scott, his residence for many years, and the place where he died. It is a grand and beautiful edifice, built somewhat in the style of an ancient castle. It is now the home of the great author's granddaughter. By the payment of a shilling a head, we gained admission, and were conducted through all but the private rooms of the family. We visited the study, the library, the parlor and other apartments, richly and curiously furnished and adorned. Many curiosities were shown us, among which were Rob Roy's mallet, the cross which Queen Mary of Scotland carried to her execution, and a blotter which had belonged to the great Napoleon.

Standing here in the place where one of the world's greatest literary geniuses died, let me tell you some things about him, which perhaps you do not know. He was born one hundred and twenty years ago. At the age of eighteen months, he became incurably lame in the right leg. He grew up, went through college and studied law. Not liking the practice of law, he devoted himself to literature. At the age of thirty he startled and electrified the world with his first great poem, the "Lay of the Last Minstrel." "Marmion" and the "Lady of the Lake" came soon after, and established him, in the judgment of the world, as the greatest living poet.

About this time he became a member of a printing firm, which, failing shortly after, involved him in debt to the amount of over two hundred thousand dollars. In this emergency he acted like a man and a Christian. He did not try to sneak out from under his obligations; but insisted that they should lie upon him, and pledged the labor of his future to the payment of every legitimate claim. Then he went to work, with all his might, and, in a surprisingly brief space of time, produced that extraordinary series of about twenty large works, known as the "Waverly Novels." They seemed to fly off from his brain and fingers, like sparks from a blacksmith's anvil.

When the last book was finished, and the copyright sold, he was able to put in the hands of his creditors the sum of two hundred thousand dollars, which he had earned with his pen in two years. It was a tremendous exertion, put forth in the midst of great domestic sorrow—the death of his wife, to whom he was passionately devoted—and cost him his life. But he died a free man—free from the disgrace of debt. He went abroad for his health, but grew rapidly worse. He was anxious to get home. His wish was gratified. He reached Abbottsford in July, 1832, and died September 21.

Just before his death he desired to be drawn into his study and to be placed by the window, where he might look out upon the beautiful Tweed. To his son-in-law, Lockhart, he expressed a wish that he would read to him. "From what book shall I read?" said he. "Do you ask that question?" said the dying potentate of the realm of literature." There is only one book. I want the Bible; read to me from that." Lockhart read the fourteenth chapter of John, which begins: "Let not your heart be troubled: ye believe in God, believe also in me. In my Father's house are many mansions: if it were not so I would have told you. I go to prepare a place for you." The sick man listened with intense interest, and when the chapter was finished, said: "Well that is a great comfort." And so he died, believing in God, believing in the Bible and believing in Jesus Christ. Who dares to say that the Christian religion is fit only for weak-minded men, timid women and immature children ?

A railroad ride of thirty seven miles brought us from Melrose to Edinburgh, which is three hundred and ninety-four miles from London. Edinburgh has been a city for about a thousand years. Its present population is two hundred and thirty thousand. It is picturesquely situated about a mile south of the Frith of Forth, a broad inlet from the North Sea. It is remarkable for the elegance and solidity of its buildings, which are all of stone.

Edinburgh is a "city set on a hill," in three respects. First, the oldest and most interesting portion of the town is literally located on a lofty elevation, which commands a magnificent view of the surrounding territory for many miles. Again, it is "a city set on a hill," whose "light cannot be hid," in the sense that it is an important center of learning, and is distinguished for the number and excellence of its literary, scientific and educational institutions. Here is the celebrated University of Edinburgh, founded in 1582, with a library of 140,000 volumes. The literary and professional men compose a large proportion of the population of the city ; and its chief business is the printing and publishing of books. The intellectual light of the capital of Scotland shines to the most distant parts of the known world.

Once more, in a religious point of view, Edinburgh "is a city set on a hill." It is very conspicuous among the cities of the world, because of the religious habits and character of its people and the surprising number and great ability of the divines and theologians whom it has produced. It has one church for every two hundred of its people. Most of the churches are of the Presbyterian order. Almost everybody goes to church. It is considered a disgrace not to attend some place of worship on the Lord's day. In the hotel where our company was entertained, family prayer is conducted every morning by the proprietor, and all the guests are invited to take part in the worship.

Edinburgh is a very beautiful city. Taking into account its picturesqueness of situation, as well as its buildings and monuments, I must agree with the unanimous verdict of travelers, with whom I have conversed, that it is the most beautiful of European cities. Imagine yourself to be standing on Princess Street, one of the main thoroughfares of the city. The street runs east and west. You are looking south. Behind you is the new town. In front is the old town. Between the two is a deep valley, which, up to your feet, is laid out in an exquisite garden, or park, stretching off to the east and west. Along the bottom of the valley runs the rail-road, with a large depot off at your left. Princess Street, on the side toward the valley, has no buildings, the park coming up to the side-walk, with a beautiful iron fence between.

In the park, just before you, rises a beautiful Gothic, brown stone monument to the memory of Sir Walter Scott. It is two hundred feet high. The base forms an arched canopy, under which is a large marble statue of Scott, in a sitting posture, with his favorite dog at his feet. From base to pinnacle, the monument, or spire, is ornamented with Gothic niches, each holding the statue of a hero or a heroine described by Scott in his poems or novels. I ascended the monument by an interior winding stair-case of two hundred and eighty seven steps. I went up one hundred and eighty feet, as high as any one can go. A gentleman, residing in the city, was my guide, here and in many other places, and pointed out from the top of the monument every important building in sight.

Resuming our places in Princess Street, and looking southward, we see, in the park near the street, a statue, on a pedestal, of David Livingstone. Across the garden-valley rises a hill, covered with buildings. Far away at the left, the hill begins, as low down as our standing place. From thence it rises gradually, till, a quarter of a mile further east than the spot where we are standing, it is an eminence nearly four hundred feet high. From thence if falls off almost perpendicularly in all directions but one. Right there stands the Castle. Away at the east, where the hill begins, are Holy Rood Abbey and Palace. Between them and the Castle, on the ridge or backbone of the hill, runs a street parallel to Princess Street, and bearing three names. Its eastern end is Canongate; its western end is Lawn Market; its middle portion is High Street.

Across the valley stretch two or three bridges. At our right, quarter of a mile away, is the Mound—a causeway of earth and masonry thrown across the valley—with a tunnel under it for the rail-road. On the mound are two fine buildings—the National Gallery and the Royal Institution.

Now turn your face to the east and walk along Princess Street. You pass many fine buildings, till, in less than half a mile, you come to Calton Hill,

Ascending to an elevation of, perhaps, one hundred feet, you find many noble buildings. They are the Royal Observatory, which I did not enter; Prof. Playfair's Monument, a beautiful little Doric temple; Nelson's Monument, one hundred and two feet high, which I ascended by a spiral stair-case of one hundred and seventy-eight steps; Dugald Stewart's Monument; and the National Monument.

This last was commenced in 1822, by King George IV. and was intended to be a copy of the Parthenon at Athens. The King's architects told him that it would cost a quarter of a million dollars. After sixty thousand dollars had been expended, and about a dozen columns had been erected, the work was abandoned. It looks like a beautiful ruin. It reminds me of the words of Christ : " Which of you, intending to build a tower, sitteth not down first, and counteth the cost, whether he have sufficient to finish it ? Lest haply, after he hath laid the foundation, and is not able to finish it, all that behold it begin to mock him, saying 'this man began to build, and was not able to finish.' "

King George began to build the National Monument, without accurately counting the cost, and was not able to finish it. Many a man begins the Christian life, without counting the cost. He thinks he can serve God and Mammon at the same time, carry heaven in one hand and the world in the other. By and by, when he finds that it takes all there is of a man to be a Christian, he concludes that he cannot afford to expend so much on a Celestial mansion, and abandons the undertaking before it is quarter finished. He makes himself a laughing stock to angels and men. Hear what the Great Teacher says in conclusion: "Whosoever he be of you that forsaketh not all that he hath, he cannot be my disciple."

Returning to our old stand in Princess Street, and looking south, as before, we see a high hill, or mountain, rising in two ridges beyond Castle Hill. The first ridge is called the Crouching Lion, from a fancied resemblance to the king of beasts at rest. The second ridge, eight hundred and twenty-two feet above the sea level, and more than seven hundred above the spot where we are standing, is Arthur's Seat.

The morning after our arrival in Edinburgh the entire party started out for a ride in two carriages called breaks. A break is a large four-wheeled conveyance, with a body like a square piano, without its legs, only much longer. The seats, from four to six in number, are raised above the box, which opens only at the rear end to receive baggage. As the seats are very high above the ground, they offer a fine opportunity to view the country through which one may be riding.

We rode out into the country, west and north, nine miles to view a new rail-road bridge across the Frith of Forth. It is more than a mile and a half long, including the approaches. It is built on the cantilever principle. It has two main spans, beside several shorter ones. Each of the long spans covers 1710 feet, which is 115 feet longer than that of the Suspension Bridge which unites the cities of New York and Brooklyn. It hangs over an arm of the sea, two hundred feet deep. It contains 54,000 tons of iron and steel, while there are 250,000 tons of solid masonry in the piers. It is held together by eight million rivets, which, if placed end to end, would reach from Edinburgh to the shores of France. The plates in its steel tubing, if laid lengthwise, would reach a distance of fifty miles. It was three years and a quarter in building; five thousand men worked upon it at one time; it cost fifteen million dollars; fifty-seven men were killed, and five hundred and eighteen were more or less injured, during its construction. Its last rivet was driven by the Prince of Wales, March 4, 1890, amid the cheers of an immense crowd and the howling of a tempest of wind. On the whole it is probably the greatest and most wonderful bridge ever built. Unlike the suspension bridge across the Frith of Tay, thirty miles north, which went down, during a terrible storm, in December, 1879, carrying a train-load of ninety passengers into the sea, it is believed that the Frith of Forth Bridge will stand for centuries.

There is only one greater bridge in the universe. That you may know what I mean, I must carry your thoughts back into the past, six thousand years. When the world was new and the golden age had not given place to the ages of mud and iron, earth and heaven had daily intercourse with each other; there was no void between them; angels flew through the air, and trod the ground, in visible form; and God himself walked in the garden, where man dwelt, and conversed with him face to face. But by and by sin came into man's heart, and instantly there was a great gulf between earth and heaven. The angels came no more; or, if they came, they could not be seen; and the human family were exiles from the Father's home, wandering about in a land of dark despair. On the dark, earth side of that gulf every human being has been born.

As we advance from the cradle toward the grave, the gulf grows wider at every step. Beyond the grave and on through eternity, the gulf is absolutely impassable. In the sixteenth chapter of Luke, the veil between time and eternity is lifted. What do we see? Wicked Dives in torment, and righteous Lazarus, with Abraham, in joy and felicity ; and we hear Dives crying : " Father Abraham, have mercy on me, and send Lazarus, that he may dip the tip of his finger in water, and cool my tongue ; for I am tormented in this flame." Listen, and hear the answer which comes over the seething bosom of the Lake of Fire : " Between us and you there is a great gulf fixed : so that they which would pass from hence to you cannot ; neither can they pass to us, that would come from thence." My friends, unless we get across the gulf, in some way, before the end of our mortal life, we are lost forever.

But is there any way to get over? Yes, Almighty God, in his infinite love, has built a bridge. The all-wise Architect drew the plans before the foundations of the world were laid. Six thousand years ago the first stone was put in its place and the first span was swung out toward earth from the celestial shore. Since its completion, millions have crossed, from darkness to light, from fear to hope, from sin to holiness, from death to life. Millions more may cross. The massive structure shows no sign of weakness or decay.

The name of the bridge is Christ. He says : " No man cometh unto the Father but by me." The bridge is free ; no toll is demanded. All may cross by simple faith in the bridge and in the word of God.

Behold the bridge ! The only approach is on this

side of the grave. Behold the Saviour of mankind. You may cross the bridge to-night. You can trust the bridge. O, trust it now. The longer you defer your crossing, the wider the gulf will look, and the greater the courage and resolution which you will require. O, that this whole congregation, or such portion of it as are on the wrong side, would arise this moment, forsake their sins and rush in a mass for the bridge! O, turn your back on the world! Turn your face toward Christ! Venture on him now! Plant your feet firmly on the bridge; and run, with all your speed, to the other shore!

We embarked on a little steam-boat and rode under and around the great bridge, viewing it from beneath and from every side. Returning to the city, we drove to Holy Rood Abbey, which is in a sadly ruined state. We were shown the spot where Queen Mary and Darnley were married, in 1565. Adjoining the Abbey is Holy Rood Palace, three hundred and ninety years old, one of the ancient residences of the Scottish kings. The building is large and grand; but its apartments are somber and gloomy, and the furnishings are faded and time-eaten. We saw Queen Mary's apartments, four rooms, one containing her bed inclosed in an iron railing.

Mary, usually called Mary Queen of Scots, was one of the most prominent historical figures of her day. She was beautiful and gifted, but unprincipled, treacherous and cruel. Her first husband, before she was queen of Scotland, was Francis II., king of France. After his death and her coronation in Scotland, she married Lord Darnley. She seemed to be more intimate with an Italian adventurer, named Rizzio, than with her husband. One night Darnley,

in a fit of jealousy, led a band of assassins up a back
stairway into Mary's apartments, and, tearing Rizzio
from her arms, dragged him into a corridor and
stabbed him to death. We saw the stairs up which
the murderers came and the blood of the murdered
man on the floor.

The horror of that night Mary never forgave nor
forgot. The son whom she bore three months afterward, James VI. of Scotland and James I. of England, could never see a drawn sword without
trembling. Mary swore vengeance on the assassins
of her favorite. A few months after, the house in
which her husband lay sick was blown up with gun-
powder and his mangled remains were found at a
distance. Six months later the royal widow married
Bothwell, who was known to have had a hand in the
murder of her hated Darnley. This was too much
for her subjects to endure. They rose in rebellion
and drove her from the throne and from Scotland.
She fled to England, where Elizabeth had her
arrested as a dangerous person. After an imprisonment of several years, Elizabeth had her tried, condemned and beheaded, on a charge of conspiracy
against the throne of England.

From Holy Rood Palace we drove up the hill, the
distance of a mile, along the street which has three
names—Canongate, High Street and Lawn Market—
past John Knox's house and St. Giles' Church (where
he preached so often) to the Castle. This is a grand
old building, now held by seven hundred English
soldiers—or Scotch, for most of those whom we saw
wore the picturesque Highland costume.

The castle was built in 617; but has been greatly
changed since then. It was formerly one of the

residences of the kings of Scotland. James VI. (afterwards James I. of England) was born here. We saw the room of his birth, and were conducted through the apartments which his mother Mary lived when the castle was her home. The ancient regalia of Scotland is kept here. It includes a crown, sceptre, and sword of state. St. Margaret's Chapel, the oldest and smallest church in Scotland, occupies the highest point of the castle-grounds. We saw the famous cannon called "Mons Meg," which weighs five tons and is four hundred years old.

We stood on the top of the highest rampart and looked down, down, almost straight down upon the city, four hundred feet below us, and away to the open country on the west ; the Crouching Lion, and Arthur's Seat, on the south ; and the Frith of Forth, on the north. We listened to the music of two large military bands. One of them was composed mainly of bag-pipe players.

Leaving the castle and the rest of the party, my ministerial comrade and I walked back down the hill, up which we had rode, to St. Giles' Church. From its pulpit John Knox used to hurl thunder and lightning, more than three hundred years ago. He is buried under the pavement in front of the church. The only thing to mark the spot is a paving stone, about twice as large as the others, with the letters " J. K.," deeply cut into its face. That is a very short epitaph for so great a man. But Knox was so great that he did not need a long inscription, or a lofty monument.

Who was John Knox? Does anyone ask that question ? He was the greatest man ever born on Scotland's soil. The Scotch are among the noblest people in the world. Scotland is the native land of stalwart manhood, freedom, independence and pure religion. And John Knox did more to make Scotland and the Scots what they are than any other man, or any ten men, who ever lived. When he came upon the stage, his countrymen were ignorant, superstitious, enslaved. When he passed away, they were intelligent, God-fearing, free. During the long conflict he was the leader of the army of reform, fighting with the word of God and prayer. Queen Mary was the leader of the army of ignorance, superstition and despotism, fighting with the sword, the rack and the fagot. You have heard the story of Knox, overheard by some of his friends, praying in his garden : " O God give me Scotland, or I die." That is the way he fought and conquered. You have heard the remark of Queen Mary : " I fear John Knox's prayers, more than I fear all the armies of England." That is the way he fought and conquered.

When Knox's body was being laid in the grave, the regent Morton said : " There lies he who never feared the face of man." Generations after, Thomas Carlyle, in reviewing his life and work exclaimed : " Honor to all the brave and true ; everlasting honor to brave old Knox, one of the truest of the true ! " I stood in no more sacred spot, in all my travels in Europe, than when I bent above the burial place of John Knox, in front of the Church of St. Giles, in the city which he helped to set on a hill.

Wednesday morning, August 27, we left Edinburgh, at half past six o'clock, and rode by rail to Sterling, thirty-six miles. Soon after starting, we crossed the Frith of Forth by the great steel, cantilever bridge, of which I spoke a few minutes ago.

We climbed the hill to Sterling Castle. This is

not equal to Edinburgh Castle ; yet it is a fine old structure, in perfect condition—the home of three hundred red-coated British soldiers. It was once the residence of the monarchs of Scotland. Bloody old tyrants most of them were. We saw the room in which James II. stabbed and killed the Earl of Douglas, four hundred and thirty nine years ago.

The view from the ramparts of the castle is said to be very fine. But there was so dense a fog that we could see nothing, After our departure, the fog departed. Two places on the highest part of the castle—overlooking the field of Bannockburn, where the English under Edward II. were beaten by the Scots under Robert Bruce, five hundred and seventy-seven years ago, with a loss of thirty thousand men—are named from two queens who greatly admired the scenery from them. The queens were Victoria, who was there in 1842 ; and Mary, who last stood there in 1532, which date is cut in the stone at the spot. James VI. was crowned in Sterling Castle, and John Knox preached the coronation sermon. We saw the pulpit used on that occasion, also Knox's Bible and communion table. In the castle yard stands a fine statue of King David Bruce.

Near the castle we visited the Gray Friars' Church and Cemetery. There I saw something which impressed me very deeply. In a space of brightest green, surrounded by a pretty iron fence, stands an exquisite, little, octagonal temple of the whitest marble, with a dome-shaped roof. The floor is some six feet above the ground. From the floor to the cornice, the walls are plate-glass, divided by graceful Corinthian columns. Within, protected from the elements by the glass, and so perfectly white, are three marble figures, of the size of life. Two are beautiful maidens, sitting with an open Bible before them. Behind stands an angel. At their feet lies a lamb. The maidens are Margaret Wilson and Margaret McLachlin ; and the monument commemorates their martyrdom.

How do you suppose they were martyred? Because they would not give up the Bible and the pure religion which it teaches, they were bound to a post, driven into the beach of the sea at low tide, and were left to be drowned by the returning waves.

Imagine the girls abandoned by all human friends, clinging to each other, and waiting for the cruel sea to come and devour them. I can see them now. I hear them triumphantly singing the praises of their Redeemer. The water reaches their feet ; it rises to their knees ; it surges up to their waists. I hear their singing more loud and clear. Now the water has reached their necks. Listen ! Do you hear the song ? It sound to me like :

> "Jesus, Lover of my soul,
> Let me to thy bosom fly,
> While the nearer waters roll,
> While the tempest still is high !
> Hide me, O my Saviour, hide,
> Till the storm of life is past."

Hold ! Do you see that big billow rolling in ? It has almost reached the girls. The last strain floats in to the shore :

> " Safe into the haven guide,
> O receive my soul at last !"

The billow rolls over their heads ; and they are singing with the saints and angels before the throne of God.

What do you think of a religious experience like that ? Do you not wish you had it ? You can have it, if you will give your hearts wholly to the Lord Jesus Christ.

XVI.

THE SCOTCH LAKES AND GLASGOW.

"From sea to sea, and from mountain to mountain."—
Micah vii., 12.

Our journey from Edinburgh to Glasgow was literally " from sea to sea and from mountain to mountain." Edinburgh is on, or near, the North Sea ; and Glasgow is on, or near, the Atlantic Ocean. Our route from the one city to the other lay, for the most part, through a wild, mountainous region.

At the close of the last discourse we had got as far on our way as the city of Sterling. Thence we rode sixteen miles, by rail, in a north-westerly direction, up the river Teith, to the village of Callander. The town stands on the banks of the river, in front of precipitous crags, overhung on the west by Mont Benledi, and horizoned all around with a mountain sky-line. It is a favorite resort for summer visitors and tourists. It contains the villa of a titled lady, standing on ground once occupied by a Roman camp.

At Callander we were transferred from coaches, drawn by the iron horses, to two breaks, drawn by horses of flesh. You will remember that I told you that a break is a four-wheeled wagon, with a body like a square piano, minus its legs, multiplied twice in length, breadth and height. Across the top runs four, or six, seats. At the rear end is a door, which opens to swallow an immense quantity of baggage. Having seen our satchels, bags and bundles disappear in the monster's black throat, we mounted the lofty seats. Immediately the driver cracked his long lash; the horses threw themselves against their collars ; and we dashed out of town, toward the west, at a furious rate.

Our route lay up the streams and lakes of Vennachoir and Achray, commanding some of the finest scenery in Scotland. First we were riding along the banks of a winding, rushing river. Then we were skirting the flowery margin of a calm, silvery lake. Then we had the companionship of a river again ; then it was a lake ; then, for the third time, it was a river. In places the road was level ; then it was up; then it was down.

In Great Britain all drivers have a peculiar habit. They walk their horses on every level, unless they are entering or leaving a city or village, and lash them into a furious gallop up and down every hill. Thus we rode from Callander, six miles and a half, to the foot of Loch Katrine. A more delightful ride could hardly be imagined. On both sides of the narrow valley rose mountain peaks and chains, of every conceivable shape. From the margins of the road to the tops of the mountains, the ground was one unbroken stretch of red. It looked as though millions of Scotchmen had been fighting here for the honor of their respective clans, and had left mountains and valleys soaked with blood. The color was that of blood, partially dried. I said to myself:

That is the appearance this whole globe would present, if all the blood of men, which men have shed in war, since the fall, were to come up to the surface of the ground into which it has soaked. This is a bloody old world. Man's chief occupation, for six thousand years, has been the shedding of blood. Take the bloodshed, the battles, the wars, the slaughters, the assassinations, the murders out of history, and there would be very little left. The red pages, in the history of every country, are ten times as many as the white.

Will war ever be a thing of the past? If a pure Christianity were to prevail everywhere throughout the world, war would, of necessity, come to an utter end. In the book from which our text is taken, and the fourth chapter, I read : "In the last days it shall come to pass, that the mountain of the house of the Lord shall be established in the top of the mountains, and it shall be exalted above the hills ; and the people shall flow into it. And many nations shall come, and say : Come, and let us go up to the mountain of the Lord, and to the house of the God of Jacob; and he will teach us of his ways, and we will walk in his paths : for the law shall go forth of Zion, and the word of the Lord from Jerusalem. And he shall judge among many people, and rebuke strong nations afar off ; and they shall beat their swords into ploughshares, and their spears into pruning-hooks : nation shall not lift up sword against nation, neither shall they learn war any more. But they shall sit every man under his vine and under his fig tree ; and none shall make them afraid : for the mouth of the Lord of hosts hath spoken it."

When will that golden age of universal peace and love be introduced? When our Lord Jesus Christ comes the second time, in the glory of his Father, with all the holy angels. Let us join with the Church of all ages and lands in the inspired prayer: "Even so, come Lord Jesus."

But what made those mountains so red? That is the question which we put to our driver. His answer was: "The heather is in bloom." "O, the heather, the heather!" we all exclaimed. "Stop driver, stop! Let us get some!" The carriage was stopped, and every passenger obtained a bunch of heather. It is a low shrub, bearing spikes of rosy flowers. It covers scores of thousands of acres of old Scotland's soil. It is not quite worthless. Bees extract honey from its blossoms; and its tops are used for oven-fuel, brooms and thatch.

The last mile of this ride lay through a narrow, rugged defile or glen, called the Trossachs. In its original condition, it was so rough, and so seamed with cross ravines, that a man could hardly crawl through on his hands and knees. Now there is a good carriage road, constructed at a heavy expense. On either side of the dark and gloomy pass towers a lofty mountain. Benawn, on the right, rises to the height of 1800 feet above the level of the sea. Benvenue, on the left, is 2386 feet high. The cleft between is just wide enough to contain the road and the river.

Having passed the Trossachs, we found ourselves at the foot of Loch Katrine. This is a most charming lake, eight miles long and three-quarters of a mile wide, winding about among the mountains from northwest to southeast. Walking out into the lake, on a beautiful rustic pier, we embarked on a graceful little steam-boat, called the "Rob Roy." The voyage was as delightful as poet or artist could imagine.

On both sides rose the mountains almost perpendicularly out of the water, their rough, dark, wooded sides contrasting strikingly with the calm blue water and calm blue sky. The sky and the lake looked so much alike, that it seemed as though they might change places without any damage or shock. Soon after starting, we passed a little emerald set in the azure of the lake, called Ellen's Isle, the central scene of Scott's poem "The Lady of the Lake." Four miles from there, on the south shore, we passed the head of an aqueduct, forty miles long, which conveys water to the city of Glasgow. It was opened, October, 1859, by Queen Victoria.

Near the head of Loch Katrine, we disembarked at a place called Stronachlachar. Stronachlachar is the most northern point which we reached in all our travels. It is in latitude fifty-six degrees and fifteen minutes; while Medina is forty-three degrees and twelve minutes. That makes a difference of thirteen degrees and three minutes. That would amount to about nine hundred miles. That is, Stronachlachar is nine hundred miles nearer the north pole than Medina is. Stronachlachar is in the latitude of northern Labrador, where perpetual winter reigns, while it enjoys summers not much shorter and cooler than ours.

How do you account for this difference in temperature between points, in the same latitude, on the western coast of Europe and on the eastern coast of America? The cause of this difference is the Gulf Stream. The Gulf Stream is a mighty river in the ocean, rising, under a tropical sun, in the Gulf of Mexico, and pouring a tremendous flood of warm water, a thousand miles wide, against the shores of the British Isles. It is an immense steam-heating apparatus, contrived, and kept in constant operation, by the power of Almighty God. If it should break down, or should be stopped one year for repairs, England, Scotland, Ireland and Wales—now so full of swarming cities, and smiling fields, and humming industry, and splendid art, and magnificent civilization—would become an almost unpeopled waste of well-nigh perpetual snow and ice.

In a sense, it is the Gulf Stream that has made English art, and English commerce, and English science, and English oratory, and English poetry, and English Christianity, and English history. What were Joseph Turner, and George Stephenson, and Isaac Newton, and Edmund Burke, and William Shakespeare, and John Wesley, and William E. Gladstone but seeds from the tree of life, which the Gulf Stream cast upon an otherwise cold and barren shore?

Whence comes the Gulf Stream? Out of the palm of the right hand of Infinite Wisdom and Power. God saw that humanity would need such a nation as the English, living apart from the rest of the world, in such a place as the British Isles. Therefore, he invented the Gulf Stream, to warm those islands so that they could support an immense population of civilized men. The summer air of Stronachlachar, contrasted with the perpetual winter of the same latitude in America, suggested these thoughts, and taught me a very impressive lesson concerning the personality, and power, and wisdom of that infinite being whom we call God.

Speaking of north and south suggests another train of thought. What is north? What is south?

North is the direction toward the north pole. South is the direction towards the south pole. How far apart are north and south? How far would you have to travel north before north would become south? If you should start here and travel directly north forty-six degrees and forty-eight minutes, you would reach the north pole. If then you should keep right on straight ahead, as soon as you passed the pole, you would be going south. A journey southward of one hundred and eighty degrees would bring you to the south pole. Passing that, without turning either to the right hand or the left, you would find yourself traveling north. Therefore the distance between the north and the south is one hundred and eighty degrees, or half the circumference of the globe, which is twelve thousand miles. Do you see clearly that the north and the south are only twelve thousand miles apart? I am sure you do.

Now how far is it from the east to the west? How far would you have to travel towards the east, before the east would become west? Reflect a moment. You start east and go around the world, never changing your course. Will east ever become west, as, in the other case, north became south? No, never. If you should circumnavigate the globe a million times, east would never become west. Therefore the distance between the east and the west is infinite.

Now turn to the twelfth verse of the one hundred and third Psalm, and read: "As far as the east is from the west, so far has he removed our transgressions from us." What idea do you get from that? I get two tremendous thoughts. The first is the wonderful scientific knowledge possessed by the man who wrote this psalm, or by the Infinite Spirit who inspired the writing. Why did not the Psalmist say : " As far as the *north* is from the *south*, so far hath he removed our transgressions from us " ? The best scientist in the world, in David's time, would have said : " The north and south are as far apart as the east and west." But inspiration did not let David fall into that blunder. If he had written : " As far as the *north* is from the *south*, so far hath he removed our transgressions from us," every modern infidel would laugh a derisive laugh and say : " That does not amount to much. The north is only twelve thousand miles from the south. If that is all your God can do, he is not much of a Saviour." But now, when the Bible says : " As far as the east is from the west," the mouth of infidelity is stopped, and the devout student of science exclaims : " Such knowledge is too wonderful for me ; it is high, I cannot attain unto it !"

The fact that David, living before the world had any real science, said " east " and " west," instead of north and south, is, to me, positive proof that he wrote under the direction of the mind of God. The Bible does not profess to be a scientific work. And yet, whenever it makes any statement bearing upon science, its language is as accurate as that of the best modern philosopher. You cannot find one scientific blunder in this whole book. If it had been written by uninspired men, it would contain hundreds of blunders, like the sacred books of India, which falsely claim to be inspired.

The other thought, suggested to me by the words north, south, east and west, is the infinite mercy and power of God, in pardoning the sins of those who sincerely repent and unfeignedly believe in him. To you who are not a Christian, duty compels me to say that all the sins you have ever committed are piled upon you, and the smallest of them is heavy enough to sink you into eternal perdition. Unless you get rid of your transgressions before you die, you will be forever excluded from the city of God. There is just one way to get rid of your sins. You must go to God for yourself, renouncing all unrighteousness, promising to serve your Creator all the rest of your life, surrendering your will utterly to his, and trusting alone in the merits of his crucified Son. Then what will take place? In a second of time God will remove *all* your transgressions as far from you as the east is from the west; he will remove them to an infinite distance, and will regard and treat you as though you had never sinned.

From Stronachlachar we rode in carriages, five miles and a half, between ranges of mountains, painted red, from a base to summit, with blooming heather, to Inversnaid. At Inversnaid we embarked on the glassy bosom of Loch Lomond, in a perfectly beautiful steamer named "The Empress." Loch Lomond is one of the most beautiful lakes in the world. It stretches north and south twenty-one miles. For thirteen miles south from its head, it is less than a mile in width. Through the rest of its length, it swells out to a breadth of about six miles, and is full of islands. The point where we took the boat is four miles from the head.

Standing at the stern, as our gallant craft steamed away, we could look back to where a huge cavern in the mountain side, called Rob Roy's cave, presents its slightly-opened lips just above the water, as though it were a gigantic monster come down to drink. Rob Roy, or Robert the Red-head, was a famous Highland outlaw, who filled all this region with the terror of his name, three hundred years ago. In muscular strength, in skill with the sword, in mental prowess and in dare-devil courage, he was unequaled in all Scotland. For many years he defied all the power of England, and was the virtual ruler of this portion of the British Empire. In this cave he stored up his plunder, and held councils with his armed clansmen. If you would know all that is known about him, and more than is known, read Scott's "Rob Roy," a book which will do you more good, and less harm, than most of the Sunday-school novels.

Loch Lomond is certainly the most beautiful body of water I ever saw. It is a silver mirror, of perfect polish, set in a frame of emerald and amethyst consisting of twenty-one mountains, rising right up from the water, and many others visible through vistas beginning with bright green, and shading off into a deeper green, and blue, and purple. These mountains have an average altitude of about two thousand feet. They are called the Alps of Scotland. They are not so lofty and grand as the Swiss Alps, but are more beautiful. The sail was a constant delight. I enjoyed it most intensely, and longed for the power to enjoy it more.

After a voyage of seventeen miles, between the mountains and among the islands, frequently darting from shore to shore to make the various landings, and after a bountiful supper on the boat, we landed at Balloch, at the foot of the lake. There we took the cars, and, after a ride of twenty miles, reached Glasgow, at eight o'clock. From Edinburgh we had traveled one hundred and nine miles, although the distance directly across the country is only fifty miles. We went to the Bath Hotel, on Bath street. The next morning we sallied out to see the city.

Glasgow is a splendid city of about eight hundred thousand inhabitants, the second in population in Great Britain and the greatest ship-building place in the world. It lies on both sides of the river Clyde, twenty one miles from its mouth. The Clyde is the most important river in Scotland. For miles, from the city down toward its mouth, its banks are one continuous ship-yard. All the way down you can see the huge skeletons of the monsters of the deep, and the same monsters in all stages of completion, from the laying of the keel to the finishing of the gorgeous inside work. The river swarms with men, all doing something about iron ships. All day long you hear the din of scores of thousands of hammers, putting heads on millions of rivets to hold together acres of iron plates, on the sides of hundreds of ships, destined to sail to every harbor on the globe. At night you see huge columns of flame shooting up toward the sky out of the chimneys of hundreds of blast-furnaces, in which a million tons of iron and steel are produced every year.

Ship-building, and the production of iron and steel, are not the only industries of Glasgow. She carries on an immense variety of manufactures, each of the most enormous proportions. Her chemical works, calico-printing establishments, breweries, glass-works and dye-houses are the wonder of the world. As a manufacturer of cotton goods, she stands among the first, having 27,000 power looms, with over two million spindles, consuming annually 125,000 bales of raw material. Her annual exports, of all kinds, amount to fifty million dollars, and her imports to thirty-five million.

The River Clyde divides Glasgow into two unequal parts, connected by ten splendid bridges. Glasgow is, for the most part, a well built city. The quays along the river are open, lined with handsome buildings, and present many fine views. In general, the streets are broad, straight, well-paved and well-lighted. The city has three fine parks, beautifully laid out, aggregating two hundred and eighty acres. Glasgow is a very religious city. It contains one hundred and seventy-five churches, of which one hundred and twenty-four are Presbyterian; twelve, Roman Catholic; five, Episcopal; seven, Baptist; other denominations, twenty-seven. Almost everybody goes to church, in Scotland's commercial metropolis. Most of the churches are large and flourishing, and the members are diligent in working for God and souls.

That religion thrives in Glasgow does not surprise us, when we reflect that the city was founded by a Christian missionary. His name was Mungo—St. Mungo, they call him now. He lived and labored nearly twelve hundred years ago. In his days most of the people of Scotland were pagans and semi-savages. Where mighty Glasgow stands was nothing but a cluster of fishermen's huts. Mungo came among them, preaching the gospel, as Jesus did among the fishermen of Lake Gennesaret. Their hearts were touched. Many of them abandoned their barbarous habits and sinful lives, and became the meek and humble followers of the Prince of Peace. Soon their huts began to give place to more substantial and elegant dwellings, grouped around a church which they helped their minister to build on the very spot where now stands the most splendid Cathedral of Scotland. Other houses were built. Trade sprung up, where fishing had been the only occupation. The population multiplied. Commerce established her throne on the banks of the Clyde. Manufactures sprung into existence. Generations and centuries came and went. And now we see the second city in size and importance, within the British Isles. All this power, wealth and magnificence had their beginning and source in the church which St. Mungo built and in the gospel which he preached. There is much in Glasgow that is evil. But all its goodness and greatness have come from the religion of Jesus Christ.

If the gospel had not been preached on the banks of the Clyde, Glasgow would not be. If the gospel had not been preached throughout the British Isles, England, Scotland, Wales and Ireland would now be covered with forests and swamps and peopled with pagans and savages. To me the history of Glasgow is a comment on the Scripture text: "Godliness is profitable unto all things, having promise of the life that now is, and of that which is to come." Godliness —which means true religion, the religion of Jesus Christ—is profitable for communities and nations.

You must have noticed the difference in wealth and power and prosperity between the Christian, and the heathen nations; between those nations which have the purest form of Christianity, and those which have a type that is more corrupt. Great Britain is, in all respects, the most powerful nation of the old world. Cross the sea into the German Empire. England and Germany are very nearly equal in stature, and breadth of shoulders, and length and strength of arms. They are both Christian nations ; their religion is Bible Christianity.

Cross the border into France. France is a great nation. But, with better soil and climate and larger territory, it is far less powerful than England or Germany. It also has a form of Christianity which is much less pure and much less like that which Christ gave to the world. That is why Wellington beat Napoleon at Waterloo, and the Prussians beat the French at Sedan. In both instances Christians, fighting with the Bible in their pockets, were too much for Christians fighting without the Bible.

From France travel south, and you find three so-called Christian nations—Spain, Portugal and Italy. You may call them powerful and prosperous ; but they are much less so than France, and their Christianity is much more corrupt than hers.

Cross the Mediterranean sea from Italy, and you find youself in the Barbary States. The people are Mohammedans, and, as a consequence, are from one-third to one-half savage. Go on eastward, through many thousand miles of savagery, and you come at length to India, where two hundred and fifty millions of people live. Till English arms and civilization and religion came, nearly all were idolaters of the most disgusting kind. What makes the difference between the wealth, and power, and enterprise, and prosperity of England and the poverty, and weakness, and stagnation, and misery of India ? The two peoples are of the same race ; and India has the advantage, a hundred times, in age, and extent of territory, and fertility of soil, and every other natural gift. The difference between the greatness of that little rocky isle, and the littleness of that immense continent of natural fertility and wealth, is the difference between a pure Christianity and a most corrupt paganism.

From what has been said, I think you can see that the nearer nations, or individuals, get to the pure religion of the Bible, the more prosperous and happy they will be. If you cannot see that, I pity your stupidity. If you do see it, and are governed by reason and not by passion, you will strive to be that kind of Christian which the Bible describes.

I was much interested in looking at the coat-of-arms, or seal, of the city of Glasgow, and in what a guide told me about it. It bears, on a shield, a tree, a bird, a fish and a bell ; and an ancient rhyme says concerning it :

> "The tree that never grew,
> The bird that never flew,
> The fish that never swam,
> The bell that never rang."

We visited the University. It was founded in 1451. It is delightfully located on a hill, in the northwestern part of the city, overlooking West End Park. Its chief building was erected in 1870, and is said to be the largest single college building in the world. It is far ahead of anything at Syracuse, or Wesleyan, or Michigan, or Cornell, or Yale, or Harvard.

We visited the Cathedral. It is one of the most attractive features of the city. It was founded seven hundred and sixty-eight years ago, and consumed thirteen years in building. Its architecture is the Early English Gothic. Its dimensions are length, three hundred and nineteen feet ; width, sixty-three ;

and height of spire, two hundred and twenty-five. It is commandingly situated on the highest ground in Scotland's metropolis. A view from its tower takes in the valley of the Clyde, with woods and hedges and pleasant fields, and the river itself, rolling away toward the ocean. The upper, or main portion of the Cathedral is very grand and imposing, but is not so extraordinary as its crypt, or underground part. Supported by its sixty-five beautiful pillars—surmounted by delicately carved capitals and graceful arches—with the light streaming in through the lancet windows, this crypt is the finest in the world. But the greatest glory of the building is its marvelous stained-glass windows, among the finest in the world. They are over eighty in number, each one giving a Bible story in pictures. A good student of Scripture could read almost the whole Bible here. One of these windows cost the enormous sum of ten thousand dollars.

This is the only cathedral in Scotland which was spared by Knox and his fellows, in the time of the reformation. It is also the only cathedral which I saw, in my European trip, which is neither Catholic nor Episcopalian. Glasgow Cathedral was built by the Catholics. It now belongs to the Presbyterians.

We traversed many streets and entered many stores, or shops, as they are always called in Great Britain. The shop windows in Glasgow are more beautiful than those in London. Glasgow is more like an American city than any other in Europe, unless, possibly, we except Liverpool.

We visited the ship-yard of the Fairfield Ship Building Company, one of the largest, if not the largest, in the world. There between 4,000 and 5,000 men are employed, in building the largest iron steam-ships. We saw all sorts of ponderous machines for rolling, and forging, and bending, and punching, and cutting plates, and bars, and beams of iron and steel. Our ears were filled with the deafening din of hundreds of men hammering rivets into place and shape. We saw men making an iron mast. It was hollow. One man had to crawl inside, and hold the red-hot rivets, while two men, on the outside, headed them down with tremendous blows of heavy hammers. That inside man, who soon loses his hearing, gets—as I was told—only about sixty cents a day. Out of that he must shelter, and feed and clothe himself and family, and educate his children, in a city where there are no free schools, and where food costs more than in Medina.

We went on board a smallish steamer, nearly done, which cost three hundred and fifty thousand dollars. They recently built a steam yacht for the Emperor of Russia, at a cost of five million dollars. While thousands of his innocent subjects—men, women and children—are traversing the weary road from their native land to far off Siberia, through drifts of snow and blinding blizzards, that infernal despot is sailing around the seas, in a pleasure boat which flashes with silver and gold wrung from them by threats and torture. How that man will tremble with terror, when he meets his victims before the great white throne of the Eternal Judge !

We saw four huge ships in process of building, each over four hundred feet long, and destined to cost nearly a million dollars. I climbed to the upper deck of one of them, as high as the eaves of a six-story house. That ship-yard reminded me of another ship-yard in which every one of us is working to-day, and every day.

This life is a ship-yard, in which you and I are building a vessel in which we shall shortly sail out upon the ocean of death. If we build a vessel according to the plan of the Supreme Ship Builder, with his help and out of the material which he supplies, we shall safely and joyously reach the shore of eternal life. But if not, the storms of an eternal winter will rend our vessel into fragments and sink our soul into the depths of bottomless despair. The ship which you are building is your character.

Are you building a true Christian character, with Christ as your model, and the Bible as your book of specifications, and the Holy Spirit as your instructor? Are you building out of the pure, solid steel of gospel repentance, and faith, and regeneration, and sanctification? If so, well. If not so, I see nothing before you but disaster, and wreck, and "the blackness of darkness for ever and ever."

XVII.

AYR AND THE ENGLISH LAKES.

" The land, whither ye go to possess it, is a land of hills and valleys, and drinketh water of the rain of heaven."—Deuteronomy xi. 11.

These words were spoken by the Lord, through Moses, to the children of Israel. The land spoken of was Canaan, or Palestine, the inheritance promised to the seed of Abraham. The same words may be used in describing the Lake Region of England. It "is a land of hills and valleys." Its hills are so high that they deserve the name of mountains. Its valleys are as beautiful as a poet's fancy or an artist's dream. It "drinketh water of the rain of heaven" in such abundance, that, collected in its valleys, under the shadow of its mountains, it holds eighteen lakes of rare and fascinating loveliness.

Turning our faces toward that land, we left Glasgow Friday morning, August 29. But before I take you to the English Lakes, I must show you another of old Scotland's sacred places. A run of forty-three miles southward, on the rails, brought us to the town of Ayr. Ayr is what Britishers call a royal burgh. It has a population of about ten thousand. It is the capital of a county of the same name. It is a seaport, at the mouth of a little river, also called Ayr.

Leaving the railway station, as soon as our train arrived, we all started, on foot, for the birth-place of the poet Burns. A walk of two miles, along a perfect road, between fields in the highest state of cultivation, often between walls of solid masonry draped with luxuriant vines, brought us to our destination. The house, in which Scotland's most popular poet first saw the light, is a very plain and humble cottage with thatched roof so low that the crown of my Derby hat almost touched it, as I stood under the eaves. Within, the walls are as rude and bare as possible. The floor consists of small, flat stones, of irregular shapes, laid, without mortar, on the ground. We paid an admission fee of twelve cents.

They showed us the room in which Burns was born, and his bed. Another room is well stored with relics of the famous bard. A lady, having charge of the museum, told us that, up to that date, she had received twenty-one thousand visitors, since the beginning of the year. For some reason, more persons visit the birth place of Burns, than that of Shakespeare, although the latter is nearer the great centers of population, and the main lines of travel, than the former. Why is this? Certainly Shakespeare was, by far the greater genius of the two. I think that the true explanation is that Burns was more the poet of the people, while Shakespeare was the poet of scholars and philosophers. Burns touched more hearts than Shakespeare, and touched them more deeply. Shakespeare may have more admirers; but there are more who love the name and memory of Burns.

When we had looked through the place, it was after eleven o'clock; and as we had had an early breakfast, we took lunch in the museum, surrounded with memorials of the poet. A walk of half a mile brought us to a ruined church called Alloway Kirk, standing near the river Doon. A small cemetery surrounds the kirk. An old man offered to be our guide. As he conducted us about, in and around the church and through the graveyard, he recited many of Burns' poems, or parts of many, in the real Scotch brogue. We showed our delight in genuine American style; and when we left him, we nearly filled his wrinkled old hands with pieces of copper. His united palms looked like the inside of a church contribution box, after the taking of a collection. Among the interesting things which he showed us were the grave of Burns' father, and the font where the infant poet was baptized. The font is a stone trough projecting through the wall of the church, so as to be filled from the outside and used from the inside.

Near the church, in a beautiful garden, is the Burns monument, a circular Greek temple, sixty feet high, built in the year 1820, at a cost of sixteen thousand dollars. We went in and saw a fine portrait of the poet, the very Bible which he presented to "Highland Mary," and many interesting relics. We also climbed to the top of the monument. Burns is not buried here; but under a more splendid mausoleum, fifty miles away, in the churchyard at Dumfries. Near the monument, in a grotto of the garden, we saw two very life-like statues—"Tam O'Shanter" and "Souter Johnnie."

A few rods away, two bridges span the Doon, called by Burns, in his poems, the "Twa Brigs." One of them is a modern structure. The other is an old-fashioned stone arch, much higher in the middle than at the ends. This is the "Auld Brig," which figures so prominently in the story of Tam O'Shanter. We crossed both bridges. On the highest part of the Auld Brig we stood a long time. We leaned over the parapet, and looked down into the silvery tide of the Bonnie Doon, flowing between its emerald banks. We thought of the great poet, standing on these same stones and enjoying this same prospect, more than a century ago. We listened while one of our number read the little poem called "The Banks of Doon," which the poet puts into the mouth of a disappointed maiden ; and then we all joined in singing the two stanzas, which begin :

> "Ye banks and braes o' bonnie Doon
>   How can ye bloom sae fresh and fair ;
> How can ye chant, ye little birds,
>   And I sae weary, fu' o' care ?"

Sit down here on this stone, and let me tell you something about Robert Burns. He was born January 25, 1759. His father was a poor man, whose life had been one long struggle with misfortune. He was, however, a man of good sense, and had picked up something of an education. He greatly desired that his children should be educated. When he was able he sent them to school ; and when he could not, he taught them himself, at home, after his day's work was ended. In after years, Robert wrote : "I am indebted to my father for most of my little pretensions to wisdom." But, so grinding was the poverty of the family, the future poet was trained to no higher avocation than the handling of the plough. At the age of fifteen, he did the work of a man. Hard work almost killed him. His naturally robust frame was overtaxed and his nervous constitution received a fatal strain. His shoulders were bowed, he became subject to violent headaches, palpitations of the heart and fits of depressing melancholy.

But overworking and underfeeding of the body could not crush, or starve, his intellect. He read every book he could borrow. He read in bed at night. He followed the plough with a book in his hand. He spent his Sundays, whenever the weather was not too severe, in the woods, reading books and studying nature. He began to manifest his poetic genius early in life. He was a born poet ; and there is an old proverb that real poets are always *born*, and never *made*. At the age of sixteen, or a little before, as he informs us, he "first committed the sin of rhyme." He kept on writing poems for eleven years, keeping his productions in his own possession. They were mostly on rural themes, and were composed while he was treading the furrow behind the plow, and perfected, and committed to writing, in his cold room by night. At the age of twenty-seven, he was guilty of a serious breach of morality, which led to such unpleasant consequences that he resolved to quit his native country and seek his fortune in America. But, before going, he determined to publish his poems. The result was a tremendous burst of applause, which resounded all through the British Isles. Old and young, grave and gay, learned and ignorant, were alike transported with wonder and delight. In a few hours the poor despised ploughman of Ayrshire became the most famous of living writers.

At once he was summoned to Edinburgh, and was feasted, praised and almost worshiped by the noblest people in that great literary center. It was at this time that Scott, then a very young man, had an opportunity of beholding and listening to the gifted stranger. He has left a very interesting account of

Burns' appearance. He was most struck with the poet's eye. He says: "I never saw such another eye in a human head, though I have seen the most distinguished men of my time. It was large and dark, and literally *glowed* when he spoke."

Burns lived but ten years after fame so suddenly burst upon him. He wrote some. He traveled a little. He received a little money for his poems. He held the position of excise-officer, with a small salary, in two different places. He became sour and melancholy, on account of his unpopularity growing out of his political opinions. At the age of thirty-seven, when his life-work ought to have been but just begun, after a brief illness, he died. If you ask what caused his early death, truth compels me to answer: Dissipation, intemperance. It is a terribly sad fact that, with all his genius—and he was one of the most brilliant geniuses the human race has ever produced—Robert Burns was a drunkard. His intemperate habits began early in life, and grew with his years. They led him into many disgraceful performances, which I will not even name. When fame brought him into greater temptations, he rapidly went on from bad to worse. As really as James A. Garfield was shot to death by Charles J. Guiteau, Robert Burns was shot to death by King Alcohol. I do not tell these things because I take delight in holding up uncleanness before your eyes, or in branding with infamy a dead man's name; but because I wish to increase your horror and hatred for intemperance. The more you admire the genius and accomplishments of the victim, the more you will oathe the vice which slew him.

It is often said, by advocates and defenders of

moderate drinking, that it is only men of weak intellects, men of no manhood, who become drunkards. They say : " Look at me ! I am a man. I have a mind. I can drink liquor, or let it alone. I shall never be a drunkard. A man who is so weak that he cannot save himself from drunkenness without being a total-abstainer is not worth saving." Was Robert Burns a mental imbecile ? Was he a man of weak intellect? Was he not worth saving from a drunkard's grave and a drunkard's doom ? If you were anything like a well-read man, you would know that an immense army of the world's greatest generals, and statesmen, and orators, and poets, and artists, and jurists, and physicians, and even divines, have gone down under the withering curse of strong drink. They thought they were strong enough to drink the cup of exhilaration, without ever touching the cup of inebriation. But their very strength was their weakness. That peculiar nervous organization which is always associated with genius, is especially susceptible to the fascinating and ruinous influences of the alcoholic bowl. The men who can drink a life-time, without ever getting intoxicated, are generally of a low intellectual rank ; they rarely make great poets, or able politicians, or successful merchants.

Where did poor Robby Burns' intemperance begin ? Where intemperance always begins—with the first glass. So far as the use of alcoholic beverages is concerned, there is no temperance but total abstinence. Temperance is the moderate use of that which is good, and total abstinence from that which is bad. That is the teaching of experience, and also of the word of God. Does not this Book say ; "Look not upon the wine when it is red, when it giveth its color in the cup, when it moveth itself aright : at the last it biteth like a serpent and stingeth like an adder "? That is God Almighty's total-abstinence-pledge—the strongest one ever written. He presents it to every man, woman and child, and commands us to sign and keep it. The word of God calls intemperance a snake ; and so it is, as millions have learned by bitter experience.

A few years ago a noted wild-beast trainer gave an exhibition with his pets in a London theatre. He put his lions, tigers, leopards and panthers through their part of the performance with perfect success, awing the audience with his wonderful nerve and his control over them. As a closing piece, he was to introduce an enormous boa-constrictor, thirty-five feet long. He had bought it when it was only two or three days old, and, for twenty-five years he had handled it daily, so that it was considered perfectly harmless and completely under his control. The curtain rose on an Indian woodland scene. The weird strains of an Oriental band steals through the trees. A rustling noise is heard. A huge serpent is seen winding its way through the underbrush. It stops. Its head is erect. Its bright eyes sparkle. Its whole body is full of life. A man emerges from the dense foliage. His eyes meet the monster's eyes. The serpent quails. The man is victor. The serpent is under the control of a master. Under his guidance and direction, it performs a series of frightful feats. At a signal from the man it slowly approaches him, and begins to coil its heavy folds around him. Higher and higher they rise till the man and serpent seem blended in one. Aloft above the man is reared its hideous head. The man gives a little scream, and the audience unite in a thunderous explosion of applause; but it freezes on their lips. The trainer's scream was a wail of death agony. Those cold, slippery folds had embraced him for the last time. They had crushed out his life, and the horror-stricken audience heard bone after bone crack as those powerful folds tightened about him. The man's plaything became his master.

In this horrible incident is presented the whole story of intemperance. The man who has swallowed the first glass of alcoholic liquor has the boa-constrictor of intemperance in his bosom. If he will strangle the monster now, he can with ease. If he permits it to live, and feeds and fondles it, he may control it for many years. But it is continually growing. And some day its deadly folds will embrace his soul and crush it into eternal death. Young man, have you begun to sport with the python of intemperance? Be warned. Now you can escape. Soon it will be too late. Soon you will be a drunkard; and it is God's unchangeable decree that "no drunkard shall inherit the kingdom of heaven."

Do you say that you did not come here to listen to a temperance lecture? You were invited to hear a sermon on the "Gospel of Foreign Travel." Temperence is a part of the gospel, and these thoughts force themselves into my mind while standing upon the "Auld Brig," in sight of the monument of that brilliant poet whom Scotch whiskey slew.

Having somewhat sated our eyes, we walked back to Ayr. There we turned our faces toward the "land of hills and valleys," which "drinketh water of the rain of heaven," where we had determined to spend our last Sabbath in Europe. About the middle of the afternoon we took the cars for Keswick, England, one hundred and thirty-six miles distant. On the way we passed through Carlisle, an English city of thirty-six thousand inhabitants, the capital of Cumberland County. Carlisle, the capital of Cumberland County, Pennsylvania, is one of its numerous namesakes. It has an old castle, in which Mary of Scotland was imprisoned by Queen Elizabeth, not long before she lost her head.

At Keswick we spent the night in a beautiful hotel, delightfully located. We were at the northern entrance of the famous English Lake Region. This district extends over a portion of three counties: Cumberland, Westmoreland and Lancaster. It contains a cluster of eighteen lovely lakes, which lie embosomed among mountains of singular beauty. The lakes oftenest visited are Windermere, the largest, Grasmere, Rydalwater, Ullswater, Derwentwater and Buttermere. The green mountains and the blue lakes are wedded to each other with rings of emerald islands and snowy vales of foaming cascades. As good a judge as Thomas Arnold says that " it is vain to talk of any earthly beauty ever equaling this country." In whatever direction the tourist may wander in the lake district, he is sure to find himself surrounded by grand and picturesque scenery.

For generations prominent men in England have spent portions of their time here ; and their elegant villas, bearing poetic names, are scattered among the valleys and along the lake shores, and crown the most conspicuous elevations. The region owes a part of its world-wide fame to the pens of gifted writers, who have here established their homes and found their graves, or have come as visitors from near or from far. Among these may be mentioned Wordsworth, Southey, Sir Christopher North, De Quincey, Dr. Arnold, Harriet Martineau and Mrs. Hemans.

Keswick is a village of three thousand inhabitants, situated on the Greta river, close to Derwentwater. It is noted for its manufacture of lead pencils. I wonder why we call them *lead* pencils. There is not a *lead* pencil in all the world, and never was. They are plumbago, or graphite, pencils. The plumbago used at Keswick is obtained from a mine on the western shore of Derwentwater. Some of our party visited the factory, and purchased pencils stamped with their own names, or the names of friends at home, whom they wished to remember with gifts.

Saturday morning we took carriages, just like the breaks of Scotland, and drove entirely around Derwentwater. I asked the driver of the carriage, in which it was my lot to ride, what he called such a wagon. He told me. I asked him to spell the word. He spelled it: s-h-e-r-r-y v-a-n-s. I afterwards learned that the true orthography is char-a-banc.

On the way around the lake we visited two waterfalls. Barrowfall and Lodore. At the latter I gazed with the greatest wonder and delight. Why ? Because, when I was six or seven years old, I read Robert Southey's poem : " How does the Water come down at Lodore ? " in my reading book at school. I was perfectly charmed with the poem. In my childish fancy I could almost see and hear the plunge and roar of the descending flood. I thought: Lodore must be the greatest natural wonder in the world. I longed to see it; I dared not hope I ever should.

And so when our carriage stopped, that Saturday morning, under the shadow of the mountain, and the driver told us that we were going to see the Falls of Lodore, O, how my heart bounded within me! I was a little boy again. The intervening years had vanished. I saw myself standing in a long line of boys and girls, in the reading class, in the old school house, with our toes on a crack in the floor. We were reading: "How does the Water come down at Lodore?" I felt the old longing. I sprang from the carriage in a second, and ran, like a boy released from school, across the field, over the big boulders and up the rocky glen, till my muscles were exhausted and my breath was gone. My feelings when, for the first time, I was approaching Niagara were less intense than when I was expecting, every moment, to find myself face to face with Lodore. And yet Lodore is but a drop compared with Niagara.

O how deep, and vivid, and lasting and tremendous are the impressions, which are made upon the mind in childhood! How infinitely important it is that those impressions be pure and elevating and divine! Is it your desire that your child shall become a temperate, virtuous, Christian man? Then begin to stamp the principles and doctrines of the Christian religion, on his mind and heart, in the earliest dawn of his intellectual and moral life. If you let the Devil have him the first seven years, the chances are that he will have him till death, and through eternity. If I am a Christian, it is chiefly because the dimmest thing in my memory, far back almost to my cradle, is the voice of my father praying to God. I do not remember the words; but the tones of his voice and the impression that he was talking to the Father above, I cannot forget.

Returning, after a ride of about ten miles, we visited the parish Church of Keswick, in whose yard sleeps the body of Southey, with this inscription on the stone: "Here lies the body of Robert Southey, LL. D., Poet Laureate, born August 12, 1774, died March 21, 1843; for forty years a resident of this parish. Also Edith his wife, born May 20, 1774, died November 16, 1837. I am the resurrection and the life, saith the Lord." On the opposite side of the stone is this: "Catharine Southey" (she was the poet's daughter) " Not to the grave, not to the grave, my soul descend to contemplate the form that once was dear—Southey."

Those last words are very full of meaning. They ought to be deeply impressed upon the mind and memory of every Christian, who mourns departed friends. Go to the grave, if you will. Strew it with flowers, if thus your affection prompts you. But never for a moment forget that not to the grave, not to the grave, is your soul to descend to contemplate the form that once was dear. The dead is not there. The dust only sleeps beneath the turf; the spirit, the real image of the Creator, has returned to God who gave it.

When we returned to our hotel, we saw floating from a tall staff in front, a large American flag. Why Brother Jonathan's ensign was there, instead of John Bull's, I do not know. Probably "mine host" depends largely, for his business, on American tourists and deems it good policy to please them thus. We, certainly, were pleased, and saluted "Old Glory" with ringing cheers and swinging hats. You will never appreciate the beauty of the "Stars and Stripes" till you see them streaming in the air of a foreign clime. Ours is the most beautiful flag in the world. God help us to preserve it from everything that can rend or pollute!

After lunch we started, some in carriages and some on foot, for Grasmere, thirteen miles away. I was one of those who rode. The ride was exceedingly enjoyable, being behind sleek and spirited horses, through a romantic and charming country, up and down and round about. About half way to our destination, off in the field at the left, unseen by us in the carriages but visited by the pedestrians, we passed a stonehenge—the remains of a temple where the Druids used to offer human sacrifices, two thousand years ago. Farther on, for miles, we saw works, in process of construction, to convey water from Lake Thirlmere, one hundred miles, to the city of Manchester. At a point where we crossed the line which divides the counties of Cumberland and Westmoreland, we saw a rude monument of an old Saxon king, slain there in battle at a time when England was divided into many kingdoms.

We reached Grasmere at half-past three o'clock, and drove to a very elegant hotel called "The Prince of Wales." There we spent Sunday, August 31. Grasmere is one of the fairest spots I have ever seen. A beautiful little lake, of irregular shape, as blue as blue can be, nestles among lofty hills as green as green can be. The place must be seen to be appreciated. The hotel stands in the midst of a lovely garden, right on the lake. On the opposite side of the hotel from the lake, clusters the village.

Sunday morning dawned clear and bright, but rather cool. At quarter to eleven o'clock, like a loyal Methodist, I attended service in the little Wesleyan

Chapel. The congregation was small. The minister and the leader of the choir were the same person. There were two sermons, one to the children, and a longer one to the adults. The message, which God's ambassador delivered, was plain and simple, and did good to my soul. After service I introduced myself to the preacher, and declined an invitation to preach in the evening.

On the way back to the hotel I stopped at St. Oswald's Church. It is a queer stone building, with little pretension to architectural beauty, and very old. Like nearly all English churches, it is surrounded by a cemetery. Following a well-beaten path, I found the grave of the poet Wordsworth. A very cheap head-stone bears this inscription :

"WILLIAM WORDSWORTH,
1850.
MARY WORDSWORTH,
1859."

In the church a mural tablet bears this inscription : "To the memory of WILLIAM WORDSWORTH, a true philosopher and poet, who, by the special gift and calling of Almighty God, whether he discoursed on man or nature, failed not to lift up the heart to holy things, tired not of maintaining the cause of the poor and simple, and so in perilous times was raised up to be a chief minister not only of noblest poesy but of high and sacred truth, this monument is placed here by his friends and neighbors in testimony of respect, affection and gratitude, anno MDCCCLI."

Wordsworth's connection with Grasmere makes it a very sacred place. Here he resided for more than half a century. He and his contemporaries and friends, Coleridge and Southey, were called "the

Lake Poets." This name was first given them, in derision, by the English aristocracy, because they were republicans in politics, and because their poetry breathed a deep sympathy with the joys and sorrows of the common people. But what was an epithet of hate became a title of honor ; and Wordsworth lived to see himself the most popular poet in the English-speaking world.

Near our hotel our attention was directed to a little cottage, called the " Dove and Bough," where Wordsworth and his wife began house-keeping. About two miles away, on an opposite hill side, we could see, peeping through the trees, a larger and finer house where he subsequently resided. Monday morning, on our way to Wintermere, we passed near the house where he spent his last years, and where he died. We all descended from our seats on the carriage and walked up the hill to the place. It is an ordinary house; but is so decked with ivy, and stands in the midst of such pleasant grounds, that it presents an exceedingly attractive appearance. We were not allowed to enter. We looked through the gate ; and I picked a little twig from a tree growing within. At another point on the road, we passed a large rock, overlooking a pleasant landscape, where the poet used to sit and study and write.

Sunday afternoon I strolled about the hotel garden, or sat on a rustic bench right by the margin of the lake. It was a time, and place, for deep and delightful meditation. I thought of my earthly home, across the mountains and the seas, where I hoped to be, worshiping with my own dear people, two weeks from that day ; and I breathed a prayer that the days on old Ocean's restless bosom might be as calm and fair as that perfect Sabbath. Then I thought of my other home, across the ocean of time, where I hoped to be when all the storms of earth are passed ; and I asked myself : how can the great God make heaven more beautiful than this beautiful Grasmere is to-day?

Sitting there, I took out my pocket Testament and deliberately read the book of Mark, without rising, in sixty-three minutes. The fact, and place, and date I entered on the margin of the gospel.

I told you that our hotel at Grasmere was called the " Prince of Wales House." It received its name, many years ago, when the Prince was its guest. In the garden stands a tall flag-staff, from which floated, all the time we were there, a white flag, bearing, in red, the coat-of-arms and motto of the Prince. The same was painted on the ground, at the base of the flag-staff, in foliage plants. What is the coat-of-arms of the Prince of Wales ? A crown, encircling three plumes. What is his motto? The German words " *Ich Dien*," which mean " I Serve."

There was an impressive lesson for me. I give it now to you. The motto of the mightiest of earthly princes, the heir apparent of the throne of the grandest of earthly empires, is, "I serve." How well he lives up to his profession, I will not undertake to tell. But perfect fidelity to that sentiment would make him the most noble and worshipful of men.

The motto of the Prince of Wales was the motto of the Prince of Heaven, the Eternal Son of God, who came down into our humanity, and died on the cross for us more than eighteen hundred years ago. He said of himself : "The Son of man came not to be ministered unto, but to minister, and to give his life a ransom for many." He carried out that idea perfectly, from the beginning to the end of his earthly life. He never did anything merely for himself. He did and suffered everything for the good of others. He was the perfect man. Perfection in us consists in imitating, with divine help, Christ's life of service for humanity.

The way to be Godlike, the way to be noble, the way to be manly and womanly, the way to rise above everything base and beastly, the only way to be happy, is to adopt, and live, the motto of the Prince of Wales, which is the motto of Christ; "*Ich Dien,*" "I Serve." If you would be great and happy in the highest degree, find, and keep, that place where, attracting the least attention to self and having the least thought of self, you can do the most for the happiness and elevation of humanity. Then you will become a Prince of God, and reign with him in glory for ever and ever.

XVIII.

CHESTER, LIVERPOOL AND HOME.

"*Return unto the land of thy fathers, and to thy kindred.*"—
Genesis xxxi., 3.

These words were from God to the Patriarch Jacob, when he had sojourned twenty-one years in Padan-aram, commanding him to go back to Canaan. We had been traveling on the continent of Europe sixty-three days; and now our original plan of travel, the voice of Providence and the love of home seemed to say to each one of us: " Return unto the land of thy fathers, and to thy kindred."

It was Monday morning. We expected to sail for America on Wednesday. So we had about three days to give to Chester and Liverpool. We left Grasmere at forty minutes past seven o'clock. We rode in two carriages, which the Scotch call breaks; and the English, char-a-bancs. The weather was pleasant, and the ride very enjoyable. After covering a distance of nine miles, we reached Wintermere, a small but beautiful village, the nearest railroad station to Grasmere. At 9:20 we were on the cars.

An uneventful ride of ninety-five miles brought us to Chester, at about one o'clock. We found entertainment at the "Golden Lion Hotel." After lunch, we started out from Foregate Street, where the hotel is situated, to see the town. Chester is a strange old city. It is the capital of the County of Chester, and is situated on the right bank of the river Dee, twenty miles from the open sea. It was founded by the Romans, as early as the year sixty-five of our era. It is surrounded with a wall of varying height, nearly two miles in circumference. It is the only city in England that still possesses its walls perfect in their entire circuit. Chester has, however, outgrown its walls, so that there are 20,000 inhabitants within the old limits, and 30,000 without. The walls have been frequently repaired; but the lower courses are believed to be as the Romans laid them, more than eighteen hundred years ago.

The old walled city is nearly square. Near the middle of each of its four sides, and facing one of the four cardinal points of the compass, is a large gateway. They are called, respectively, North Gate, East Gate, Bridge Gate and Water Gate. From each gate, into the city, runs a street. The four streets meet, at a cross, in the center of the city, dividing the old town into four blocks. The four streets are named from the four gates—North Gate Street, East Gate Street, Bridge Gate Street and Water Gate Street.

These four streets exhibit Chester's most characteristic feature, "the Rows." I presume you have all heard of the Chester Rows; but few of you have any definite idea of what they are. I will try to make you see them. Along the streets where the Rows are, all the buildings stand out flush with the curbstones, or nearly so, leaving no room for sidewalks, where you would expect to find them. There are sidewalks, however. Where are they? They take the place of the first or second (usually the second) story of the houses. The sidewalks are *in* the houses.

You walk on the house floor. Over your head is a ceiling, above which is the next story of the building. On one side of you, is a partition, with windows and doors. In there the people live, or carry on trade. There are the shops and stores. On the other side you look out upon the street, with nothing to obstruct your vision but a railing and the posts which hold up the building.

Such are the famous "Chester Rows." Through them you can walk two miles, protected from sun, and rain, and dust, and mud. They are a fulfillment of Bellamy's prophecy, in the book called "Looking Backward," that, one hundred years from now, all city side-walks will be covered with roofs, so that umbrellas and parasols will no longer be needed. Chester is the nicest city in the world for shopping. If American ladies knew how convenient its Rows are, it seems to me they would all desire to remove to the banks of the Dee.

Our hotel "the Golden Lion," was just outside the wall on Forgate Street, a few hundred feet east of East Gate. In going forth to view the town, the first thing which we purposed to do was to walk around the city on the wall. We went up on a flight of stone steps near East Gate. Then, starting with our faces toward the south, we walked completely around the the city on the top of the wall, on a stone path four and one-half feet wide, and about three feet below the parapet. In some places the wall is fifty feet above the ground outside ; and in other places, it is as low as ten or fifteen feet. The material of the wall is a beautiful red sand-stone. It was built as a defense ; it is carefully preserved as a relic of the past. Chester expects never to see war again. If she should, her walls would be no protection whatever against the big guns of the present age. We had not gone far on the wall, when we were obliged to clamber down into the street, and pass around a considerable stretch which had fallen down, and which a large gang of men were engaged in rebuilding.

At the southeast corner, we came upon the river, which skirts the south wall, and had its company as far as the south-west corner. There we found the Castle, a huge mass of walls and towers, within whose court we saw the red-coated soldiers of Queen Victoria performing their evolutions. All along the western wall, we were in plain sight of the mountains of Wales.

Across the north-western corner, piercing the wall in two places, runs a rail-road. The ramparts tremble every time the iron horse goes snorting and thundering through. What would the brave men who piled up these stones do and say, if raised from the dead, they could see a flying locomotive with its train of cars? How strangely the dead past and the living present are linked together in weird, old Chester!

At the northwest angle is the Water Tower. It contains a museum of curiosities, and a queer old man who has charge of them. The tower stands at some distance from the wall, with a double wall connecting it with the main fortification. At the point of junction is a smaller tower, beneath which we entered an old dungeon, in which political prisoners used to be confined. On the level ground outside the walls, between the rail-road and the Water Tower, are the remains of an old Roman bath-house, and many broken columns of a temple, or other building, erected by the conquerors of the world two thousand years ago.

At the walled city's northeast angle is Phœnix Tower. It is also called King Charles' Tower, because, in the war between the people and the aristocrats of England, Charles I. stood here one day, and, with his heart full of shame and despair, saw the army of Cromwell defeat the royal army, at Rossland moor, two miles away. That was two hundred and forty-six years ago. A quarter of a mile more of walking brought us to our starting point. One walk around Chester's walls did not satisfy me. I repeated it in the afternoon ; and again Tuesday morning, before breakfast.

Descending from the wall we visited the Cathedral. It is a grand and massive old sandstone church, three hundred and seventy-five feet long, lifting an enormous square tower one hundred and twenty-seven feet toward the sky. In the choir is some of the very finest oak carving in the world. It represents years of labor by scores of the most gifted artists. In the lady's chapel—which means that part of the church especially dedicated to the Virgin Mary—a verger directed my attention to a tomb said to contain the remains of Werbergha, the patron saint of Chester, and then informed me that she is buried in two other places in England. That means that three places claim the honor of holding her ashes, and that no one but God and his angels know which is really her grave. It makes no difference to her where she was buried. If you die in the faith of Jesus Christ, it will make no difference to you where your body shall find a resting place. At the end of the world, on the morning of the resurrection, when Christ comes the second time, he will find the ashes of St. Werbergha and of all his saints, no matter where the convulsions of nature or the malice or carelessness of men may have scattered them.

On the wall of the north aisle we saw eight very fine mosaics—that is pictures made of little pieces of colored stone, inlaid so as to look, at a little distance, exactly like pictures painted on canvas. They are each about four feet square. They represent respectively: "Abraham offering Isaac," "The Burial of Sarah," "The finding of Moses," "Aaron and Hur holding up the hands of Moses," "David before Saul with the head of Goliath," "David mourning for Absalom," "The Angel feeding Elijah" and "Elijah meeting Ahab." The spaces between these pictures are filled with smaller mosaics of Abraham, Moses, David and Elijah.

I said to myself, as I stood looking at these wonderful productions: Where and what, would the world's art be without religion? Without religion, the world's art would not deserve the name of art. Nearly all the great paintings and statues of all nations have represented religious subjects. Art has drawn more themes, and more inspiration, from the Bible than from all other sources. The Bible is the best text-book the world has ever had, or ever will have, not only on religion, but also on history, and biography, and science, and philosophy, and poetry, and oratory, and art. Aside from its infinite value as a spiritual guide, the Bible is worth more to mankind, as an intellectual instructor, than all other books put together.

In the nave of the Cathedral, at the front, are suspended two flags, which were carried at the battle of

Bunker Hill, by a British regiment recruited at Chester. If I had spoken what was in my heart, I should have said : Old flags, if our Yankee grandfathers' gun-powder had not given out, that June day, you would not be hanging here, but in some hall or museum over on my side of the Atlantic Ocean.

There are many interesting old houses in Chester. Chief among them is the " God's Providence House," as they call it. It is three stories high, and stands with its gable facing the street. On the ground floor is a harness-shop. The front of the second story is occupied by the side-walk, or " Row," with a furniture store opening upon it. The third story and gable-end are richly ornamented with stucco panels and wooden stiles. Under the third story window is an inscription, running across the entire front, which reads : "God's Providence is mine Inheritance."

The story is that a fearful plague visited Chester in 1647 and 1648. It raged, with terrible fury, for ten months, sweeping off into the grave more than two thousand victims. It visited every house in the city but one. The one which it spared was this very house at which we are now looking. The man who lived here two hundred and forty-four years ago was a Christian, a man strong in faith and mighty in prayer. He believed that it was through the providence of God, in answer to his prayers, that the plague did not enter his dwelling. So, when the peril had passed, he put up this inscription, as a perpetual testimony to the love and mercy and power of the Almighty : " God's Providence is mine Inheritance." Can you say : " God's providence is mine inheritance " ? Do you believe in the providence of God, whereby he watches over his children and makes all things contribute to their highest welfare? Do you believe that " all things work together for good to them that love God?" I do; and, if I did not, it seems to me I should wish I had never been born. This doctrine is clearly taught in the Bible, and in the experiences of myriads of Christians. John Fletcher, one of the fathers of Methodism and one of the saintliest preachers and mightiest theologians that ever lived, when a young man, was in the city of Lisbon, about to sail for Brazil, on a voyage of ambition and adventure. On the very morning when he expected to depart, the maid who waited on him at breakfast spilled a considerable quantity of hot water upon him, and scalded him so badly that he had to go to bed in the surgeon's care. Before he recovered, the ship sailed, leaving him behind, and was never heard from again. What was the spilling of that water, which saved Fletcher's life? Was it a lucky accident? Taken with the loss of the ship, in which it prevented him from sailing, was it a wonderful coincidence? No. It was a providence. God, foreseeing the wreck of the ship, brought about the spilling of the water on purpose to save the life of a man, for whom he had planned a useful and honorable future.

When the Asiatic cholera was raging in the city of New York, many years ago, and all who could were fleeing from the pest-ridden place, a Christian man sat in his house, after his wife and children had retired for the night, perplexed with anxious thoughts. Should he stay where he was, and where his business interests and his duties were, or should he take his loved ones and fly to some sheltered spot far in the north or west? He desired to know, and to do, the will of God. In a spirit of prayer and trust and obedience, he opened his Bible at random and his eyes fell on these words : " He that dwelleth in the secret place of the Most High shall abide under the shadow of the Almighty. I will say of the Lord, he is my refuge and my fortress, my God ; in him will I trust. Surely he shall deliver thee from the snare of the fowler, and from the noisome pestilence. He shall cover thee with his feathers, and under his wings shall thou trust ; his truth shall be thy shield and buckler. Thou shalt not be afraid for the terror by night ; nor for the arrow that flieth by day ; nor for the pestilence that walketh in darkness ; nor for the destruction that wasteth at noon-day. A thousand shall fall at thy side, and ten thousand at thy right hand ; but it shall not come nigh thee. Only with thine eyes shalt thou behold and see the reward of the wicked. Because thou hast made the Lord, which is my refuge, even the Most High, thy habitation, there shall no evil befall thee, neither shall any plague come nigh thy dwelling."

His resolve was taken. He knew that that was a message from God to him. He closed the book. He went to bed and slept till morning, without a fear or care. He and his household remained in the city, and not one of them was harmed.

Was it a coincidence that he read the ninety-first Psalm ? Was it an accident that the cholera passed him by, while it entered almost every other home ? Let atheists answer : " Yes." Let all who believe that there is a God say : " No ! It was an overruling providence that guided that man's eyes to that particular psalm, and impressed him to remain in the city, and shielded him and his loved ones there."

Such thoughts came to me, as I stood in the street, in Chester, in front of that old house, and read the inscription : " God's providence is mine inheritance."

All this sight-seeing took place on Monday. Tuesday morning I visited St. John's Church. A portion fell long years ago. The rest has been repaired and preserved. A part of the nave, preserved in almost its original perfection, was erected in the year 1070. In the ruined chapter house, formerly occupied as a dwelling, I was shown the room in which De Quincey wrote "The confessions of an English Opium-Eater."

The Grosvenor Museum was the next attraction. It contains a large and exceedingly interesting collection of Roman remains, dug up in Chester. They are such articles as sepulchral tablets, altars, fragments of statues and columns, sections of exquisite mosaic floors, pottery and coins. They are the relics of a civilization which flourished in England more than two thousand years ago.

One very curious thing which I saw in this museum was a scold's-bridle, such as was used in England centuries ago. It consists of an iron band, which was made to pass around the face and fasten behind. In front, projecting inward so as to hold the lips apart and nearly fill the mouth, is a large piece of iron welded to the band. Two other bands pass over the head to hold the instrument in its place.

The wearing of such a thing as that would seem a very severe punishment. But is it any worse than the scold deserves ? How much of ruin and misery a scolding tongue can cause, only the Infinite Mind can know. Much of the drunkenness and debauchery which curse society have their source in the domestic scold, who turns home into hell, and drives husband

and sons, for relief, into the cooler and more comfortable hell of the saloon. If all the scolds in America were condemned to wear bridles, millions of dollars would have to be invested forthwith in buildings and machinery for their manufacture.

But if I were the Czar of America, I would let the scolds go, till I had put a bridle on the mouth of every slanderer and tattler. They are as much worse than the scold, as the cyclone, which demolishes your house, is worse than the March gale, which merely rattles your windows. The slanderer and his right hand supporter, the tattler, blast and destroy everything, in this life, which is most precious and beautiful, and inflict wounds which time can never heal. Every man who holds any public position must expect to have lies invented and circulated about him. All he can do is to bear the wrong in silence, leaving his vindication to time and to God; for, for every lie which he undertakes to hunt to its hole and destroy, ten other lies will leap out of the slanderer's poisoned throat and start on their career of havoc and destruction. Therefore, if I could, I would stop every lie, before it starts, by putting a Chester bridle on the mouth of every slanderer and tattler, of both sexes.

About six miles from Chester are two princely residences, with surrounding grounds, which we intended to visit. Two things kept us from making ,the excursion—the weather was too foul for a pleasure ride ; and the thought of starting for sweet home the next day almost took away our desire for further sight-seeing. The places to which I refer are Eaton Hall, the palace of the Duke of Westminster and Hawarden, the residence of Gladstone.

The Duke of Westminster is, with perhaps one exception, the richest man in England. His Eaton Hall estate comprises an expanse of lawns and gardens and fields and forests, measuring twelve miles long and eight miles wide. He also owns a large part of the city of London. His entire income is said to be seven dollars and a half a minute, or ten thousand and eight hundred dollars a day.

The richest individual in the world is an American. He lives in New York. His name is Jason Gould. He is worth two hundred and fifty million dollars. He made every cent of that vast fortune himself. Can you take in the meaning of those figures—two hundred and fifty million dollars? Why, if Adam had lived till the present time, and had saved forty thousand dollars every year, he would not be as rich to-day as is Mr. Gould. But let me assure you that the poorest pauper, who has the love of God in his heart, and the assurance that his name is written in heaven, is richer than all the money-kings of earth combined, provided they know not Christ. Jay Gould is worth two hundred and fifty millions to-day. But how much would he be worth, if he should cross the river of death to-morrow? He cannot carry his gold with him into eternity; and, if he could, it might melt in his hands.

Tuesday afternoon we left Chester, by rail, and reached Liverpool, twenty-one miles distant, at fifteen minutes past five o'clock. We went to the Stork Hotel and spent the night. Liverpool is the third largest city in Great Britain. It has a population of about six hundred thousand. It is situated on the right bank of the Mersey River, which flows almost directly north, and empties into the Irish Sea. As a commercial city Liverpool stands second in the world, London being first. Although Liverpool is an old town, its greatness is of recent origin. Nearly one-half of all the products exported from England are shipped from this port. The greater portion of the emigrants coming to America sail from here. Ten transatlantic lines of steamers, employing the largest and finest vessels, are established in this vast emporium. All this business began with a little American steamer, the first which ever crossed the ocean, named the *Savannah*. It sailed from Savannah, Georgia, May 6, 1819, and had a passage of twenty-six days. It had been declared, by wise men, that no ship could ever cross the Atlantic by steam, because it would be impossible to carry a sufficient supply of coal to last through the voyage. The Savannah carried over a copy of the book containing the demonstration of that proposition.

Liverpool has many great public works. One of the most wonderful of these is a tunnel under the river, connecting the city with the suburb Brinkenhead. The tunnel is two miles and a half long, is wide enough for a double line of railway track and cost more than four million dollars. Liverpool has the finest docks in the world, excepting only those of London. Altogether they cost one hundred and twenty-five million dollars. The largest of them, Alexandra Dock, is the largest in the world. Its size is so great that twenty-one vessels of the greatest length and tonnage can, at the same time, discharge or load their cargo at its quay. The docks extend up and down the river a distance of seven miles, and are always filled with shipping. Along the docks are rows of warehouses, in which the produce of half the world is stored.

We spent about eight hours, viewing the interesting sights of Liverpool. It is well-built, and is as clean as a purely commercial city could be expected to be. It looks more like an American than an English town. The first building which we visited was St. George's Hall. Its foundation stone was laid June 28, 1838, the coronation day of Queen Victoria. It is used for legislative and judicial purposes and for public entertainments. All political gatherings are rigidly ruled out. The structure is one of which the city may well feel proud, and holds a high rank among the buildings of modern times. Entering, you ascend a flight of stone steps, reaching almost the entire length of its east front, and pass under a lofty portico, supported by sixteen Corinthian columns, each sixty feet high. The center of the building is occupied by the great hall, one hundred and sixty-nine feet long and eighty-five feet wide, with galleries seventy-four feet high, all overarched with a solid vault of masonry. It will comfortably seat about six thousand persons. It is finished, with great richness, in polished granite columns, marble balustrades and pavements, and polished brass doors with elegant foliated tracery. A corridor runs around the hall, communicating with the various accessory rooms.

In front of St. George's Hall stand equestrian statues of the Queen and her husband, Prince Albert. The latter is exceedingly pleasing to behold. But the Queen is disfigured by an insignificant-looking hat which she wears on her head.

Just north of St. George's Hall we visited the Free Public Library and Museum, and the Walker Art Gallery. In the museum I saw the largest and finest collection of stuffed birds that I ever saw. It is perfectly immense. It must contain scores of thousands of specimens, from the gigantic condor of the Andes, down to the tiniest humming bird.

Another exhibit, which I studied with great interest, was a collection of glass imitations of all the largest diamonds in the world. Though of small intrinsic value, they accurately represent the size, shape and color of the originals. The largest stood for the Mattan Diamond, the largest and most valuable in the world. It is shaped like a pear, somewhat elongated from stem to blow. A line, drawn through it between those points, would measure about two inches and a half. It was discovered in Borneo in 1776, and became the property of a prince, or Rajah, of that country. Two men-of-war, with stores and amunition complete, and quarter of a million dollars in money, were offered, by the Dutch Government, for the gem and refused by the Rajah, who replied that the fortunes of his family depended upon its possession. That little piece of transparent carbon, which you could hide in one hand, is estimated to be worth three million and a half of dollars.

Looking into that casket of diamonds, I recalled the words of our Lord : " The kingdom of heaven is like unto a merchant man seeking goodly pearls ; who, when he had found one pearl of great price, went and sold all that he had, and bought it." The goodliest pearl in the world is the diamond. Therefore, we may say that the pearl, for which the merchant gave all he had, was a diamond. The diamond in the parable represents experimental religion. If you have embraced the religion of Jesus Christ, as a definite and

personal experience, you have a diamond which is
worth infinitely more than all the gems of earth ; and,
if the Devil asks you to sell it for the baubles of this
world, you ought to say to him as the Rajah of Mattan said of his diamond : " My fortunes for time and
eternity depend upon my possession of this treasure.
I will not sell it."

At four o'clock, Tuesday afternoon, we boarded
a little steamboat, and were carried out into the river
to the great Inman steamer City of New York, which
was lying at anchor, waiting for the tide to rise, that
she might get over the bar into the ocean. Going on
board that great floating palace, we found our stateroom ; and got our baggage in place ; and hunted up
our deck chairs and sea-rugs, which had been
expressed from Antwerp, where we had left them
sixty-six days before ; and put things to rights ; and
had dinner—a most sumptuous banquet ; and sat on
deck till dark, watching the swarming ships, and
eying our great rival, the Teutonic, of the White Star
Line ; and went to bed.

At eleven o'clock, the tide having risen, the noble
ship weighed anchor and put out to sea. The next
morning we were out of sight of land. The sea was
smooth, the sky was bright, and everybody was gay
and happy.

At about noon we entered the harbor of Queenstown, on the southern coast of the far-famed Emerald
Isle. That was my first glimpse of Ireland, and I had
a great desire to go on shore. But that was impossible. Our ship did not make her dock but anchored
in the offing till the mails, which left Liverpool after
she did, and came a shorter way partly by land and
partly by water, were brought out in a tug. Then
we steamed out into the ocean, leaving the Teutonic

at anchor where we saw her when we entered Queenstown harbor.

Our voyage of three thousand and twenty-seven miles was now fairly begun. It would be superfluous to describe our return voyage, as it would be mainly a repetition of the outward voyage, which was described with considerable minuteness. We had good weather all the time, with the exception of the third day when the sea was decidedly rough, and most of the passengers paid a heavy tribute to old Neptune. I described the City of New York in connection with a description of the Red Star Ship Westernland, on which we made the outward passage.

Wednesday morning, September 10, I came on deck in time to witness the birth of as fine a day as I ever saw. One of the officers told me that the Teutonic, which had not till then been in sight since we left her at Queenstown, had passed us in the night. At the breakfast table my opposite (not a member of our party) was very glum and cross. He had wagered money on the speed of our ship, and had lost. When I went on deck, I could dimly see the shores of Long Island. O how happy I was to see the land—the land of my home and my birth! It seemed to me that that was the most beautiful morning I had ever seen. It was indeed glorious.

As the day advanced and the shores grew nearer, the forward deck was crowded with passengers. They were the gayest company I ever saw. Everybody was congratulating everybody else that home was so near. "How beautiful! how beautiful!" was on every tongue, as we saw the coasts of New York and New Jersey almost embracing each other, at Sandy Hook, amid a crowd of steamers and white-winged sailing vessels. Soon we were over the bar, where the water is twenty-one feet deep at low tide, and we were in the finest harbor on the globe. It was pleasant to hear the foreigners on board praise our harbor and speak contemptuously of the little mud-holes, called harbors, of European countries.

I must not take time to describe our sail up the harbor, past the islands and forts and through the fleets of ships coming and going. In due time our monster vessel, with the help of a little tug, swung into her slip crowded with people waving handkerchiefs and shouting recognition to their friends on our decks, and we were at home.

Like that, only more glorious, will be the faithful Christian's entrance into the harbor of Heaven. We have been sailing on the ocean of time for many weary years. If we are on board the "Old Ship Zion," Heaven cannot be far away. Some bright morning you will come on deck—the rolling deck of disease or sudden accident, or old age—and catch a glimpse of the evergreen shore of immortality. The sight will fill your soul with joy unspeakable and full of glory. Soon, without a pang of regret but with shouts of ecstasy, you will smoothly sail over the bar of death into the harbor of eternal life. Then, between banks of glittering emerald and among islands of ruby and amethyst, you will move up to the golden wharf crowded with angels and saints waving and shouting you "Welcome!" In that glittering throng you will recognize many of the friends of earth, who have long been awaiting your coming. Brightest of all will beam your Saviour's face; and, as you step on the eternal shore, he will clasp you in his arms of almighty love and say: "Home at last!"

THE END.

www.ingramcontent.com/pod-product-compliance
Lightning Source LLC
Chambersburg PA
CBHW021152230426
43667CB00006B/359